E. M. Forster

A Passage to India

A CASEBOOK

EDITED BY

MALCOLM BRADBURY

MACMILLAN

First published 1970 by
THE MACMILLAN PRESS LTD
Houndmills, Basingstoke, Hampshire RG21 2XS
and London
Companies and representatives
throughout the world

ISBN 0–333–05177–7

Printed in Hong Kong

Eleventh reprint 1994

TO NICHOLAS BROOKE

CASEBOOK SERIES

JANE AUSTEN: *Emma* David Lodge
JANE AUSTEN: *'Northanger Abbey'* & *'Persuasion'* B. C. Southam
JANE AUSTEN: *'Sense and Sensibility'*, *'Pride and Prejudice'* & *'Mansfield Park'*
  B. C. Southam
BECKETT: *Waiting for Godot* Ruby Cohn
WILLIAM BLAKE: *Songs of Innocence and Experience* Margaret Bottrall
CHARLOTTE BRONTË: *'Jane Eyre'* & *'Villette'* Miriam Allott
EMILY BRONTË: *Wuthering Heights* Miriam Allott
BROWNING: *'Men and Women'* & *Other Poems* J. R. Watson
CHAUCER: *Canterbury Tales* J. J. Anderson
COLERIDGE: *'The Ancient Mariner'* & *Other Poems* Alun R. Jones & W. Tydeman
CONRAD: *'Heart of Darkness'*, *'Nostromo'* & *'Under Western Eyes'* C. B. Cox
CONRAD: *The Secret Agent* Ian Watt
DICKENS: *Bleak House* A. E. Dyson
DICKENS: *'Hard Times'*, *'Great Expectations'* & *'Our Mutual Friend'* Norman Page
DICKENS: *'Dombey and Son'* & *'Little Dorrit'* Alan Shelston
DONNE: *Songs and Sonets* Julian Lovelock
GEORGE ELIOT: *Middlemarch* Patrick Swinden
GEORGE ELIOT: *'The Mill on the Floss'* & *'Silas Marner'* R. P. Draper
T. S. ELIOT: *Four Quartets* Bernard Bergonzi
T. S. ELIOT: *'Prufrock'*, *'Gerontion'* & *'Ash Wednesday'* B. C. Southam
T. S. ELIOT: *The Waste Land* C. B. Cox & Arnold P. Hinchliffe
T. S. ELIOT: *Plays* Arnold P. Hinchliffe
HENRY FIELDING: *Tom Jones* Neil Compton
E.M. FORSTER: *A Passage to India* Malcolm Bradbury
WILLIAM GOLDING: *Novels 1954–64* Norman Page
HARDY: *The Tragic Novels* R. P. Draper
HARDY: *Poems* James Gibson & Trevor Johnson
HARDY: *Three Pastoral Novels* R. P. Draper
GERARD MANLEY HOPKINS: *Poems* Margaret Bottrall
HENRY JAMES: *'Washington Square'* & *'The Portrait of a Lady'* Alan Shelton
JONSON: *Volpone* Jonas A. Barish
JONSON: *'Every Man in his Humour'* & *'The Alchemist'* R. V. Holdsworth
JAMES JOYCE: *'Dubliners'* & *'A Portrait of the Artist as a Young Man'* Morris Beja
KEATS: *Odes* G.S. Fraser
KEATS: *Narrative Poems* John Spencer Hill
D.H. LAWRENCE: *Sons and Lovers* Gamini Salgado
D.H. LAWRENCE: *'The Rainbow'* & *'Women in Love'* Colin Clarke
LOWRY: *Under the Volcano* Gordon Bowker
MARLOWE: *Doctor Faustus* John Jump
MARLOWE: *'Tamburlaine the Great'*, *'Edward II'* & *'The Jew of Malta'* J. R. Brown
MARLOWE: *Poems* Arthur Pollard
MAUPASSANT: *In the Hall of Mirrors* T. Harris
MILTON: *Paradise Lost* A. E. Dyson & Julian Lovelock
O'CASEY: *'Juno and the Paycock'*, *'The Plough and the Stars'* & *'The Shadow of a
  Gunman'* Ronald Ayling
EUGENE O'NEILL: *Three Plays* Normand Berlin
JOHN OSBORNE: *Look Back in Anger* John Russell Taylor
PINTER: *'The Birthday Party'* & *Other Plays* Michael Scott
POPE: *The Rape of the Lock* John Dixon Hunt
SHAKESPEARE: *A Midsummer Night's Dream* Antony Price
SHAKESPEARE: *Antony and Cleopatra* John Russell Brown
SHAKESPEARE: *Coriolanus* B. A. Brockman

SHAKESPEARE: *Early Tragedies* Neil Taylor & Bryan Loughrey
SHAKESPEARE: *Hamlet* John Jump
SHAKESPEARE: *Henry IV Parts I and II* G.K. Hunter
SHAKESPEARE: *Henry V* Michael Quinn
SHAKESPEARE: *Julius Caesar* Peter Ure
SHAKESPEARE: *King Lear* Frank Kermode
SHAKESPEARE: *Macbeth* John Wain
SHAKESPEARE: *Measure for Measure* C. K. Stead
SHAKESPEARE: *The Merchant of Venice* John Wilders
SHAKESPEARE: *'Much Ado About Nothing' & 'As You Like It'* John Russell Brown
SHAKESPEARE: *Othello* John Wain
SHAKESPEARE: *Richard II* Nicholas Brooke
SHAKESPEARE: *The Sonnets* Peter Jones
SHAKESPEARE: *The Tempest* D. J. Palmer
SHAKESPEARE: *Troilus and Cressida* Priscilla Martin
SHAKESPEARE: *Twelfth Night* D. J. Palmer
SHAKESPEARE: *The Winter's Tale* Kenneth Muir
SPENSER: *The Faerie Queene* Peter Bayley
SHERIDAN: *Comedies* Peter Davison
STOPPARD: *'Rosencrantz and Guildenstern are Dead', 'Jumpers' & 'Travesties'*
  T. Bareham
SWIFT: *Gulliver's Travels* Richard Gravil
SYNGE: *Four Plays* Ronald Ayling
TENNYSON: *In Memoriam* John Dixon Hunt
THACKERAY: *Vanity Fair* Arthur Pollard
TROLLOPE: *The Barsetshire Novels* T. Bareham
WEBSTER: *'The White Devil' & 'The Duchess of Malfi'* R. V. Holdsworth
WILDE: *Comedies* William Tydeman
VIRGINIA WOOLF: *To the Lighthouse* Morris Beja
WORDSWORTH: *Lyrical Ballads* Alun R. Jones & William Tydeman
WORDSWORTH: *The 1807 Poems* Alun R. Jones
WORDSWORTH: *The Prelude* W. J. Harvey & Richard Gravil
YEATS: *Poems 1919–35* Elizabeth Cullingford
YEATS: *Last Poems* Jon Stallworthy

Issues in Contemporary Critical Theory Peter Barry
Thirties Poets: 'The Auden Group' Ronald Carter
Tragedy: Developments in Criticism R.P. Draper
Epic Ronald Draper
Poetry Criticism and Practice: Developments since the Symbolists A.E. Dyson
Three Contemporary Poets: Gunn, Hughes, Thomas A.E. Dyson
Elizabethan Poetry: Lyrical & Narrative Gerald Hammond
The Metaphysical Poets Gerald Hammond
Medieval English Drama Peter Happé
The English Novel: Developments in Criticism since Henry James Stephen Hazell
Poetry of the First World War Dominic Hibberd
The Romantic Imagination John Spencer Hill
Drama Criticism: Developments since Ibsen Arnold P. Hinchliffe
Three Jacobean Revenge Tragedies R.V. Holdsworth
The Pastoral Mode Bryan Loughrey
The Language of Literature Norman Page
Comedy: Developments in Criticism D.J. Palmer
Studying Shakespeare John Russell Brown
The Gothic Novel Victor Sage
Pre-Romantic Poetry J.R. Watson

CONTENTS

ACKNOWLEDGEMENTS

E. M. Forster, *The Hill of Devi* (Edward Arnold (Publishers) Ltd); *Writers at Work: the 'Paris Review' interviews*, ed. Malcolm Cowley (Martin Secker & Warburg Ltd and the Viking Press Inc.; © Paris Review Inc. 1957, 1958); 'Forster's "Wobblings" ', from *Aspects of E. M. Forster* (Mr Oliver Stallybrass and Edward Arnold (Publishers) Ltd); 'Mr E. M. Forster's New Novel', from the *Spectator* (28 June 1924) (Mr L. P. Hartley); Ralph Wright, New Novels review, from *New Statesman*, XXIII (21 June 1924); J. B. Priestley, review of five novels, from *London Mercury*, LVII (July 1924) (A. D. Peters & Co.); Peter Burra, Introduction to *A Passage to India* (Everyman Library edition) (Mrs Helen P. Moody); Virginia Woolf, 'The Novels of E. M. Forster', from *The Death of the Moth and Other Essays* (Mr Leonard Woolf and the Hogarth Press Ltd; © Harcourt, Brace & World Inc. 1942); Lionel Trilling, *E. M. Forster* (Chatto & Windus Ltd; © New Directions Publishing Corporation 1943); E. K. Brown, *Rhythm in the Novel* (University of Toronto Press); Reuben A. Brower, *The Fields of Light* (© Oxford University Press Inc. 1951); Gertrude M. White, '*A Passage to India*: Analysis and Revaluation', from *PMLA* LXVIII (September 1953) (Modern Language Association of America); James McConkey, 'The Prophetic Novel: *A Passage to India*', from *The Novels of E. M. Forster* (Cornell University Press; © Cornell University 1956); Frederick C. Crews, '*A Passage to India*', from *E. M. Forster: The Perils of Humanism* (Oxford University Press and Princeton University Press); an abridged version of John Beer, 'The Undying Worm', from *The Achievement of E. M. Forster* (Chatto & Windus Ltd and Barnes & Noble Inc.); Frank Kermode, 'The One Orderly Product', from *Puzzles and Epiphanies: Essays and Reviews 1958–1961* (Routledge & Kegan Paul Ltd and Chilmark Press Inc.).

GENERAL EDITOR'S PREFACE

EACH of this series of Casebooks concerns either one well-known and influential work of literature or two or three closely linked works. The main section consists of critical readings, mostly modern, brought together from journals and books. A selection of reviews and comments by the author's contemporaries is also included, and sometimes comments from the author himself. The Editor's Introduction charts the reputation of the work from its first appearance until the present time.

What is the purpose of such a collection? Chiefly, to assist reading. Our first response to literature may be, or seem to be, 'personal'. Certain qualities of vigour, profundity, beauty or 'truth to experience' strike us, and the work gains a foothold in our mind. Later, an isolated phrase or passage may return to haunt or illuminate. Where did we hear that? we wonder – it could scarcely be better put.

In these and similar ways appreciation begins, but major literature prompts to very much more. There are certain facts we need to know if we are to understand properly. Who were the author's original readers, and what assumptions did he share with them? What was his theory of literature? Was he committed to a particular historical situation, or to a set of beliefs? We need historians as well as critics to help us with this. But there are also more purely literary factors to take account of: the work's structure and rhetoric; its symbols and archetypes; its tone, genre and texture; its use of language; the words on the page. In all these matters critics can inform and enrich our individual responses by offering imaginative recreations of their own.

For the life of a book is not, after all, merely 'personal'; it is more like a tripartite dialogue, between a writer living 'then', a reader living 'now', and whatever forces of survival and honour link the two. Criticism is the public manifestation of this dialogue, a witness to the continuing power of literature to arouse and excite. It illuminates the possibilities and rewards of the dialogue, pushing 'interpretation' as far forward as it can go.

And here, indeed, is the rub: how far can it go? Where does 'interpretation' end and nonsense begin? Why is one interpretation superior to another, and why does each age need to interpret for itself? The critic knows that his insights have value only in so far as they serve the text, and that he must take account of views differing sharply from his own. He knows that his own writing will be judged as well as the work he writes about, so that he cannot simply assert inner illumination or a differing taste.

The critical forum is a place of vigorous conflict and disagreement, but there is nothing in this to cause dismay. What is attested is the complexity of human experience and the richness of literature, not any chaos or relativity of taste. A critic is better seen, no doubt, as an explorer than as an 'authority', but explorers ought to be, and usually are, well equipped. The effect of good criticism is to convince us of what C. S. Lewis called 'the enormous extension of our being which we owe to authors'. A Casebook will be justified only if it helps to promote the same end.

A single volume can represent no more than a small selection of critical opinions. Some critics have been excluded for reasons of space, and it is hoped that readers will follow up the further suggestions in the Select Bibliography. Other contributions have been severed from their original context, to which some readers may wish to return. Indeed, if they take a hint from the critics represented here, they certainly will.

A. E. DYSON

INTRODUCTION

E. M. FORSTER had not published a work of fiction for fourteen years when, in 1924, he produced his fifth and most famous novel *A Passage to India*. The book was acclaimed and it is now recognized as one of the great classics of the twenties and of the twentieth century. Even so, Forster has not followed it with another novel. He celebrated his ninetieth birthday on 1 January 1969; but the book he published forty-five years earlier is the most recent novel we have to remember him by. And so we regard him very much as a novelist of the earlier part of the century. Most of his writing in fact belongs to the Edwardian period, and in a television interview of a few years back he rather gave the impression that this was his essential fictional world: '. . . I think one of the reasons why I stopped writing novels is that the social aspect of the world changed so much. I had been accustomed to write about the old-fashioned world with its homes and its family life and its comparative peace. All that went, and though I can think about the new world I cannot put it into fiction.' But of course *A Passage to India* is not that kind of book; it is one of the most inclusive and ranging novels ever written. It is hardly about homes, family life and peace; it is hardly – in its central political and spiritual themes – old-fashioned. And as it is adventurous in matter, so it is in technique. It represents, in fact, a marked change from anything Forster had ever done before, and shows him confronting a new kind of experience in a new way. Three years after it appeared, Forster published another book, *Aspects of the Novel* (1927), a discussion of the novel-form as such. What is particularly striking about the book is that it represents a profound attempt to reconcile modernism, formalism, experimentalism in the novel with its simple atavistic functions of telling a story and creating interesting characters. Forster's stress in the work is that the novel must deal both with 'life by time' and 'life by value', must deal both in material and spiritual matters. Forster had always done this in his fiction; but *A Passage to India* surely represents his profoundest and fullest effort, humanly and technically, at the task.

Forster himself seems not to have thought so. He is said to have felt on finishing the book that it was a failure; and the novel of his he most prefers is the earlier *The Longest Journey*. But with some important exceptions most critics, from the time of its appearance up to today, have tended to regard *A Passage to India* as the culmination of Forster's career. Lionel Trilling picked out *Howards End* as 'undoubtedly Forster's masterpiece'; Rose Macaulay appears, in her *The Writings of E. M. Forster* (1938), to prefer the earlier novels for their social comedy; Angus Wilson shares the author's preference for *The Longest Journey*. Otherwise criticism of Forster has tended more and more to focus on this book: perhaps even to an unfair extent. In doing so, however, it may simply have proved a point Glen O. Allen made about the novel: that in the years since its publication it has enjoyed the somewhat paradoxical status of 'being valued without being understood'.[1] It is certainly true that few other novels have produced such a *variety* of reading and emphasis, such a critical multiplicity of opinion. The range of emphases has been extraordinarily wide. Some critics have seen it as eminently a social comedy, others as a religious novel. Some have seen it as very much a novel of a traditional type, drawing on the techniques of Victorian fiction to establish a wide social panorama and a close relationship between author and reader; others have seen it as eminently a modernist or symbolist novel. Some critics have seen it as a statement of twentieth-century liberal hope, a novel about the joining together of faiths, creeds and races; others have seen it as a profound statement of twentieth-century despair and nihilism. The book may have been widely liked; it has certainly been very differently read, as this collection of essays shows.

[1] Glen O. Allen, 'Structure, Symbol and Theme in E. M. Forster's *A Passage to India*', *PMLA* LXX (Dec 1955) 934–54.

How and when was the book written? Even this question can encourage different interpretations: since it does make a difference whether we consider the book as a novel of the twenties, responding to the pessimistic collapse in the progressive dreams of the pre-war period, or as a novel that comes out of the same fictional environment as his earlier four books, all published in the Edwardian period. The novel was certainly written 'across' the war, and must inevitably have been affected by it; I would myself say that the war has a great deal to do with its vision, and that in that sense it is very much a novel of the 1920s, when fiction shows a marked, experimental turn away from confidence in the onward march of society and history.

In April, 1922, [reports Rose Macaulay[1]] Mr Forster wrote in his diary: 'Have read my Indian fragment with a view to continuing it.' The Indian fragment had been written after the 1912 visit; it expanded, through 1922 and 1923, into the novel *A Passage to India*, which bears obvious marks of originating from two different periods in the uneasy social history of Indian and Anglo-Indian[2] relationships. . . . A good many things had happened to Indians and to British India in the ten years between Mr Forster's two visits; the date of the novel is apparently approximately that of the earlier visit. . . . The European war is apparently still ahead.

Actually, Forster indicates in his notes to the new Everyman edition of the novel that the war Aziz foresees is the Second World War; but Miss Macaulay's point has imaginative truth. A good deal of what is in the book must draw on pre-war India. Forster started his first version of the book during or after the visit he made to India in 1912–13. He then set it aside, and partly because of the war. After the war was over, in 1921, he returned to India, to

[1] Rose Macaulay, *The Writings of E. M. Forster* (1938).
[2] i.e. English resident in India. 'Since I am dealing with past events, my vocabulary is often antiquated. For instance I call English people "Anglo-Indians". And throughout I use "India" in the old, and as it seems to me the true, sense of the word to designate the whole subcontinent.' E. M. Forster, in Preface to *The Hill of Devi* (London and New York, 1953). So do many of the critics and reviewers in this volume; and so, of course, does Forster in *A Passage to India* itself.

act as private secretary to the Maharajah of the state of Dewas Senior.[1] This second visit made him return to the story, but it also made him revise it. In part this must have been normal authorial dissatisfaction; it also must have been due to the fact that India had indeed changed, as he himself noted in his comment on writing the novel (see p. 27 below). The record of the manuscript, which is discussed by Oliver Stallybrass in this Casebook (pp. 32–43), is revealing. It shows that, although Forster made considerable changes in the earlier 1913 draft he did not discard it, nor completely restructure the whole book imaginatively. It also shows that Forster seems to have 'stuck' at the point of the incident in the caves, and was apparently uncertain how he would develop or explain these events: especially with regard to Aziz and Adela. Indeed, Forster's decision to intensify the sinister uncertainty of the double incident in the caves probably explains the basic reinvigoration that the book was given when Forster picked it up again. All this does suggest that in some of its detail and its imaginative assumption the novel is pre-war. It also suggests that the novel reflects new obsessions and observations Forster brought to the novel in coming back to it – and which were the result not only of revisiting India, but also of being exposed to the new facts of life in the English 1920s.

Whatever explanation one gives, though, I think we do need to accept that *A Passage to India* is considerably different from any of Forster's earlier works. Forster was born in 1879, and his most crucial creative period was before the First World War. He had acquired many important ideas and influences at Cambridge, notably from the philosophy of G. E. Moore and the kind of environment, stressing good personal relations and hopeful humanism, which produced it. His early novels are social comedies that bear a marked debt to Samuel Butler and Meredith, and they are clearly linked to – however much they may vary from – the tradition of comedy of manners-and-morals so important to the nineteenth-century English novel. All of Forster's earlier novels had come out in a fairly brief period, between 1905 and

[1] The two visits are both recorded in his memoir *The Hill of Devi* – a book which provides useful background for the novel.

1910. The first three – *Where Angels Fear to Tread* (1905), *The Longest Journey* (1907) and *A Room with a View* (1908) – are social-moral comedies of great distinction. That is to say, they explore critically a relatively stable social world, in which the Forsterian virtues and values – the worth of the developed over the undeveloped heart; the worth of spontaneous passion over calculating moralism; the worth of giving oneself to the risks of the imagination and of the unseen – are explored amidst a group of characters in many ways conventionally upper middle class, whose dilemmas are really those of falling in love, making marriages and having property. Forster's distinction in these novels really comes from two linked sources. The first is the sheer *complexity* of his moral and cultural critique. His attitudes are liberal, humanist, reformist, romantic; and yet they are constantly being questioned from the standpoint of a quizzical moral realism by the author himself. The second perhaps explains the first; for it becomes apparent through these novels that what marks Forster's work is not only spiritual and moral curiosity but also spiritual and moral control, a kind of good sense which has to do with the way in which art can be considered to be *true*. Art may illuminate our lives by fantasy; or by making elegant formal orders; or by pursuing, finally, a standard of wisdom and truth. Forster clearly believes it should do the last of these things; and hence his conviction that art has a humanist power, has a central role to perform in the culture as a whole. This humanist view of art, and this moral scepticism, is apparent in all of Forster's novels; which in one sense can be taken as the adventures of the liberal humanist mind in this century.[1] But first with *Howards End* (1910), and then, more fundamentally, with *A Passage to India*, these emphases change, even if the basic themes remain. *Howards End* is very much a Condition-of-England novel, and its subject is the romantic, organic wholeness of the community. 'Only connect! . . . and human love will be seen at its height' is the theme that runs through it; the seen and

[1] This aspect of Forster is magnificently elaborated in Lionel Trilling's *E. M. Forster* (New York, 1943; London, 1944). Brian Cox interestingly attacks it in *The Free Spirit* (Oxford, 1963).

the unseen, the public and the private, the prose and the passion
must all be drawn together, and the feminine, modern intelligentsia and the new businessmen, the two main groups of the
novel, must come together and try to see things whole. But
Forster at the same time shows a process of historical acceleration
at work which clearly threatens his characters and his hopes for
them. The 'sense of flux' is growing, the 'civilization of luggage'
is advancing, and English society is moving into a new phase in
which hope and fulfilment seem less possible. And this sense of
serious historical unease is obviously even greater in *A Passage
to India*. And at the same time this is linked with a principle of
spiritual vacancy: the 'panic and emptiness' of *Howards End*
which of course returns more bleakly in the Indian novel. The
fear that the world is not made for man and does not instruct man
is an important turn-of-the-century dilemma in art, because it is
the disillusionment of romanticism. And this becomes a sharpen-
ing theme in Forster's later novels. So these uneasy elements that
had become marked in *Howards End* are surely much more fully
developed still in *A Passage to India* – a book that, it seems to
me, challenges itself in all sorts of directions in pursuing Forster's moral realism to the most profound questioning of hope,
meaning and connection that he ever produced.

A Passage to India is both a very full and genial book, and a very
bleak one. It contains some of Forster's richest and most extended social observation, and also one of the darkest evocations
of anarchy and historical disorder we have had in fiction, in its
dark discovery in the caves: 'Everything exists; nothing has
value.' This may seem to be a judgement that it was fashionably
easy to come to in the 1920s (or indeed for that matter now).
But Forster doesn't come to it easily, and he creates its meaning
by giving in his novel a world sufficiently vast and various for us
to recognize the way in which all faith can be challenged. For
he creates a world in which men believe so many things, where
spirit is held to take so many forms, and where man and his
meanings are utterly dwarfed by a nature that seems to lie beyond
the rule of men, civilization or even time itself. The novel begins

by placing man in India and then in the universe, spatial and temporal; and it continues to do so. It is not simply in that dark vision, which in any case is not the only vision in the novel, but in the making of a large fictional world in which that vision can have a meaning, that *A Passage to India* acquires its remarkable grandeur. And that world which any vision worthy of being a vision in the book must include is not just a religious world, a world of belief; nor just a natural world, or a social world or a political world. All of these things are there, and being there they must be put in relation. In each of these worlds, the moral and spiritual contradictions are seen, explored, worked; and so the novel is 'stretched out' to a vast inclusiveness. The inclusiveness may mean anarchy; but, again, the vision of anarchy in the cave is not the whole book. For the traditional Forster hope – 'Only connect' – is clearly present even in this unconnected and contingent world. Forster seeks to make even this full, varied and yet in many ways meaningless world fall into relation. Against Mrs Moore's vision of nothingness, there is Godbole's vision of completeness. And, just as he creates two such visions, Forster also creates two 'tones' in the novel by which we might see these: one which is 'poetic' and the other which is 'comic', one which sees muddle as mystery and the other which sees mystery as muddle.

All this is why *A Passage to India* is a large, mysterious and modern book: why, in fact, it is difficult to read. As we start reading it, it leads our human sympathies gently and easily, with a familiar Forster charm; and we will not find it a difficult novel in the sense, say, that *Ulysses* is. The problems, as they develop, are really problems of emphasis. For instance, it is in many respects a political novel – as Peter Burra put it, 'a novel no student of the Indian question could disregard'. But at the same time we must feel that, although politics matter in this book, they are only a part of what matters, for Forster is concerned with moving beyond the public world to a personal world – that world of personal relationships and of 'good will plus culture and intelligence' that we associate with Mrs Moore at the beginning and with Fielding. On the other hand, that cultured humanism itself has some severe challenges in the novel; for it would seem that it depends upon a norm of man centred in the Mediterranean, and it is severely challenged by India. And of course it is challenged not just by Indian politics, by the problems of the Imperial relationship; but also by the land, by geography and nature. So, as we move beyond the social and public web, with its imagery of nets, prisons, order and system, into a more 'natural' world where the truth of the heart can be expressed and indoors and outdoors meet, we start to find a freer world and then begin to find that it is not, entirely, free. The more natural world is also a world in which men can be 'mud, moving'; in which nature can be implacable; and in which the rejection of order and rationality can lead to a fatalistic acceptance of misery and worthlessness. For man is dwarfed, here in India, and nature different. The orders, judgements and values that seem familiar in England (those, for instance, of Forster's own earlier novels) obviously cannot serve as they did. And gradually we find that this is a novel in which the human world, and humanism itself, are placed against larger forces. A central character, Mrs Moore, dies suddenly; the human sequence of events starts to give way to a less direct sequence of themes and patterns; and then, in its muddled way, humanity seems to come back at the end. But the place, the conditions affecting relationship, even some of the characters, are new. And the novel ends on a discouragement to the human relationships. Is it simply a political discouragement, which would leave an historical hope in the air? It is in fact more, for the earth and the sky are also discouraging. But perhaps they are simply reminding us that human life is not all, and that we will all connect one to another in a world beyond? That would be hopeful too, but there is also the suggestion that we do not know that there is such a world beyond; that human life is all there is, and so the true relationship will never be given.

The question of what aspect of the novel, what mode in it, is dominant, is one that has bewildered critics greatly, and this volume will show some of the results. My own views are developed in the last essay in this Casebook (pp. 224–42), but they will be seen to disagree with several of the essays before it. And disagreement will undoubtedly continue as the importance and fascination of the novel grows increasingly apparent. On the whole, modern criticism has tended to take what I have said so far, as recognizable; and to proceed onward from there. In my own essay in this volume I have distinguished between the 'human plot' and the 'verbal plot' of the novel. The distinction in fact applies perfectly well to all novels; but it has a special significance for symbolist or modernist works because of their preoccupation with unifying the *form* of the action, its rhetorical design rather than its human logic. It would seem to me fairly evident that putting the 'human' and the 'verbal' plots of the novel into right relation is the great critical task. Generally the earlier critics tended to emphasize the social and political aspects of the book – as Trilling does (pp. 77–92). But Trilling suggests (in this fairly early piece (1943)) that the novel had an unusual imbalance between the plot and the story: 'The characters are of sufficient size for the plot; they are not large enough for the story – and that indeed is the point of the story.' More recently, when the novel has been subjected to a great deal of close analysis, the formal problems of the novel have been much discussed. In particular, two emphases have emerged. One derives from a sense that the book is a novel of 'mystery' and has a revelation to make; the other, not unrelated to the first, derives from Trilling's sense that there is an unusual constructional principle involved. So there has been growing stress on Forster's formal effects; in particular, on the way our attention is persistently directed toward repetitions, parallels, recurrences, symbols. Peter Burra noticed this in the 1930s (pp. 61–72), and indeed Forster draws attention to this way of developing a novel in his own *Aspects of the Novel* (1927). He praised Burra's observation, and it has since been extensively developed in criticism. As Burra and more systematically E. K. Brown (pp. 93–113) point out, themes run on, thoughts and insights pass mysteriously from character to character and become part of the narrative voice. This tends to diminish our sense of the characters as individuals, and to enhance our sense of the common world they share and the rhythms and themes that run through it. Brown suggests that this gives a quality of numinous or prophetic vision to the entire work. Other critics have gone even further. They have held that the universe of the novel is invested with a philosophy – some have said the Hindu philosophy, or the Godbole philosophy.[1] Wilfred Stone is not the only critic to see the book moving toward a vision of universal oneness: 'There is no getting out of this, our common boat. Not only are we related, each to each, as persons, but we partake also of the earth, sky, and water, of mud, temples, and bacteria; of oranges, crystals, and birds – and of the unseen as well.'[2]

On the other hand, critics such as James McConkey (pp. 154–64) and Reuben A. Brower (pp. 114–31) find that rhythm and symbol are crucial features of the novel, but they doubt whether this points to a vision of universal wholeness. As Brower puts it: 'Forster's pattern leads to no such resolution. Playing, sometimes capriciously, with every possible meaning of an experience, he cannot reach conclusions.' And another kind of question is raised by Frank Kermode's brief but highly interesting essay (pp. 216–23). Kermode points out that Forster's aesthetics are basically symbolist and share a great deal with the movement of aesthetics in the early part of the century. But he also reminds us that Forster, while stressing that art is the 'one orderly product' and must have artistic wholeness, has said that this depends considerably on 'faking'. In short, the real effort of the artist's imagination goes into bringing the materials of his world into totality or aesthetic consonance. Kermode stresses the range of experience Forster attempts to cover, but he questions whether the totality can really enter the world, can come under the rule of time. Another way of posing the problem is to say that, although an artist may believe that there is a pattern in things, a sense of a whole beyond the parts, he may believe this either formally or spiritually, so to

[1] One bold critic, though, has suggested that Godbole is a somewhat evil character. David Shusterman, 'The Curious Case of Professor Godbole: *A Passage to India* Re-examined', in *PMLA* LXXVI (Sept 1961) 426–35.

[2] Wilfred Stone, *The Cave and the Mountain: A Study of E. M. Forster* (Stanford and London, 1966).

speak. There can be that patterning which is characteristic of what we do when we create art; that making of form, which shows that art is different from life, and can transcend time as we cannot. Or there can be that patterning which amounts to the novelist's asserting that he has a meaning, possesses a t uth; there is a way in which men may know that these consonances are there in the universe. As perhaps we can now see, these amount to two very different interpretations of the novel, even though they may develop from some of the same premises.

These more modern emphases on the technique of *A Passage to India* are of great significance in illuminating the novel. It is, however, important to remind ourselves that we do not *have* to accept their premises completely. There has been a strong tendency in modern criticism to become obsessed by symbols; to read all novels as symbolist constructs; and indeed to regard the 'human plot' as necessarily created by the 'verbal plot', since by logical necessity all novels are made of words. Indeed they are. And indeed *A Passage to India* is a technically self-conscious and sophisticated book. But important as these symbolist readings are in demonstrating the complexity of this or any novel, they tend, often, to demonstrate only one kind of complexity. Thus it becomes possible to suggest that if we can show that the imagery of sun and moonlight run through the novel, we have shown more than if we illustrate just how dense and thorough Forster's representation of Indian society is. Certainly India, and its life in the period of the British Raj, is, for Forster, something more than just a 'symbolic' landscape. A great deal of his imaginative energies go into creating it, and the book creates an intense experience of his own when confronted by India. His India is not divorced from demonstrable social fact. Far from it, indeed; it is given with a great historical and sociological awareness. Equally Forster's attentiveness to the character and characteristics of Indian communities, religions, customs and mores is always apparent. In short, there is another kind of complexity in the book – the complexity of a densely created society and a densely created web of relationships – which is fundamental to the book. Nor is all this passingly illustrative, the background simply to

larger themes. Few critics, in fact, have satisfactorily dealt with
the way in which the book, if it is in certain respects a symbolist
novel, is also a comic one. Lionel Trilling and Frederick C.
Crews have written best about this aspect of Forster, though
they have not really stressed it strongly with regard to this particular work. For of course comedy here means more than his
detached but profoundly observant awareness of manners; it also
means his capacity for ironically questioning his own larger
gestures. That irony is touched on in several essays. But it is
precisely Forster's capacity for filling out the world in its human
detail as a recognizable world of foibles and manners that makes
his novel – at least for this reader – so much denser and fuller than
Virginia Woolf's novels of the twenties, to which, otherwise, it
bears a real resemblance. As Forster himself points out in *Aspects
of the Novel*, a 'rigid pattern' can shut the door on life. It so
'leaves the novelist doing exercises, generally in the drawing
room. . . . To put it in other words, the novel is not capable of
as much artistic development as the drama: its humanity or the
grossness of its material (use whatever phrase you like) hinder it.'
Certainly a satisfactory appraisal of *A Passage to India* will
depend upon our realizing how much realism as well as symbolism there is in it. And Forster, in *Aspects of the Novel*, emphasizes
how in some sense his idea of rhythm and *leitmotif* is a technical
resistance *against* too much formal ordering. In brief, we do not
need to go all the way with the novelists who emphasize these
elements and then deduce a philosophy from them. It may in fact
all be an enabling technique designed to serve other interests.
'Life by time' is, surely, made to live with 'life by value'.

So critics have disagreed, and we in turn may disagree with the
critics. I have tried, in these introductory comments, not to
suggest a conclusion about the book; rather to indicate what
complicated problems the book has set for those who have tried
to read it closely. Is it primarily a novel of 'rhythm' – or a novel
of society and politics and human relationships? Is it an optimistic novel, pointing to the unity hidden behind all things, or a
pessimistic one? But whatever we decide about such questions,

we will, I think, be likely to grant that *A Passage to India* is
a remarkable modern novel. To put it like that is to raise questions not just about what the book is in itself – but how it com-
pares with the other great English novels of the century. It does,
I had better say, seem to me among the greatest: along with
Women in Love or *Lord Jim* or *Ulysses*. It has their fullness of
imaginative force. It assimilates many of the technical aspects of
twentieth-century modernism in art – the sense that art, faced
by social confusion, can produce coherence chiefly through the
exploration of its own symbolic ordering powers – and also many
of its intellectual aspects – its sense of progressive despair or
failed hope through history, its search for a new historiography
for an ominous century. But of course that quality of moral
balance, which (as I said earlier) is one essential aspect of Forster's
liberalism, informs this book too. If it abounds in contradictions,
it withdraws from extremities. The qualities of living intelligence
and questioning control, which in the liberal notion should shine
through works of art, remain vivid and strong. The book
touches us not only through its fullness, and its artistry; it also
touches us through its decency. And that, too, seems a very
important thing for us to say about it.

MALCOLM BRADBURY

PART ONE

Composition: 1912–24

E. M. Forster

I BEGAN this novel before my 1921 visit [to India], and took out the opening chapters with me, with the intention of continuing them. But as soon as they were confronted with the country they purported to describe, they seemed to wilt and go dead and I could do nothing with them. I used to look at them of an evening in my room at Dewas, and felt only distaste and despair. The gap between India remembered and India experienced was too wide. When I got back to England the gap narrowed, and I was able to resume. But I still thought the book bad, and probably should not have completed it without the encouragement of Leonard Woolf. . . .

(from *The Hill of Devi*, 1953)

P. N. Furbank and F. J. H. Haskell

INTERVIEWERS. To begin with, may we ask you again, why did you never finish 'Arctic Summer'? [This was an unfinished novel by Forster, written before *Howards End*; he gave a reading from it at the Aldeburgh Festival in 1951.]

FORSTER. I have really answered this question in the foreword I wrote for the reading. The crucial passage was this:

. . . whether these problems are solved or not, there remains a still graver one. What is going to happen? I had got my antithesis all right, the antithesis between the civilized man, who hopes for an Arctic Summer in which there is time to get things done, and the heroic man. But I had not settled what is going to happen, and that is why the novel remains a fragment. The novelist should, I think, always settle when he starts what is going to happen, what his major event is to be. He may alter this event as he approaches it, indeed he probably will, indeed he probably had better, or the novel becomes tied up and tight. But the sense of a solid mass ahead, a mountain round or over or through which (*he interposed*, 'in this case it would be *through*') the story must somehow go, is most valuable and, for the novels I've tried to write, essential.

INTERVIEWERS. How much is involved in this 'solid mass'? Does it mean that all the important steps in the plot must also be present in the original conception?

FORSTER. Certainly not all the steps. But there must be something, some major object towards which one is to approach. When I began *A Passage to India* I knew that something important happened in the Marabar Caves, and that it would have a central place in the novel – but I didn't know what it would be.

INTERVIEWERS. But if you didn't know what was going to happen to the characters in either instance, why was the case of *A Passage to India* so different from that of 'Arctic Summer'? . . . In both cases you had your antithesis.

FORSTER. The atmosphere of 'Arctic Summer' did not approach the density of what I had in *A Passage to India*. Let me see how to explain. The Marabar Caves represented an area in which concentration can take place. A cavity. (*We noticed that he always spoke of the caves quite literally – as for instance when he interrupted himself earlier to say that the characters had to pass 'through' them.*) They were something to focus everything up: they were to engender an event like an egg. What I had in 'Arctic Summer' was thinner, a background and colour only. . . .

INTERVIEWERS. . . . What was the exact function of the long description of the Hindu festival in *A Passage to India*?

FORSTER. It was architecturally necessary. I needed a lump, or a Hindu temple if you like – a mountain standing up. It is well placed; and it gathers up some strings. But there ought to be more after it. The lump sticks out a little too much.

INTERVIEWERS. To leave technical questions for a moment, have you ever described any type of situation of which you have had no personal knowledge?

FORSTER. The home-life of Leonard and Jacky in *Howards End* is one case. I knew nothing about that. I believe I brought it off.

INTERVIEWERS. How far removed in time do you have to be from an experience to describe it?

FORSTER. Place is more important than time in this matter. Let me tell you a little more about *A Passage to India*. I had a great deal of difficulty with the novel, and thought I would never finish it. I began it in 1912, and then came the war. I took it with me when I returned to India in 1921, but found what I had written wasn't India at all. It was like sticking a photograph on a picture. However, I couldn't *write* it when I was in India. When I got away, I could get on with it. . . .

INTERVIEWERS. A more general question. Would you admit to there being any symbolism in your novels? Lionel Trilling rather seems to imply that there is, in his books on you – symbolism, that is, as distinct from allegory or parable. 'Mrs Moore', he says, 'will act with a bad temper to Adela, but her actions will somehow have a good echo; and her children will be her further echo. . . .'

FORSTER. No, I didn't think of that. But mightn't there be some of it elsewhere? Can you try me with some more examples?

INTERVIEWERS. The tree at Howards End? [A wych-elm, frequently referred to in the novel.]

FORSTER. Yes, that was symbolical; it was the genius of the house. . . .

INTERVIEWERS. Do you pre-figure a shape to your novels?

FORSTER. No, I am too unvisual to do so. (*We found this surprising in view of his explanation of the Hindu festival scene, above.*)

INTERVIEWERS. Does this come out in any other way?

FORSTER. I find it difficult to recognize people when I meet them, though I remember about them. I remember their voices.

INTERVIEWERS. Do you have any Wagnerian leitmotiv system to help you keep so many themes going at the same time?

FORSTER. Yes, in a way, and I'm certainly interested in music and musical methods. Though I shouldn't call it a system. . . .

INTERVIEWERS. We have got a few more questions about your

work as a whole. First, to what degree is each novel an entirely fresh experiment?

FORSTER. To quite a large extent. But I wonder if experiment is the word?

INTERVIEWERS. Is there a hidden pattern behind the whole of an author's work, what Henry James called 'a figure in the carpet'? (*He looked dubious.*) Well, do you like having secrets from the reader?

FORSTER (*brightening*). Ah now, that's a different question. . . . I was pleased when Peter Burra [who wrote the Introduction to the Everyman edition; see pp. 61–72 of this volume] noticed that the wasp upon which Godbole meditates during the festival in *A Passage to India* had already appeared earlier in the novel.

INTERVIEWERS. Had the wasps any esoteric meaning?

FORSTER. Only in the sense that there is something esoteric in India about all animals. I was just putting it in; and afterwards I saw it was something that might return non-logically in the story later.

INTERVIEWERS. How far aware are you of your own technical cleverness in general?

FORSTER. We keep coming back to that. People will not realize how little conscious one is of these things; how one flounders about. They want us to be so much better informed than we are. If critics could only have a course on writers' *not* thinking things out – a course of lectures . . . (*He smiled.*)

INTERVIEWERS. You have said elsewhere that the authors you have learned most from were Jane Austen and Proust. What did you learn from Jane Austen technically?

FORSTER. I learned the possibilities of domestic humour. I was more ambitious than she was, of course; I tried to hitch it on to other things.

INTERVIEWERS. And from Proust?

FORSTER. I learned ways of looking at character from him. The modern subconscious way. He gave me as much of the modern way as I could take. I couldn't read Freud or Jung myself; it had to be filtered to me.

INTERVIEWERS. Did any other novelists influence you technically? What about Meredith?

FORSTER. I admired him – *The Egoist* and the better constructed bits of the other novels; but then that's not the same as his influencing me. I don't know if he did that. He did things I couldn't do. What I admired was the sense of one thing opening into another. You go into a room with him, and then that opens into another room, and that into a further one.

INTERVIEWERS. What led you to make the remark quoted by Lionel Trilling, that the older you got the less it seemed to you to matter that an artist should 'develop'.

FORSTER. I am more interested in achievement than in advance on it and decline from it. And I am more interested in works than in authors. The paternal wish of critics to show how a writer dropped off or picked up as he went along seems to me misplaced. I am only interested in myself as a producer. What was it Mahler said? – 'anyone will sufficiently understand me who will trace my development through my nine symphonies'. This seems odd to me; I couldn't imagine myself making such a remark; it seems too uncasual. Other authors find themselves much more an object of study. I am conceited, but not interested in myself in this particular way. Of course I like reading my own work, and often do it. I go gently over the bits that I think are bad.

INTERVIEWERS. But you think highly of your own work?

FORSTER. That was implicit, yes. My regret is that I haven't written a bit more – that the body, the corpus, isn't bigger. I think I am different from other writers; they profess much more worry (I don't know if it is genuine). I have always found writing pleasant, and don't understand what people mean by 'throes of creation'. I've enjoyed it, but believe that in some ways it is good. Whether it will last, I have no idea.

(an interview with Forster at King's College,
Cambridge, 20 June 1952, published in
*Writers at Work: the 'Paris Review'
interviews*, ed. Malcolm Cowley, 1958)

Oliver Stallybrass

E. M. FORSTER once referred to the 'satisfaction' with which
'experts in psychology, and collectors, and researchers into the
process of creation' regard the 'wobblings of authors' as exhibited
in their manuscripts.[1] These people, or those of them within
striking distance of Austin, Texas, have since 1960 been able to
extend their satisfaction to Forster's own 'wobblings'; for in that
year the Humanities Research Center at the University of Texas
acquired from the London Library all the extant manuscripts of
A Passage to India. Since 1965 some of this satisfaction has been
available also to anybody with the patience to unravel Robert L.
Harrison's ingeniously tangled skein of *textus receptus* and
manuscript variants.[2]

This account of the manuscripts may appropriately start with
the circumstances in which they crossed the Atlantic. In 1960 the
London Library, faced with acute financial difficulties, hit on the
idea of an auction sale, all the objects to be sold being specially
presented by members and well-wishers of the Library. E. M.
Forster had been a life member since 1904 and a committee member from 1933 to 1948, and had once described the Library as
catering 'neither for the goose nor for the rat, but for creatures
who are trying to be human. The desire to know more, the desire
to feel more, and, accompanying these but not strangling them,
the desire to help others: here, briefly, is the human aim, and the
Library exists to further it' (*Two Cheers for Democracy*, London,
1951, pp. 313–14). Now he underlined these memorable words
by presenting the manuscripts of his masterpiece. They formed
the sale's *pièce de résistance*, and at £6500 established a new record
price for a manuscript by a living author.

At that time I happened to be Chief Cataloguer at the London
Library; but my cataloguing activities were restricted, during one
of the happiest months of my life, to producing the draft of a
single entry for the Christie sale catalogue. This rate of progress
is not quite as reprehensible as it may seem: the more than 500
pieces of paper of all shapes and sizes arrived in no discernible

order, often had totally unrelated matter on their two sides, and altogether formed a gigantic jigsaw puzzle, some of whose pieces, Forster suggested in a letter, 'you may feel tempted to lose'. Piety prevailed, however, and only two blank pieces of paper and a few rusty paper-clips were discarded.

As publicity for the sale I had been encouraged to write a newspaper article on the manuscripts, and this appeared in the *Guardian*, 20 June 1960. In writing it I assembled much more material than I was able to incorporate in 1000 words, and it is this material, checked and revised in the light of Harrison's indispensable work, which forms the basis of the present essay. The only other published account of the manuscripts, apparently, apart from Harrison's own Introduction with its chapter-by-chapter commentary, is an appendix in George H. Thomson's *The Fiction of E. M. Forster*.[3] This is a valuable study, but its emphases are closely related to a particular interpretation of the novel, and there is room for a more general account of the manuscripts.

I use the plural advisedly: for the first fact to emerge clearly, when I began my sorting operations, was that I was dealing not only with the 'final' manuscript, but with a large quantity of earlier draft material as well. The second discovery was the need for those quotation marks round 'final'. The word has to be used, since Forster insists that there was no later manuscript; but it blurs the remarkable divergence between the manuscripts and the published version, between the jigsaw puzzle and the picture on the lid.

There were, in these circumstances, at least two possible assembly methods open to me. The one I chose was to start by assembling a version which should be (*a*) as complete and (*b*) as late, i.e. as close to the published text, as possible. In most cases there was no conflict between these two aims; but occasionally I had to use my judgement in assigning priority to one or the other. Thus, where an accidental gap of a mere three words could be avoided only by substituting an earlier version of the page in question, it seemed reasonable to accept the tiny gap; where, on the other hand, two consecutive pages of the generally latest version included, on the back of one, a later draft of one sentence of the other, it would have been absurd to reject a complete page for the sake of one sentence.

At the end of this stage I had assembled a version of the novel which, though written (as we shall see) over a decade and containing some inconsistencies, notably over names, is virtually continuous and complete. Many passages present in the published version are absent there – and vice versa – but of definite lacunae there are only six, all minor ones. Three are caused by the loss of, probably, one leaf in each case, and two by the imperfect dovetailing of an interpolated passage; while the sixth, already mentioned, represents a mere three words inadvertently omitted in rewriting.

Physically, this version consists of 399 single leaves, mostly folio or double folio torn in two – though sixty-six leaves have been reduced to a variety of sizes by the author's habit of tearing off, usually at the bottom, material which has been rewritten on another leaf. It is important to note that Forster, in this novel at any rate, never continues on the verso of a leaf, but always on a new recto. Nevertheless, eighty of these 399 leaves bear some writing on their versos. In a very few cases a passage has been written on a verso for interpolation in the following recto; in a few others a verso contains a *later version* of part of the following recto; and a few versos contain working notes or even, occasionally, extraneous matter, such as two fragments (*MPI* 725) of what Forster has identified as abortive attempts at short stories, and also, rather curiously, a transcription of the final dialogue passage from Lawrence's *Women in Love* (*MPI* 724–5).[4] The great majority, however, of these eighty used versos contain discarded draft material, sometimes deleted, sometimes not. In most cases these early drafts on what are now to be regarded as versos relate to the same general area of the book as their rectos, though there are some notable exceptions (e.g. *MPI* 452–3).

It will make for ease of reference if I adopt the terms used by the Humanities Research Center[5] and by Harrison (both of whom appear to have found my classification acceptable),[6] and refer to the main manuscript, just described, as MS. A. MS. B is the name given to the 101 remaining folio manuscripts leaves, including nineteen with versos utilised, which represent in the main variants of passages found in the rectos, and sometimes also the versos, of MS. A. Between MS. B and the versos of MS. A there seems to be no radical distinction – merely the fortuitous one of which discarded leaves came to Forster's hand, and at what stage. Indeed, one continuous fragment (*MPI* 693–7) consists of A387v, B97, A388v, A393v, and B98, and illustrates neatly the problem of classification and the value of Harrison's work in reuniting fragments which I was forced to sunder.

With MS. B my method was to assemble the longest possible continuous passages, and arrange these in the order of their starting-points, in so far as I could determine these with any precision in relation either to MS. A or to the published book. No doubt some of my decisions were arbitrary, and in at least one case (B11; *MPI* 244–5) mistaken; in another (B59; *MPI* 239 and 328–9) it looks as if at some stage a leaf has got turned over so that as regards its 'recto', though not its 'verso', it is badly misplaced.

In addition to the manuscripts proper there is a typescript carbon of nineteen quarto sheets known as MS. C. This includes a discarded epigraph to part I,[7] but consists mainly of a version, intermediate between MS. A and the published book, of various passages, the longest being from chapter xxxvi;* also a typescript half-title page with autograph dedication, and a handwritten title-page which is clearly related to the typescript, and of which I shall have more to say.

Finally there are four folded double folio leaves of corrections and addenda, to which likewise I shall return.

As we have seen, a feature of the version represented by the rectos of MS. A in their final state (and *a fortiori* of earlier versions) is its wide divergence from the published text. Chapter xxxii is unique in diverging only by one word, while a few others, notably I and xxvii–xxxi, offer only minor variants. Elsewhere, not only do the division and even the order of chapters vary – in MS. A chapter vii precedes chapters v and vi – but the entire text

* Chapter numbers refer to the published book, not the manuscripts.

shows so many changes that but for Forster's statement to the
contrary it would be tempting to postulate a later manuscript
version between this one and the author's typescript, which seems
to have constituted the final copy.

Instead, Forster must have made extensive alterations, either
in producing the typescript, or on the typescript, or both. There
are, in fact, several pieces of evidence which between them show
clearly that he did both: the state of a number of the typescript
leaves; the four leaves containing notes, some precise, others less
so ('the whole of this Ch [i.e. XIII] . . . is not quite right'), of
alterations, made or about to be made, on the numbered typescript pages; and those places (*MPI* 4, for example) where, it
seems, Forster grew dissatisfied while typing a page, and re-
drafted a sentence or two on the preceding verso. That he also
retyped some leaves from a corrected carbon copy, and sent the
new leaves to the publisher at a late stage, is suggested by two
typescript leaves of MS. C which, though different from the
book, have evidently been in the hands of the publisher or even
of the printer; and this hypothesis is confirmed by other evidence,
for which I am indebted to Mr B. W. Fagan, among the records
of the London publisher Edward Arnold. Yet another indication
of the complex operations involved in the production of this
novel is the handwritten title-page (MS. C), the joint work of
author and publisher, bearing a pencilled note in the author's
hand: '*Uncorrected Typescript*. N.B. *Edith* Quested becomes
Adela about page 40. *Khan* Bahadur *Nawab* Bahadur in Ch xx' –
a note which suggests, among other things, that the earlier chapters were probably typed out before the later ones were written.

This leads to the question of chronology. The author stated at
one point 'Green ink chapters written *c*. 1913. Adela as Edith or
Janet. Ronnie [*sic*] as Gerald. Rest written 1922–1923', but later
agreed that this description is not quite accurate. First, Ronny
Heaslop, while his surname varies, nowhere appears as Gerald.
Second, the last page of the manuscript is dated 21 January 1924.
Finally, the green-ink–black-ink distinction needs modifying.
The chapters written entirely or substantially in green ink are
I–VII (chapter II having in black ink eight octavo leaves evidently

written at the same period as the rest, and one short interpolated passage); in addition there are green-ink leaves in the main manuscript of chapter XII, and among the supplementary material for chapters VIII, XII and XIV. Now, it seems unlikely that after a decade the author should again have been using green ink, but spasmodically this time instead of consistently. On the other hand, parts at least of the manuscript of chapter VIII, being based on a story about an animal charging a car which the author heard during his second visit to India in 1921[8] (the first had been in 1912–13), must date from the later period. Graphology might settle the question, but other evidence – watermarks, the political flavour of a paragraph in chapter IX (*PI* 111), and the appearance in chapter VIII, for the first time and in full measure, of truncated leaves[9] – suggest that it would be more correct to say 'chapters I–VII and subsequent green-ink leaves written *c.* 1913, rest written 1922 or 1923 to 1924'. In this case, eleven leaves are all that remain of the earlier version for chapters VIII–XIV; though it is possible that chapters IX–XI, which are not essential from a structural point of view, had no existence until the later period. The interesting points in any case are the long interval, and the fact that each creative period followed a visit to India.

Apart from a few pages which are evidently fair copies, the manuscripts are untidy. Mention has already been made of the various sizes to which many leaves have been reduced. Sometimes the matter discarded in this way has first been deleted, sometimes not, and, since the tear is often roughly made, occasional un-deleted but redundant words are to be found. There is much deletion and correction, some of it in pencil, and, to quote the author again, 'scriggles . . . surge up from the margin, they extend tentacles, they interbreed'.[10] Apart from 'scriggles', the margins contain occasional dates (unreliable: two consecutive dates in chapter XX read 9/7/23 and 10/6/23), tallies of words, and question marks, some of which suggest factual points to be verified, others perhaps a vague dissatisfaction. A few chapters have their pages numbered in pencil, but the majority have only what appears to be an indication of how many pages they contain, or once contained, while the numbering of the chapters themselves is erratic and shows traces of alteration, some of it done by the author immediately before delivery to the London Library. As for the actual handwriting, this undoubtedly comes into the category of 'cacography if there is such a word'. (There is.)

The main impression conveyed by the manuscripts, and by their divergences from the book, is of an author who writes fast, and uses the physical act of writing as part of 'the process of creation', not as a mere recording technique. Speed would account for some curious spelling mistakes and for such slips as 'service' for 'surface', 'break' for 'brake', 'their' for 'there', and 'parents' pupils' for 'pupils' parents' (*MPI* 79) – this last, it is amusing to note, occurring in three other fragments (*MPI* 39, 40, 42) as a deliberately introduced slip of the tongue. It is fascinating to compare these first and final versions – some passages have as many as five drafts – and to see a touch of irony added, a wrong note eliminated, an inert snatch of dialogue springing suddenly to life. An author's 'improvements' are not always accepted as such by all his readers – Henry James is a case in point – but few are likely to quarrel with the judgement revealed in the following changes:

'... Mrs Turton takes bribes, red-nose is apparently still a bachelor.' (*MPI* 8)
'*... Mrs Turton takes bribes, Mrs Red-nose does not and cannot, because so far there is no Mrs Red-nose.*' (*PI* 13)

... a family marriage that had been celebrated with imperfect solemnity. (*MPI* 12)
... a family circumcision that had been celebrated with imperfect pomp. (PI 15)[11]

'... the verandah is good enough for an Indian and Mrs Callander takes my carriage and cuts me dead. ...' (*MPI* 28; Aziz is speaking)
'*... the verandah is good enough for an Indian, yes, yes, let him stand, and Mrs Callendar takes my carriage and cuts me dead. ...*' (*PI* 25)

... in case the natives should see the Englishwomen acting. ... (*MPI* 35)
... lest the servants should see their mem-sahibs acting. ... (*PI* 26)

One touch of regret – not conversational regret, but the stab that goes down to the soul – would have made him a different man, and she would have worshipped him. (*MPI* 89)
One touch of regret – not the canny substitute but the true regret from the heart – would have made him a different man, and the British Empire a different institution. (*PI* 54)

He was inaccurate because he desired to honour her. (*MPI* 343)
He was inaccurate because he desired to honour her, and – facts being entangled – he had to arrange them in her vicinity, as one tidies the ground after extracting a weed. (*PI* 165)

. . . he chose to pretend that Mr Das had a sense of justice equal to his own. (*MPI* 471)
. . . he liked to maintain that his old Das really did possess moral courage of the Public School brand. (*PI* 224)

Her particular brand of sensations and opinions – why should they claim so much importance in the world? (*MPI* 476)
Her particular brand of opinions, and the suburban Jehovah who sanctified them – by what right did they claim so much importance in the world, and assume the title of civilisation? (*PI* 226-7)

One could multiply such examples endlessly. In addition, there is a general tendency to convert narrative into dialogue – though occasionally the reverse happens, as when 'a shapeless discussion occurred' (*PI* 47) replaces the actual discussion (*MPI* 72) – and to eliminate explanatory comment of the 'he was lying' type (*MPI* 607). Some passages in the book – including the famous jest about the 'pinko-grey' races (*PI* 66) and the speech of Aziz about the need of Indians for 'kindness, more kindness, and even after that more kindness' (*PI* 122) – are absent from the manuscripts; while the latter contain much material that was finally rejected. Forster's admirers are likely to relish many such passages as the account of Fielding's past (*MPI* 107-9), that of the chauffeur's origins (*MPI* 168), and the rumours of Adela's death: 'By four o'clock Adela was dead or dying all over the Civil Station and as far as the Railway. North of the railway she was known to be ill. . . .' (*MPI* 395). They may even be tempted to feel that too many babies have gone out with the bathwater;

but in most cases they will probably agree that the interests of economy and form have rightly prevailed.

Some of the changes affect the characterisation perceptibly. Aziz appears to have been observed with almost complete clarity from the outset, but Fielding would have been a subtly different person if he had been allowed to retain his motor-bicycle (*MPI* 219), to smoke cigarettes instead of a pipe (*MPI* 409; *PI* 194), and to practise the characteristic Wilcox ritual of looking at his watch (*MPI* 79; cf *Howards End* (1947 ed.) pp. 107, 201, 222, 232). Adela (alias Violet, alias Janet, alias Edith) is more aggressive in the earlier manuscript chapters – 'she had little self-control and had learnt[12] at Cambridge that one ought to show when one's bored' (*MPI* 82) – more like the suffragette *manquée* of the 1960 London stage production. Other examples are noted by Harrison.

Inconsistencies of name are not without significance: at one stage Ronny bore the surname Moore, which, combined with other evidence, suggests that at that period part III of the novel had not been projected. The numbering and renumbering of chapters have already been mentioned, and have their own interest: one most effective change, isolating and emphasising as it does the almost personal power of the climate, is the renumbering of what was originally a single chapter as the present chapters IX, X, and XI.

Turning to more obvious structural issues, we find in almost every chapter variants of incident: both the engagement and its rupture, for example, are treated very differently in the manuscripts, so is the 'bridge party', so is the trial; above all, so is the expedition to the Marabar caves. It is an interesting fact that, of the 101 leaves of MS. B, no less than fifty-five represent earlier drafts of chapters XIV–XVI, and it is clear that this central episode caused the author an unusual amount of trouble; it seems probable, indeed, that this is one reason why the book was not completed around 1913. (Another may have been the need to refresh his memory of Indian English.) These drafts vary greatly from each other and from the book. In one version (*MPI* 310) the famous account of the echo is given in the form of a dialogue, in the first cave, between Aziz and Adela (Edith); in another (*MPI*

337–8) the echo is linked with Fielding's reflections, not Mrs Moore's, and it is Fielding, not Aziz, who finds the field-glasses, while the two men have apparently been acquainted long enough for Aziz to have 'compelled' Fielding to learn the four lines of Persian poetry which are quoted in chapter 11 (*PI* 22) but are not in MS. A at that point. Some of the writing illustrates well the modest beginnings from which so much of the impressive final version emerges: in one early four-leaf draft Adela, in a supposedly hysterical state, is actually made to say something as wooden and unconvincing as 'Miss Derek, I have been lacking in sympathy myself all my life, I feel' (*MPI* 316).

This fragment of four leaves is perhaps the most intriguing in the entire trove, for it answers unequivocally the question which, *pace* the confident conclusions of some critics, the author has so scrupulously refrained from answering in the book: whether (ignoring the more implausible explanations) Adela was the victim of hallucination or of attempted assault by somebody other than Aziz. In this early stage of the book's genesis, at least, there *was* an assault (*MPI* 315); as is confirmed elsewhere in some working notes headed 'Situation at the catastrophe' (*MPI* 723). This is one of a number of notes scattered around the versos and margins, of which two others may be mentioned as examples of the light they shed on the author's discarded intentions and his methods: the remarkable 'Aziz & Janet drift into one another's arms – then apart' (*MPI* 722), and the marginal note against McBryde's appearance in chapter xviii, 'Introduce him earlier' (*MPI* 364) – as is duly done in chapter v of the book.

Finally the manuscripts shed light on one or two doubtful readings in the published texts. The curious use of 'draggled' (*PI* 220) in the apparent sense of 'tangled' is confirmed (*MPI* 464), as is the substantival use of 'beat up' (*PI* 275; *MPI* 588) where 'heat up' might have been expected – though this may be one of those slips of the pen to which I have referred. On the other hand, future editions of *A Passage to India* will surely have to correct 'Others praised Him without attributes' (*PI* 327) to '... with attributes' (*MPI* 698), 'half dead' (*PI* 331) to 'half deaf' (*MPI* 706), and 'fifty five-hundred' (*PI* 335; *MPI* 716) to the reading from MS. B, 'fifty or five-hundred' (*MPI* 717).[13]

The paramount interest of the manuscripts, however, is the remarkable light they throw on 'the process of creation' and on one of the great English novels; and I cannot end this essay without expressing the hope that other manuscrips of the same author will one day enter the public domain.

SOURCE: *Aspects of E. M. Forster* (1969).

NOTES

1. *The Library*, ser. 5, vol. XIII (1958) 142–3. Forster was reviewing *Authors at Work: an address delivered by Robert H. Taylor at the opening of an exhibition of literary manuscripts at the Grolier Club together with a catalogue of the exhibition by Herman W. Liebert and facsimiles of many of the exhibits* (New York, 1957).

2. *The Manuscripts of 'A Passage to India'* (University Microfilms, Ann Arbor, Mich., 1965), referred to in this essay as *MPI*. Another abbreviation used is *PI* for *A Passage to India* (1947).

3. Wayne State University Press, Detroit, 1967, pp. 261–72. John Colmer has also made use of the manuscripts, or rather of Harrison's edition of them, in *E. M. Forster: A Passage to India* (Arnold, 1967).

4. Though I should not have needed help over this identification, I am in fact indebted for it to Elizabeth Heine of the University of Hawaii.

5. To whose Director and staff I am grateful for answering some of my many questions.

6. Harrison, indeed, appears to endow MS. A with a more unitary status than it possesses when he suggests that 'the direction of the book was fairly well established at the time of writing MS. A' (*MPI* xix). I return later to the complicated question of chronology.

7. The epigraph, of which another version is found on A32v, reads:
Four men went to pray.
The first said to the Muezzin, 'Surely it is not the hour for prayer yet?'
The second said to the first, 'Do not blame the Muezzin.'
The third said to the second, 'Do not blame him for blaming the Muezzin.'
The fourth said, 'Thank God, I am not as these other three.'
The prayers of all four were unheard.

Jalaluddin Rumi

8. See *PI* (Everyman's Library ed., repr. 1957) p. xxix; and *The Hill of Devi* (London, 1953) 89–90.

9. This habit of decapitating (or more commonly depeditating) partially rewritten leaves, in order to use the versos of the discarded segments, may have been acquired under wartime conditions in Egypt; the late H. E. Wortham, who edited the *Egyptian Mail* at the time, told me that Forster's contributions were often written on the backs of envelopes.

10. *The Library*, ser. 5, vol. XIII (1958) 142–3.

11. This alteration may reflect the difference between what was felt mentionable in print in 1913 and in 1923; just as the omission, on which Forster himself has commented (*Abinger Harvest* (1953 ed.) pp. 173–4), from the second edition of *Sense and Sensibility* of a sentence containing the words 'natural daughter' reflected a change in the opposite direction.

12. Perhaps from Stewart Ansell.

13. For drawing my attention to all these points I am indebted to George H. Thomson. In the last example the actual reading of MS. B is '50 or 500'.

Virginia Woolf

MORGAN [Forster] said he felt 'This is a failure,' as he finished the *Passage to India.*

> (from *A Writer's Diary*,
> ed. Leonard Woolf, 1953)

PART TWO

Contemporary Reception: 1924

D. H. Lawrence

(Letter to Martin Secker from Del Monte Ranch, Questa, 23 July 1924)

Dear Secker,

Am reading *Passage to India*. It's good, but makes one wish a bomb would fall and end everything. Life is more interesting in its undercurrents than in its obvious; and E.M. does see people, people and nothing but people ad nauseam . . .

(Letter to John Middleton Murry from Del Monte Ranch, Questa, 3 October 1924)

. . . I'm glad you like the Hopi Dance article. All races have one root, once one gets there. Many stems from one root: the stems never to commingle or 'understand' one another. I agree Forster doesn't 'understand' his Hindu. And India to him is just negative: because he doesn't go down to the root to meet it. But the *Passage to India* interested me very much. At least the repudiation of our white bunk is genuine, sincere, and pretty thorough, it seems to me. Negative, yes. But King Charles *must* have his head off. Homage to the headsman . . .

(from *Collected Letters of D. H. Lawrence*,
ed. Harry T. Moore, 1962)

L. P. Hartley

OF all the novels that have appeared in England this year, Mr Forster's is probably the most considerable. If it had merely been up to his standard, its pre-eminence would scarcely have been challenged; and in its scope and its effect it surpasses his previous books. In them, delightful as they were, evidences of

partiality, imperfect sympathy, eccentricity of outlook so pro-
nounced as sometimes to seem an obsession, spoiled the exquisite
flavour and distinction of his work. Perhaps spoiled is too strong
a word; but they gave it a partisan air, almost an air of propaganda; as though it were Mr Forster's mission to show that all
the evil in the world came out of Philistinism, suburbanism and
the Public Schools. One trembled for the stupid well-meaning
person who blundered into Mr Forster's pages, disturbed his
fawns at their play, and recommended corporal punishment for
them. Such a one did not get off lightly.

Some such distinction between types Mr Forster preserves in
his last, and as we think his best, book. The Anglo-Indians stand
for much that Mr Forster dislikes: insensitiveness, officialdom,
stupidity, repressiveness, rudeness. The Indians are the children
of Nature, affectionate, courteous, eager, irresponsible, wayward.
Mr Forster's heart lies with them, but his sympathy does not
blind him to the defects of their qualities; their impracticability,
their double-dealing, conscious and unconscious, the crust of
shallow intrigue which makes action, when they take it, of none
effect. Nor does he fail to do justice to the redeeming qualities of
their rulers. They are, of course, the qualities that make themselves felt in a crisis; and a crisis is foreign to the spirit of the
East, which does not so much rise as sink to an emergency.

A Passage to India is much more than a study of racial contrasts and disabilities. It is intensely personal and (if the phrase
may be pardoned) intensely cosmic. The problem of the English
in India lies midway between these two greater considerations,
linking them up and illuminating them. To the question, can
the English as a foreign ruling caste arrive at a working arrangement with the Indians? Mr Forster answers perfunctorily, No.
And to the question (more interesting to the novelist), can an
individual Englishman with the best will in the world reach
terms of intimacy with an Indian similarly disposed? Mr Forster
again seems to say, with infinite hesitation and regret, that he
cannot:

'Why can't we be friends now?' said [Fielding] holding him
[Aziz] affectionately. 'It's what I want. It's what you want.'

But the horses didn't want it—they swerved apart; the earth didn't want it, sending up rocks through which riders must pass single file; the temples, the tank, the jail, the palace, the birds, the carrion, the Guest House that came into view as they issued from the gap and saw Mau beneath: they didn't want it, they said in their hundred voices, 'No, not yet,' and the sky said, 'No, not there.'

All the characters except perhaps Fielding, the unconventional Anglo-Indian schoolmaster whom the ladies of the station in their spiteful way called 'not quite pukka', are at the mercy of their moods and nerves. Most novelists take it as a postulate that personality is capable of little variation, that it is within narrow margins determinable and accountable, and on this assumption work out problems of relationship to a logical conclusion. Mr Forster sees human beings very differently. They have little sure hold over themselves; they are subject to skiey influences and 'dangers from the East'; they reach out for a prevailing mood and find it gone. They are infinitely receptive and 'suggestible'. Hence their failure to come into touch with each other. They desire the most intimate spiritual contacts, but they have no assurance of success because they do not know, from one moment to another, where the weight of their desires will lie: gravity pulls their personalities this way and that, they cannot count on themselves. The 'incident' of the Marabar Caves would have been a strain on the most tough-minded person; its effect on the two sensitive ladies who had come out, with the best will in the world, to find what India meant, was little short of disintegrating. It is the central fact of the book, this gloomy expedition arranged with so much solicitude and affection by Dr Aziz to give his guests pleasure. A lesser novelist than Mr Forster could have shown everything going wrong, could have emphasized the tragic waste of Aziz's hospitality and kind intentions, could have blamed Fate. But no one else could have given the affair its peculiar horror, could have so dissociated it from the common course of experience and imagination, could have left it at once so vague and so clear. Unlike many catastrophes in fiction, it seems unavoidable whichever way we look at it; we cannot belittle it by saying that the characters should have behaved more sensibly, the sun need not have been so hot or the scales weighted against happiness. And not only by the accident of the caves does Mr Forster illustrate the incalculable disastrous fluctuations of human personality, but he subtly works in the black magic of India, crudely presented to us in a hundred penny-dreadfuls about the stolen eyes of idols and death-bearing charms.

A Passage to India is a disturbing, uncomfortable book. Its surface is so delicately and finely wrought that it pricks us at a thousand points. There is no emotional repose or security about it; it is for ever puncturing our complacence, it is a bed of thorns. The humour, irony and satire that awake the attention and delight the mind on every page all leave their sting. We cannot escape to the past or the future, because Mr Forster's method does not encourage the growth of those accretions in the mind; he pins us down to the present moment, the discontent and pain of which cannot be allayed by reference to what has been or to what will be. The action of the book is not fused by a continuous impulse; it is a series of intense isolated moments. To overstate the case very much, the characters seem with each fresh sensation to begin their lives again. And that perhaps is why no general aspect or outline of Mr Forster's book is so satisfactory as its details.

(from the *Spectator*, 28 June 1924)

Ralph Wright

IT is a commonplace exaggeration among reviewers to say that the literary world has been waiting breathlessly for Mr X's new book. Thirteen years have passed since Mr Forster's last novel appeared, and even a literary world cannot maintain its breathlessness for so long as that. Yet Mr Forster has never been forgotten, and there are a good many people who, whenever they have found themselves re-reading his earlier books, have felt a certain grudge against an author they knew to be still young for ceasing to try and produce the novel they were persuaded he alone, as representative of his generation, was likely to give them.

Now this generation, we all know, has many faults, but it has above other more brilliant ages one clear virtue, that of truthfulness. Not Truth with a large T perhaps, but at all events a desire to state the facts of a case as fairly and dispassionately as possible. It may not be so interested as other generations in the meaning of the universe, but it tries harder to find out what is happening and has happened. Why, even its historians view the past no longer as a lesson book.

Mr Forster has other great merits as a novelist, but if there is one that stands out far ahead of the others, it is this sensitiveness to truth. He does mean to find out about the characters who in life and still more in novels, are usually viewed as backgrounds against which the more heroic and adorable people can display the obvious virtues. It is not so much that he wishes to stand up for the unpopular; that after all is merely the old game reversed; he is not seeing what can be said for them, he is merely trying to see what they are really like. Of course to do this successfully requires an extremely sensitive mind and a very accurate and subtle sense of words. But these in Mr Forster's case are, one feels, secondary, though all important, things; what comes first is this desire to know how people think and feel and act in relation to one another.

In *A Passage to India* he has chosen a subject of enormous difficulty. Race feeling, or the violent reaction from what seems the intolerable race feeling of our fellows, is strong in every one of us. It is almost impossible to start a conversation on India, at dinner or in a railway carriage, even in this country, without producing a heated quarrel. For in the case of India there is much more than even race feeling, which is strong enough, to disturb us. There is our behaviour to a conquered country. There is a ticklish question of conscience. There is great ignorance. There is a quite genuine hatred of muddling, and a suspicion that whatever we do, go or stay, we shall produce disaster. It is race feeling multiplied by the old Irish situation multiplied by money. There

is hardly one man in a million who can keep his head when the
subject turns up, or one man in a hundred thousand who will try
to. And it is on this almost fratricidal subject that Mr Forster
has chosen to be fair. At least we can be certain of one thing,
that patriots on neither side will bless him for it.

The opening of the book is admirably planned. We are shown
a group of educated Indians discussing quite calmly whether or
not friendship with an Englishman is a possibility. We are used
to this discussion the other way on; and the dispassionateness of
the shifted angle sets the tone of the book from the outset. The
conversation is desultory. It is not, one feels, a set piece of propaganda. The characters are not speaking to an audience and there
are no points to score. And almost at once one falls into Mr
Forster's mood of refusing to score a point for either side, of
realising that there is an interest in people for their own sake and
not as representatives of political idealisms or pawns in the hands
of political or commercial forces. The English are treated as
fairly as the various Indians, they remain even, in spite of their
superior attitude, on the whole the most sympathetic to us.

He spoke sincerely. Every day he worked hard in the court
trying to decide which of two untrue accounts was the less untrue,
trying to dispense justice fearlessly, to protect the weak against
the less weak, the incoherent against the plausible, surrounded
by lies and flattery. That morning he had convicted a railway
clerk of over-charging pilgrims for their tickets, and a Pathan of
attempted rape. He expected no gratitude, no recognition for this,
and both clerk and Pathan might appeal, bribe their witnesses
more effectually in the interval, and get their sentences reversed.
It was his duty. But he did expect sympathy from his own people,
and except from new-comers he obtained it.

The new-comers are his mother and the girl to whom he is
expecting to become engaged. Both of them are anxious to see
India with their own eyes, to judge for themselves, to be fair.

On the Indian side we have among others the Mohammedan
Aziz, a doctor, and the almost incomprehensible Hindoo, Godbole. Aziz seems almost as if he were a portrait, so clearly seen is
he, in his enthusiasms, his volatile feeling, his vagueness, his

quickness to take unreasoning offence, his folly and his limitations. 'He was sensitive rather than responsive. In every remark
he found a meaning, but not always the true meaning, and his
life though vivid was largely a dream.'

For a time all goes on as usual. The mother and the girl make
the acquaintance of Dr Aziz. There is a ridiculous 'Bridge party',
a party meant to bridge the gulf between the English and the
Indians, which naturally only serves to emphasize it. And then
a terrible thing happens. Aziz is accused of an assault upon the
girl. What actually happened we never really know. We only
know that Aziz is innocent, and that one of those ghastly moments
of tension in India between the two populations has arisen:

> The collector could not speak at first. His face was white,
> fanatical, and rather beautiful – the expression that all English
> faces were to wear at Chandrapore for many days. Always brave
> and unselfish, he was now fused by some white and generous
> heat; he would have killed himself, obviously, if he had thought
> it right to do so.

An Englishman with a fair mind dares to take the Indian's side:

> The collector looked at him sternly, because he was keeping
> his head. He had not gone mad at the phrase 'an English girl
> fresh from England', he had not rallied to the banner of race. He
> was still after facts, though the herd had decided on emotion.
> Nothing enrages Anglo-India more than the lantern of reason
> if it is exhibited for one moment after its extinction is decreed.
> All over Chandrapore that day the Europeans were putting aside
> their normal personalities and sinking themselves into their com-
> munity. Pity, wrath, heroism, filled them, but the power of
> putting two and two together was annihilated.

This event, which one is inclined to resent as melodramatic
at first, is of the utmost importance in the scheme of the book.
The evil·thing has happened thereby. Individuals have ceased
their individual existence for the time being, and become part of
one of the herds. Unreason is loose, Indians and English become
angry and futile in equal measure though in different ways. Only
old Godbole, the learned Hindoo, remains unmoved. And he,

though he knows what has happened, asks blandly and politely if the party which has led up to this has been a success? The whole community is momentarily mad, and phrases and catchwords rule the minds of men.

Further than this into the plot it is hardly fair to Mr Forster's readers to go. It is enough to show the problem he has set himself, and stress the sympathy and fairness of his treatment. And this fairness is no judicial fairness. Nothing is further from his mind than the delivery of a judgment. The whole aim is sight and insight – the distinguishing of the individual problem from the obscuring mass.

M. Gide in an excellent passage on Proust tells us how a lady he knew had suffered from bad sight as a child. It was not until she reached the age of twelve that her parents realised this and gave her spectacles. 'Je me souviens si bien de ma joie,' he reports her conversation. 'Lorsque, pour la première fois je distinguai tous les petits cailloux de la cour.' It is in this power of distinguishing 'tous les petits cailloux' where most people see nothing but masses that Mr Forster's special talent seems to lie. And it is from this ability that his special kind of fairness takes its birth. Again and again, even in such a tempting ground as that of the relations between Indian and Anglo-Indian, he refuses to generalise. That he leaves to his characters, and it is clear that it is from this habit of thinking in generalisations that most of their troubles spring. And naturally he comes forward with no solution. At the end of the book we are left with a scene of reconciliation between Dr Aziz and Fielding, the Englishman who had taken his part, and with whom he had subsequently quarrelled:

'Why can't we be friends now?' said the other, holding him affectionately. 'It's what I want. It's what you want.' But the horses didn't want it – they swerved apart; the earth didn't want it, sending up rocks through which riders must pass single file; the temples, the tank, the jail, the palace, the birds, the carrion, the Guest House, that came into view as they issued from the gap and saw Mau beneath: they didn't want it, they said in their hundred voices, 'No, not yet,' and the sky said, 'No, not there.'

The book seems to me to be a real achievement. There are

things in it that I would have otherwise. There is a queer kind of mystery connected with the caves, where the terrible thing occurred, which is never cleared up. This in itself would hardly matter. What does seem to me to matter is a kind of mystical attitude to the caves, a suggestion of nameless horror that it is *impossible* to explain. I do not believe in nameless horrors, and I suspect Mr Forster of doing so. Again, there is no one in the book that one can really care for. But that, on second thoughts, I would perhaps not have altered. It is, I think, an integral part of the book. Its reason is the same as that which refuses to allow Mr Forster to give his heroine any physical attractions. It is a fear of loading the dice.

But even a reader who insists that some characters in a novel should engage his sympathy completely cannot miss the peculiar merits of the book. It is written with great care. It is so full of knowledge and so beautifully perceptive. It is most delicately written. We have had a long time to wait since *Howards End*, and if Mr Forster continues to write like this the waiting is worth it. *A Passage to India* is a better book than any earlier ones. It is as sensitive as they were, it is far better proportioned, and the mind which made it is more mature.

(from the *New Statesman*, XXIII, 21 June 1924)

J. B. Priestley

MR E. M. FORSTER has had a **very** different fate from that of any other member of that group of promising, brilliant young novelists, the 'coming men' of 1910–12. Many of his colleagues, instead of writing themselves 'in', have by this time succeeded in writing themselves out. Mr Forster, after the publication of his very successful *Howards End*, apparently stopped writing fiction, and this new story of Anglo-Indian life is the first novel he has produced for at least twelve years. His return should be regarded by every intelligent reader of fiction as an event. He has brought back his own exquisite **sanity** into the English novel, and his curious sensitiveness, honesty and, perhaps above all, his civilising quality (for surely he is the most civilised writer we have), make some of our more recent discoveries among novelists look very cheap. Once more we are given a real novel, an honest thing in three dimensions, and not an amusing literary gesture, a bag of coloured tricks, seven shillings worth of careless and dishonest autobiography served up with sixpenny worth of creative effort. Everything is present, ideas, character, action, atmosphere – a genuine civilised narrative. While I enjoyed every moment of this book, however, I cannot help feeling sorry that Mr Forster did not choose to mirror contemporary English society in that astonishingly just and sensitive mind of his. Anglo-India is caught here, I imagine, as it has never been caught before, and its sharp divisions, its crushing institutionalism and officialism, its racial and herd thought and emotion, provide an excellent background for Mr Forster's somewhat elusive philosophy of personal relationships. But it is too much of a 'special case', and unless we too happen to be Anglo-Indians, Mr Forster's little thrusts are too apt to give us the pleasant task of applauding the discovery of weaknesses outside ourselves instead of the less pleasant but more salutary and exciting business of acknowledging our own weaknesses. But how cunningly the scene is presented, and with what extraordinary justice. Two ladies arrive from England, one, Mrs Moore, the old mother of the district magistrate, the other, Miss Quested, his prospective wife, and their presence in Chandrapore, their desire to know 'the real India', and their distrust of the official Anglo-Indian attitude have the same effect as a stone flung into a pool. Mr Forster has distributed his interest, so that this is nobody's story, or rather it is everybody's. Person after person; Mrs Moore, old, weary of the needless complications, the fussiness of life, looking for an hour or so of quiet with the huge staring universe; Miss Quested, so curiously barren like all her kind, who laboriously desire to do right without really spending themselves; young Heaslop, the conscientious Indian civilian, only frustrated by the knowledge of his own rectitude; Aziz, the Europeanised Oriental, drifting, emotional, and only contemptible when glimpsed against a background that is not his; and so on and so forth; person after person is brought before us in the shifting and re-shifting of the action, and everyone is treated as real persons should be treated – with a certain detached sympathy that is the very height of human justice. So, too, group after group, Anglo-Indians, Moham-medans, Brahmans, are similarly caught. And what a wealth of ideas and impressions the narrative holds, from such flicks of the whip as these:

They [the Anglo-Indians] had started speaking of 'women and children' – that phrase that exempts the male from sanity when it has been repeated a few times. Each felt that all he loved best in the world was at stake, demanded revenge, and was filled with a not unpleasing glow, in which the chilly and half-known fea-tures of Miss Quested vanished, and were replaced by all that is sweetest and warmest in the private life. 'But it's the women and children,' they repeated, and the Collector knew he ought to stop them intoxicating themselves, but he hadn't the heart . . .

– to such characteristic passages of dialogue and subtle impression as this:

'But it has made me remember that we must all die: all these personal relations we try to live by are temporary. I used to feel death selected people, it is a notion one gets from novels, because some of the characters are usually left talking at the end. Now "death spares no one" begins to be real.'
'Don't let it become too real, or you'll die yourself. That is the objection to "meditating upon death. We are subdued to what we work in. I have felt the same temptation, and had to sheer off. I want to go on living a bit." '
'So do I.'
A friendliness, as of dwarfs shaking hands, was in the air. Both man and woman were at the height of their powers – sensible, honest, even subtle. They spoke the same language, and held the same opinions, and the variety of age and sex did not divide them. Yet they were dissatisfied. When they agreed, 'I want to go on liv-ing a bit,' or, 'I don't believe in God,' the words were followed by a curious backwash as though the universe had displaced itself to fill up a tiny void, or as though they had seen their own gestures from an immense height – dwarfs talking, shaking hands and

assuring each other that they stood on the same footing of insight. They did not think they were wrong, because as soon as honest people think they are wrong instability sets up. Not for them was an infinite goal behind the stars, and they never sought it. But wistfulness descended on them now, as on other occasions; the shadow of the shadow of a dream fell over their clear-cut interests, and objects never seen again seemed messages from another world.

It is some time since I read *Howards End*, and it has not been possible for me to read it again for the purpose of comparison, a matter of some interest after such a long silence on the part of an author. Writing, then, after such a long interval, I can only suggest that a certain curious evocative power, a certain unusual and very characteristic pregnancy of style, which was at its height in the earlier work, has not been here entirely recaptured. On the other hand, this is the more rounded, complete and satisfying narrative, if only because it never for a moment ceases to be entirely convincing, whereas in *Howards End*, the two most important incidents in the narrative, the seduction of one sister and the marriage of the other, never failed to leave me frankly incredulous. No, Mr Forster has not returned to disappoint us. Unlike his Anglo-Indian males, he is one of those fortunate few who are able to allow nothing to 'exempt them from sanity', and now that he has come back, as a novelist, to a world that is even more insane and even more in need of his clear-sighted exquisite charity, than the world he stopped writing about so many years ago, now that he has returned we should celebrate the event. In that neurotic's home and that dreary smoking-room which together represent contemporary fiction, a window has been opened and once more we can catch a glimpse of the mountains and the stars.

(from the *London Mercury*, LVII, July 1924)

PART THREE
More Recent Studies

Peter Burra

FROM 'THE NOVELS OF
E. M. FORSTER'* (1934)

... [Forster's novels] are eminently works of art, the reason lying in the close attention he has given to the qualities which he describes as Pattern and Rhythm. By that he means the various devices by which the different parts of the novel can be linked up with one another. Their effectiveness depends, he points out, on the memory of the reader, and his power to recognize the significance of incidental detail; and

the final sense (if the plot has been a fine one) will not be of clues and chains, but of something aesthetically compact, something which might have been shown by the novelist straight away, only if he had shown it straight away it would never have become beautiful.

Mr Forster has developed the art of clues and chains to an unusual extent. In its simplest form it consists of throwing in hints that are a preparation for events that follow probably much later. They are generally so casually introduced that we hardly observe them; hence a full appreciation of his novels depends absolutely on a second reading. For example, the deaths of Mrs Wilcox, Leonard Bast, and Mrs Moore appear when we come upon them to be too sudden for credibility – the author had finished with them, so they died. In point of fact, they are quite deliberately

* This essay was reprinted as the Introduction to the Everyman edition of *A Passage to India* (1942), to which Forster provided some notes. He praised Burra's critical sensitivity and said of this essay (of which we here have a part): 'I have re-read it with pleasure and pride, for Burra saw exactly what I was trying to do; it is a great privilege for an author to be analysed so penetratingly, and a rare one.'

prepared for by earlier remarks on the state of their healths which
at the time were too commonplace for us to see their significance.
Another good instance occurs in *Where Angels Fear to Tread*.
Philip is asking Caroline about her conversation with Gino. 'And
of what did you talk?' 'The weather – there will be rain, he says,
by tomorrow evening . . .' etc. The torrential storm which results
in the carriage accident in which Gino's child dies is thus prepared for seventy pages before it occurs.

This simple ruse, whose purpose is to give tightness to the
plot itself, develops into another ruse which Mr Forster rather
curiously calls rhythm, but which might more aptly be termed
leit-motif. The example which he gives is the little tune of Vinteuil in Proust, and its significant reappearances. The *leit-motif*
need not in itself be peculiarly significant, but by association
with its previous appearance accumulates meaning each time it
recurs. In *The Longest Journey* there are several examples – the
star Orion is one of them, and recurs somewhat like violets in
A Room with a View. A more structural *motif* in the former book
is the level crossing near Cadover. When Rickie and Agnes
arrive at Mrs Failing's, Stephen tells them accusingly that their
train ran over a child at the crossing. There follows some futile
badinage as to what has happened to the child's soul, which
Stephen cannot endure. ' "There wants a bridge," he exploded.
"A bridge instead of all this rotten talk and the level crossing." '
It appears later that a second child had been rescued by Stephen
himself. The crossing is passed and repassed by Rickie later in
the book, each time with the memory of death. At the end he is
killed there himself, wearily saving Stephen, whom he finds drunk
across the line. And in the concluding chapter we learn in a casual
remark from Stephen that the railway has been bridged. A train
is heard passing across the final darkness. The sense of completion is extraordinary.[1] The images which are used as *leit-motifs*
fall very little short of becoming symbols. Mr Forster nowhere
uses symbols as Mrs Woolf does, translating an inarticulate idea
into an image; but he constantly uses images to suggest, by
association, more than they themselves signify.

In *A Passage to India*, one of the most 'aesthetically compact' books ever written, whose thought, like music's, cannot be fixed, nor its meaning defined, there is an extreme instance of one passage calling back to another. Mrs Moore returns home to bed at the end of the first day in the book. She is alone. 'Going to hang up her cloak, she found that the tip of the peg was occupied by a small wasp. . . . "Pretty dear," said Mrs Moore to the wasp. He did not wake, but her voice floated out, to swell the night's uneasiness.' The scene is simply a beautiful detail, and connects, apparently, on to nothing. But pages and years later, after her death, old Professor Godbole, who had once sung to her at a tea party, hits on an image in his wandering thoughts which, with extraordinary suggestiveness, calls us back to that scene.

Covered with grease and dust, Professor Godbole had once more developed the life of his spirit. He had, with increasing vividness, again seen Mrs Moore, and round her faintly clinging forms of trouble. He was a Brahman, she Christian, but it made no difference, it made no difference whether she was a trick of his memory or a telepathic appeal. It was his duty, as it was his desire, to place himself in the position of the God and to love her, and to place himself in her position and to say to the God: 'Come, come, come, come.' This was all he could do. How inadequate! But each according to his own capacities, and he knew that his own were small. 'One old Englishwoman and one little, little wasp,' he thought, as he stepped out of the temple into the grey of a pouring wet morning. 'It does not seem much, still it is more than I am myself.'

Such beauty is not to be reckoned.

Most important of all, he uses buildings and places and the names of places – such places as can be appropriately associated with a recurring idea, and thus take on significance as symbols – to be the framework of his books. The Room with a View and Howards End represent thoughts which stamp their pattern on the story. *The Longest Journey* and *A Passage to India*, with there three parts – 'Cambridge, Sawston, Wiltshire'; 'Mosque, Caves, Temple' – are planned like symphonies in three movements that are given their shape and their interconnections by related and contrasted localities. In the later book the 'Marabar caves' are the

basis of a *tour de force* in literary planning. They are the keynote
in the symphony to which the strange melody always returns.
During the first half of the book constant reference to them
directs attention forward to the catastrophe. After this, every
reference to them directs our attention back to the centre, to the
mystery which is never solved. The three structures, Mosque,
Caves, Temple, are outward shapes of a man's spiritual adventures, but only by actual association in the story; pure symbolism
would involve an unwanted unreality.

This, then, is what gives to the raw material of his stories such
distinction – the quality which he comprehensively calls Rhythm,
which means the use of *leit-motif* phrases and images to link up
separated parts, with the additional function of dramatic irony
and symbolism. This it is which gives pattern to the most diffuse
of all forms. This device – of *motifs*, irony, and symbols – is, in
fact, the modern equivalent of the classical unities, an invention of
the greatest value, having all the classical advantages and none
of their so severe limitations.

Mr Forster, we said, was a musician who chose the novel
because he had ideas to utter which needed a more distinct
articulation than music could make. He is interested passionately
in human beings; not only in the idea of them – which is pre-
sumably what most novelists mean when they lay claim to that
passion – but in their actual living selves. His observation is so
close, his power to describe so exact, that although we can see
into their secret lives – which, as he says, it is the novelist's unique
privilege to discover – his characters are as elusive, as incompletely realized, as our own living friends. He describes with
extraordinary insight personal experience in relation to social; the
social setting is for him an item which cannot be omitted in the
analysis of a whole man. Hence the novel of social comedy,
instead of a purer, more musical form.

'A proper mixture of characters,' he tells us, is one of the most
important ingredients of the novel. As a vehicle for conveying
ideas everything depends on that. It is the nature of the mixture
that distinguishes Mr Forster's work; which is built invariably
round the – generally violent – clash of opposites. In *Where*

Angels Fear to Tread the clash is between the world of conventional morality and a world more akin to Nature. To heighten the contrast the conflicting elements are vested in England and Italy. 'More than personalities were engaged . . . the struggle was national.' It is a fight between North and South, between Culture and the Beast. Culture and the Beast are again the conflicting opposites in *The Longest Journey*. Here the clash is between Rickie and Stephen, who eventually find that they are children of one mother – the one educated at Cambridge, the other brought up among shepherds in the Wiltshire downs. In both these books the violence of the plots, which we have already noticed, derives directly from the violence of this clash of opposites. In the next, *A Room with a View*, the clash is more quietly, more subtly presented, and the plot is at the same time a subtle one. Again a contrast is made between England and Italy; but, except in so far as the carriage-driver 'Phaethon' and his lover 'Persephone' bear on the story, the countries do not coincide with the opposites. The conflict is less externalized and takes place inside Lucy, in her struggle to choose between Cecil Vyse and George Emerson, between the 'medieval' self-conscious life of culture and emancipated athletic honesty; between pretended feelings and true feelings.

Howards End is as violent as the earlier books. It is an extremely complicated piece of work, but (to state the conflict for the moment as simply as possible) it can be described as the clash between the business life and the cultured life; between 'Wilcoxes' and 'Schlegels' (the names come to be used almost as symbols of the two ways of living); between 'the outer life of telegrams and anger' and the life of 'personal relations'. Again the author adds a deliberate detail for the sake of heightening the contrast – the Wilcoxes are English to the backbone, the Schlegels are of German origin.

In *A Passage to India*, which did not appear till fourteen years later, the clash seems at first sight to be a purely racial one. The distinction between types is less prominent, the political passion that describes the disastrous anomaly of the British in India is more obvious. The propagandist element in the book is

undeniable, but one can hardly conclude that it was written with
that for its final purpose. For one thing, in the last part of the
book – 'Temple' – the problem is a different one. 'For here the
cleavage was between Brahman and non-Brahman; Moslems and
English were quite out of the running, and sometimes not mentioned for days.' The intrusion of the English at Mau is incidental
and designed only to reintroduce what is the real theme of the
book – the friendship of Fielding and Dr Aziz. The rocks that
rise between them on their last ride together, the horses that
swerve apart – they symbolize Indian differences, it is true, but
differences that are not more great, only more particular, than
the differences that exist between any two men, between Philip
and Gino, Rickie and Stephen, Schlegels and Wilcoxes. Once
again, therefore, the author's interest is in the clash of human
beings, the struggle which any one individual must endure if he
is to achieve intimacy with any one other. The fundamental
personal difference is again deliberately heightened by an external
circumstance – the difference of race.

Before we proceed to reject these analyses as being too bare to
convey even a half-true impression, another aspect of the clash,
which is common to them all, must be referred to. Mr Forster
introduces into each of these five books what one can only
describe as an elemental character; one who sees straight through
perplexities and complications, who is utterly percipient of the
reality behind appearances, both in matters of general truth and
of incidents in the story. Their greater wisdom, their particular
knowledge, put into ironic contrast the errors and illusions of the
rest. They are Gino, Stephen, George (together with his father),
Mrs Wilcox, and Mrs Moore. In the case of the men the stress is
laid on the athletic, of the women on the intuitive. The latter,
Mrs Wilcox and Mrs Moore, play a distinctly minor part in their
stories. It is curious to find vested in middle-aged women the
elemental quality which is more obviously associated with the
athletic, but we find it also in some of Shakespeare's heroines.
Both discover on particular complicated occasions an unques-
tioning certainty about the truth of an event. Of Helen Schlegel's
secret love of Paul 'Mrs Wilcox knew . . . though we neither of

us told her a word, and had known all along'. So of Dr Aziz, 'Of
course he is innocent,' says Mrs Moore. Very few words are
spoken by either of them. They both seem to have withdrawn
from a world whose little stupidities and illusions have ceased
to affect them except as they distract their inner life. They are
both curiously mysterious, their personalities conveying with an
astonishing force far more than there is actual evidence for. Mrs
Wilcox 'was not intellectual, not even alert, and it was odd that,
all the same, she should give the idea of greatness. Margaret, zig-
zagging with her friends over Thought and Art, was conscious
of a personality that transcended their own and dwarfed their
activities.' One rather strange accident attaches to both of them:
they belong to the enemy's camp – that is to say, to the side of
the clash with which we are least likely to sympathize. In fact,
Mrs Moore's Anglo-Indian setting does not call for our sympathy
at all. They thus prepare the way for the merge of opposites to
which we return later. Some of the mystery attaches as well to
the three men. They are strange because in the middle of a social
comedy they prefer to dispense with the disguises which the rest
wear. As the Rev. Arthur Beebe remarks: 'It is so difficult – at
least I find it difficult – to understand people who speak the
truth.'

By the very nature of the conflict which he arranges it is clear
how much store Mr Forster sets by the athletic. The one chance
which puts the deformed Rickie in the way of salvation is that
'he had escaped the sin of despising the physically strong – a sin
against which the physically weak must guard'. In the person of
Stephen physical strength is exalted into the most exciting beauty
and the whole novel reminds one constantly of the work which
Lawrence produced a few years later. When he makes his first
appearance, a third of the way through the book, the writing is
lifted up like music to herald his approach. He is the product of an
intensely passionate imagination working upon closely recorded
detail of behaviour and conduct. He is life, at the centre and at the
circumference – he is the world's essential simplicity, transformed
by the author's vision. His significance is clear to the reader at
once; no other character – except Mrs Failing when the mood is

on her – perceives it, until Ansell, the articulate philosopher, sums him up:

A silence, akin to Poetry, invaded Ansell. Was it only a pose to like this man, or was he really wonderful? He was not romantic, for Romance is a figure with outstretched hands, yearning for the unattainable. Certain figures of the Greeks, to whom we continually return, suggested him a little. One expected nothing of him – no purity of phrase nor swift-edged thought. Yet the conviction grew that he had been back somewhere – back to some table of the gods, spread in a field where there is no noise, and that he belonged for ever to the guests with whom he had eaten.

Gino and George Emerson are very different people, but they represent the same athletic honesty. Gino was 'majestic; he was a part of nature.' 'Centuries of aspiration and culture' were defenceless against the impulses he aroused. The quality in George is contrasted with its absence in Cecil, whom Lucy is engaged to marry. At the beginning of the book it is latent but undeveloped in George, but each of his rare meetings with Lucy draws it out. Lucy comes to connect Cecil with a drawing-room that has no view, George is associated with a room with a view that looks out over life. Lucy and George meet from time to time, but always appear to be looking at each other 'across something' – across 'the rubbish that cumbers the world', across the little bundles of clothes which they strip for bathing, and which break into speech (the fancy reminds one of Daudet) 'proclaiming: "No. We are what matters. Without us shall no enterprise begin. To us shall all flesh turn in the end." ' And George, to whom physical nakedness has given a new certainty, greets her 'with the shout of the morning star'; and eventually beseeches her to turn from the pretence of Cecil to his own manhood. Lucy cannot admit to herself that he is right, till a few minutes later Cecil is asked to make up a four at tennis.

Cecil's voice came: 'My dear Freddy, I am no athlete. As you well remarked this very morning, "There are some chaps who are no good for anything but books"; I plead guilty to being such a chap, and will not inflict myself on you.'

The scales fell from Lucy's eyes. How had she stood Cecil for a moment? He was absolutely intolerable, and the same evening she broke her engagement off.

The athletic fitness of Gino, Stephen, and George is stressed in another significant way. Each realizes – exceptionally, we are given to understand – 'that physical and spiritual life may stream out of him for ever'. Stephen 'would have children: he, not Rickie, would contribute to the stream; he, through his remote posterity, might be mingled with the unknown sea.' 'Ah, but how beautiful he is!' says Gino, bathing his baby. 'And he is mine; mine for ever. Even if he hates me he will be mine. He cannot help it; he is made out of me; I am his father.' And the story of George and Lucy ends: 'Youth enwrapped them; the song of Phaethon announced passion requited, love attained. But they were conscious of a love more mysterious than this. The song died away; they heard the river, bearing down the snows of winter into the Mediterranean.'

Gino, Stephen, George – these are heroes. They represent the same elemental quality as Mrs Woolf's Percival in *The Waves*. But whereas Percival is presented as an adored, desired opposite, a symbol of the unattainable, Mr Forster brings in these characters to make a clash, to conflict with the other side. Mr Forster describes the clash of opposites, but not only the clash; he describes the merge as well. He realizes that, having regard to their common humanity, no two types, however much opposed, can be considered as absolutely distinct. Hence his point of view is constantly shifting – each side is alternately presented for sympathy, first impressions are contradicted, confirmed, contradicted again, so that a close attention and memory are required to add up the final sum. We cannot doubt that what is urged upon us in *The Longest Journey* is the return to Nature – what is emphasized is the value of the earth. Yet the tragedy does arise from Rickie's faith in her, learnt through Stephen, from his magnificent refusal to heed his aunt's warning 'Beware of the Earth'. When it comes to 'warnings', Mrs Herriton, Mrs Failing, Mrs Wilcox, the Anglo-Indians, people whom imagination has never visited, are always – right. It is in *Howards End* that our impressions are likely to become most confused. 'Wilcoxes' and 'Schlegels' are presented with as exact a balance of sympathy as is possible – much as Shakespeare presents Richard II and Bolingbroke, for example, or the royalists and the rebels, in *Henry IV, Part I*. So that it almost depends on the personal feeling of the reader to incline the scale finally either way.

In *Howards End* the two opposing points of view are woven across each other so closely that it is hardly possible to detach the threads. Two families, the Schlegels and the Wilcoxes, come into contact with each other as a result of a chance meeting. 'Schlegels' consist of two sisters and a brother – Margaret, Helen, and the youthfully aesthetic Tibby. Their spiritual home is Queen's Hall, and they hold vaguely advanced opinions. 'Wilcoxes' make money; 'they are keen on all games', and they 'think charm in a man is rather rot'. The trouble begins when Helen and Paul think they are in love with one another – an illusion which does not last more than a few hours.

'To think that because you and a young man meet for a moment, there must be all these telegrams and anger,' supplied Margaret.

Helen nodded.

'I've often thought about it, Helen. It's one of the most interesting things in the world. The truth is that there is a great outer life that you and I have never touched – a life in which telegrams and anger count. Personal relations that we think supreme, are not supreme there. There love means marriage settlements, death, death duties. So far I'm clear. But here's my difficulty. This outer life, though obviously horrid, often seems the real one – there's grit in it. It does breed character. Do personal relations lead to sloppiness in the end?'

'Oh, Meg, that's what I felt, only not so clearly, when the Wilcoxes were so competent, and seemed to have their hands on all the ropes.'

'The world would be a grey bloodless place,' comments the author, 'were it entirely composed of Miss Schlegels. But the world being what it is, perhaps they shine out of it like stars.' Such is his detachment. The two elements continue to play

upon each other, and the greatness and limitations of each
are revealed with an astonishing clearness. Helen withdraws
further into the 'personal life', but for Margaret the 'outer life'
gradually becomes a 'real force', something that she could not
attain to. She sees that it represents a 'spirit without which life
might never have moved out of protoplasm'. Finally she becomes
Mr Wilcox's second wife. Then when the crisis of the book is
reached and a catastrophe occurs, Wilcoxes are seen in all their
weaknesses – they fail because they have never known the 'personal life'. It seems for the moment as if the author is going to
separate them, suggesting that it is impossible to reconcile such
opposites, and that 'those who stray outside their nature invite
disaster'. But life returns to the normal. Margaret still accepts
Mr Wilcox. And at the very end, as tragedy goes off into the past,
and much pain has been suffered and many wrongs have been
revealed – 'Nothing has been done wrong,' she says to him with
the final wisdom of acceptance.

For love, she sees, is a greater thing than opinions. What a
folly it were to ruin the rare possibility of intimacy with any man,
for so imaginary a cause as one's personal beliefs. The man himself is the important element, and not the way he thinks, nor the
work he does. 'I can't bother over results,' she once remarked
regarding the British Empire, 'they are too difficult for me. I can
only look at the men. An empire bores me, so far, but I can
appreciate the heroism that builds it up.' Again: 'She hated war
and liked soldiers – it was one of her amiable inconsistencies.'
It is possible that in that inconsistency Mr Forster is enunciating
his philosophy as definitely as he has done anywhere. You may
be a convinced rebel – but do not pretend that you can resist
empire builders. You may be a pacifist – but you are laying a false
emphasis on consistency if you allow that to affect your appreciation of soldiers. What a man thinks and the way of life he goes
will inevitably clash with other thoughts and different ways. But
the man himself is more than his opinions or the accidents that
attach to him. It is possible for Schlegels to accept Wilcoxes, it is
possible for Englishmen to ride with Indians. And the final
wisdom is to grant that 'nothing has been done wrong'.

The words have – to use a phrase of Mrs Woolf's – the weight of the whole book behind them. They ring with that prophetic 'tone of voice' which sounds right through his masterpiece *A Passage to India* – the tone in which the great writers of tragedy have spoken their last words of reconciliation. They rise up – as he says of great poetry – from that anonymous part of a man which 'cannot be labelled with his name. It has something in common with all other deeper personalities, and the mystic will assert that the common quality is God.'

So that in the end it will be more true to say that, after all, if Mr Forster's novels 'tell a story' as they do, they are these more desirable things as well – 'melody' and 'perception of the truth'. No words can describe them; the melody cannot be heard through any medium but its own. All I have attempted here is some indication of the shape and the mode. Much that is most remarkable in his writing has scarcely been commented upon: his dazzling humour, acute and delicate satire that never misses its mark, his vivid characterization, whether in the 'flat' or the 'round'; his faultless sense of the style appropriate to individuals, especially in regard to their tricks of speech – these and other arts give the actual texture of his work its distinction. But these are stamped with his name. It is the Anonymous Prophecy that will remain with us, the transcendent beauty of the Mosque and Temple, and the athletic body of Stephen. It would be perhaps merely stupid to ask, in conclusion, for more. It is possible that the mind which saw so visionarily the significance of Stephen, and which could tell the Wilcoxes that 'nothing has been done wrong', has achieved their own wisdom; that the organism, being perfectly adjusted, is silent.

SOURCE: *The Nineteenth Century and After* (Nov 1934), reprinted as the Introduction to the Everyman edition of 1942.

NOTE

1. One is reminded of *Anna Karenina*. But there the accident at her first entrance *suggests* to her mind the way of her suicide at the end. Here it is a purely chance circumstance – an aesthetic irony such as Hardy delighted in.

Virginia Woolf

[None] of the books [he wrote] before *Howards End* and *A Passage to India* altogether drew upon the full range of Mr Forster's powers. With his queer and in some ways contradictory assortment of gifts, he needed, it semeed, some subject which would stimulate his highly sensitive and active intelligence, but would not demand the extremes of romance or passion; a subject which gave him material for criticism, and invited investigation; a subject which asked to be built up of an enormous number of slight yet precise observations, capable of being tested by an extremely honest yet sympathetic mind; yet, with all this, a subject which when finally constructed would show up against the torrents of the sunset and the eternities of night with a symbolical significance. In *Howards End* the lower middle, the middle, the upper middle classes of English society are so built up into a complete fabric. It is an attempt on a larger scale than hitherto, and, if it fails, the size of the attempt is largely responsible. Indeed, as we think back over the many pages of this elaborate and highly skilful book, with its immense technical accomplishment, and also its penetration, its wisdom, and its beauty, we may wonder in what mood of the moment we can have been prompted to call it a failure. By all the rules, still more by the keen interest with which we have read it from start to finish, we should have said success. The reason is suggested perhaps by the manner of one's praise. Elaboration, skill, wisdom, penetration, beauty – they are all there, but they lack fusion; they lack cohesion; the book as a whole lacks force. Schlegels, Wilcoxes, and Basts, with all that they stand for of class and environment, emerge with extraordinary verisimilitude, but the whole effect is less satisfying than that of the much slighter but beautifully harmonious *Where Angels Fear to Tread*. Again we have the sense that there is some perversity in Mr Forster's endowment so that his gifts in their variety and number tend to trip each other up. If he were less scrupulous, less just, less sensitively aware of the different aspects of every case, he could, we feel, come down with greater force on one precise point. As it is, the strength of his blow is dissipated. He is like a light sleeper who is always being woken by something in the room. The poet is twitched away by the satirist; the comedian is tapped on the shoulder by the moralist; he never loses himself or forgets himself for long in sheer delight in the beauty or the interest of things as they are. For this reason the lyrical passages in his books, often of great beauty in themselves, fail of their due effect in the context. Instead of flowering naturally – as in Proust, for instance – from an overflow of interest and beauty in the object itself, we feel that they have been called into existence by some irritation, are the effort of a mind outraged by ugliness to supplement it with a beauty which, because it originates in protest, has something a little febrile about it.

Yet in *Howards End* there are, one feels, in solution all the qualities that are needed to make a masterpiece. The characters are extremely real to us. The ordering of the story is masterly. That indefinable but highly important thing, the atmosphere of the book, is alight with intelligence; not a speck of humbug, not an atom of falsity is allowed to settle. And again, but on a larger battlefield, the struggle goes forward which takes place in all Mr Forster's novels – the struggle between the things that matter and the things that do not matter, between reality and sham, between the truth and the lie. Again the comedy is exquisite and the observation faultless. But again, just as we are yielding ourselves to the pleasures of the imagination, a little jerk rouses us. We are tapped on the shoulder. We are to notice this, to take heed of that. Margaret or Helen, we are made to understand, is not speaking simply as herself; her words have another and a larger intention. So, exerting ourselves to find out the meaning, we step from the enchanted world of imagination, where our faculties work freely, to the twilight world of theory, where only our intellect functions dutifully. Such moments of disillusionment have the habit of coming when Mr Forster is most in earnest, at the crisis of the book, where·the sword falls or the bookcase drops. They bring, as we have noted already, a curious insubstantiality into the 'great scenes' and the important figures. But they absent themselves entirely from the comedy. They make us wish, foolishly enough, to dispose Mr Forster's gifts differently and to restrict him to write comedy only. For directly he ceases to feel responsible for his characters' behaviour, and forgets that he should solve the problem of the universe, he is the most diverting of novelists. The admirable Tibby and the exquisite Mrs Munt in *Howards End*, though thrown in largely to amuse us, bring a breath of fresh air in with them. They inspire us with the intoxicating belief that they are free to wander as far from their creator as they choose. Margaret, Helen, Leonard Bast, are closely tethered and vigilantly overlooked lest they may take matters into their own hands and upset the theory. But Tibby and Mrs Munt go where they like, say what they like, do what they like. The lesser characters and the unimportant scenes in Mr Forster's novels thus often remain more vivid than those with which, apparently, most pain has been taken. But it would be unjust to part from this big, serious, and highly interesting book without recognizing that it is an important if unsatisfactory piece of work which may well be the prelude to something as large but less anxious.

Many years passed before *A Passage to India* appeared. Those who hoped that in the interval Mr Forster might have developed his technique so that it yielded rather more easily to the impress of his whimsical mind and gave freer outlet to the poetry and fantasy which play about him were disappointed. The attitude is precisely the same four-square attitude which walks up to life as if it were a house with a front door, puts its hat on the table in the hall, and proceeds to visit all the rooms in an orderly manner. The house is still the house of the British middle classes. But there is a change from *Howards End*. Hitherto Mr Forster has been apt to pervade his books like a careful hostess who is anxious to introduce, to explain, to warn her guests of a step here, of a draught there. But here, perhaps in some disillusionment both with his guests and with his house, he seems to have relaxed these cares. We are allowed to ramble over this extraordinary continent

almost alone. We notice things, about the country especially,
spontaneously, accidentally almost, as if we were actually there;
and now it was the sparrows flying about the pictures that caught
our eyes, now the elephant with the painted forehead, now the
enormous but badly designed ranges of hills. The people too,
particularly the Indians, have something of the same casual,
inevitable quality. They are not perhaps quite so important as
the land, but they are alive; they are sensitive. No longer do we
feel, as we used to feel in England, that they will be allowed to go
only so far and no further lest they may upset some theory of the
author's. Aziz is a free agent. He is the most imaginative character
that Mr Forster has yet created, and recalls Gino the dentist in his
first book, *Where Angels Fear to Tread*. We may guess indeed
that it has helped Mr Forster to have put the ocean between him
and Sawston. It is a relief, for a time, to be beyond the influence
of Cambridge. Though it is still a necessity for him to build a
model world which he can submit to delicate and precise criticism, the model is on a larger scale. The English society, with all its
pettiness and its vulgarity and its streak of heroism, is set against
a bigger and more sinister background. And though it is still true
that there are ambiguities in important places, moments of imperfect symbolism, a greater accumulation of facts than the
imagination is able to deal with, it seems as if the double vision
which troubled us in the ealier books was in process of becoming
single. The saturation is much more thorough. Mr Forster has
almost achieved the great feat of animating this dense, compact
body of observation with a spiritual light. The book shows signs
of fatigue and disillusionment; but it has chapters of clear and
triumphant beauty, and above all it makes us wonder, What will
he write next?

Source: 'The Novels of E. M. Forster', in *The Death of the
Moth and Other Essays* (1942).

Lionel Trilling

A PASSAGE TO INDIA (1943)

THE years between 1910 and 1914 were the vestibule to what Forster has called 'the sinister corridor of our age'. *Howards End* records the sense of Germany's growing strength; Mr Schlegel, father of Helen and Margaret, had voluntarily exiled himself from the old Germany of philosophers, musicians and little courts and he spoke bitterly of the new imperialism to which 'money [was] supremely useful; intellect, rather useful; imagination, of no use at all'.

Not many books of the time were so precisely sensitive to the situation, yet a kind of sultry premonitory hush comes over literature in these years. The hope of the first decade of the century has been checked. The athletic quality of intelligence which seemed to mark the work of even five years earlier has subsided.

In 1910, following the publication of *Howards End*, Forster projected two novels but wrote neither. The next year he finished a play, *The Heart Of Bosnia*, which, by his own account, was not good, although it almost reached the stage in 1914; plans for its production were abandoned at the outbreak of war and the manuscript was lost by the producer. In 1912, Forster, in company with Dickinson and R. C. Trevelyan, sailed for India. Dickinson, travelling on one of the fellowships established by Albert Kahn in the interests of international understanding, had official visits and tours to make and the friends separated at Bombay. But their itineraries crossed several times and they spent a fortnight as guests of the Maharajah of Chhatarpur, who loved Dickinson and philosophy – ' "Tell me, Mr Dickinson, where is God?" ' the Maharajah said. ' "Can Herbert Spencer lead me to him, or should I prefer George Henry Lewes? Oh when will Krishna come and be my friend? Oh Mr Dickinson!" '

The two travellers came away from India with widely different feelings. Dickinson, who was to love China, was not comfortable in India. Displeased as he was by her British rulers, he was not pleased with India itself. 'There is no solution to the problem of governing India,' he wrote. 'Our presence is a curse both to them and to us. Our going away will be worse. I believe that to the last word. And *why* can't the races meet? Simply because the Indians *bore* the English. That is the simple adamantine fact.' It is not an enlightening or even a serious view of the situation, and Forster, dissenting from it, speaks of the 'peace and happiness' which he himself found in India in 1912 and again on his second visit ten years later.

The best fruit of the Indian journey was to be *A Passage To India*, but meanwhile Forster wrote several short pieces on Indian life of which two, 'The Suppliant' and 'Advance, India!' (both reprinted in *Abinger Harvest*) admirably depict the comic, sad confusion of a nation torn between two cultures.

He began to sketch the Indian novel, but the war postponed its completion for a decade. And the war quite destroyed the project for a critical study of Samuel Butler, with whose mind Forster's has community at so many points. But the war, which sent Forster to non-combatant service in Egypt, developed in him the interest in Imperial conduct and policy which the Indian tour had begun. Hitherto Forster's political concern had been intense but perhaps abstract; now it became increasingly immediate. The three Egyptian years gave him not only the material for two books and many essays, but also a firm position on the Imperial question. . . . In 1922 Forster made a second journey to India and took up again the Indian story he had projected. *A Passage To India* appeared with great success in 1924.

A Passage To India is Forster's best-known and most widely read novel. Public and political reasons no doubt account for this; in England the book was a matter for controversy and its success in America, as Forster himself explains it, was due to the superiority Americans could feel at the English botch of India. But the public, political nature of the book is not extraneous; it inheres in the novel's very shape and texture.

By many standards of criticism, this public, political quality works for good. *A Passage To India* is the most comfortable and even the most conventional of Forster's novels. It is under the control not only of the author's insight; a huge, hulking physical fact which he is not alone in seeing, requires that the author submit to its veto-power. Consequently, this is the least surprising of Forster's novels, the least capricious and, indeed, the least personal. It quickly establishes the pattern for our emotions and keeps to it. We are at once taught to withhold our sympathies from the English officials, to give them to Mrs Moore and to the 'renegade' Fielding, to regard Adela Quested with remote interest and Aziz and his Indian friends with affectionate understanding.

Within this pattern we have, to be sure, all the quick, subtle modifications, the sudden strictnesses or relentings of judgment which are the best stuff of Forster's social imagination. But always the pattern remains public, simple and entirely easy to grasp. What distinguishes it from the patterns of similarly public and political novels is the rigor of its objectivity; it deals with unjust, hysterical emotion and it leads us, not to intense emotions about justice, but to cool poise and judgment – if we do not relent in our contempt for Ronny we are at least forced to be aware that he is capable of noble, if stupid, feelings; the English girl who has the hallucination of an attempted rape by a native has engaged our sympathy by her rather dull decency; we are permitted no easy response to the benign Mrs Moore, or to Fielding, who stands out against his own people, or to the native physician who is wrongly accused. This restraint of our emotions is an important element in the book's greatness.

With the public nature of the story goes a chastened and somewhat more public style than is usual with Forster, and a less arbitrary manner. Forster does not abandon his right to intrude into the novel, but his manner of intrusion is more circumspect than ever before. Perhaps this is because here, far less than in the English and Italian stories, he is in possession of truth; the Indian gods are not his gods, they are not genial and comprehensible. So far as the old Mediterranean deities of wise impulse and loving intelligence can go in India, Forster is at home; he thinks they can go far but not all the way, and a certain retraction of the intimacy of his style reflects his uncertainty. The acts of imagination by which Forster conveys the sense of the Indian gods are truly wonderful; they are, nevertheless, the acts of imagination not of a master of the truth but of an intelligent neophyte, still baffled.

So the public nature of the novel cannot be said to work wholly for good. For the first time Forster has put himself to the test of verisimilitude. Is this the truth about India? Is this the way the English act? – always? sometimes? never? Are Indians like this? – all of them? some of them? Why so many Moslems and so few Hindus? Why so much Hindu religion and so little Moslem? And then, finally, the disintegrating question, What is to be done?

Forster's gallery of English officials has of course been disputed in England; there have been many to say that the English are not like that. Even without knowledge we must suppose that the Indian Civil Service has its quota of decent, devoted and humble officials. But if Forster's portraits are perhaps angry exaggerations, anger can be illuminating – the English of Forster's Chandrapore are the limits toward which the English in India must approach, for Lord Acton was right, power does corrupt, absolute power does corrupt absolutely.

As for the representation of the Indians, that too can be judged here only on *a priori* grounds. Although the Indians are conceived in sympathy and affection, they are conceived with these emotions alone, and although all of them have charm, none of them has dignity; they touch our hearts but they never impress us. Once, at his vindication feast, Aziz is represented as 'full of civilization . . . complete, dignified, rather hard' and for the first time Fielding treats him 'with diffidence', but this only serves to remind us how lacking in dignity Aziz usually is. Very possibly this is the effect that Indians make upon even sensitive Westerners; Dickinson, as we have seen, was bored by them, and generations of subjection can diminish the habit of dignity and teach grown men the strategy of the little child.

These are not matters that we can settle; that they should have arisen at all is no doubt a fault of the novel. Quite apart from the fact that questions of verisimilitude diminish illusion, they indicate a certain inadequacy in the conception of the story. To represent the official English as so unremittingly bad and the Indians as so unremittingly feeble is to prevent the story from being sufficiently worked out in terms of the characters; the characters, that is, are *in* the events, the events are not in them: we want a larger Englishman than Fielding, a weightier Indian than Aziz.

These are faults, it is true, and Forster is the one novelist who could commit them and yet transcend and even put them to use. The relation of the characters to the events, for example, is the result of a severe imbalance in the relation of plot to story. Plot and story in this novel are not coextensive as they are in all Forster's other novels. (I am not using plot and story in exactly the same sense that Forster uses them in *Aspects Of The Novel*.) The plot is precise, hard, crystallized and far simpler than any Forster has previously conceived. The story is beneath and above the plot and continues beyond it in time. It is, to be sure, created by the plot, it is the plot's manifold reverberation, but it is greater than the plot and contains it. The plot is as decisive as a judicial opinion; the story is an impulse, a tendency, a perception. The suspension of plot in the large circumambient sphere of story, the expansion of the story from the center of plot, requires some of the subtlest manipulation that any novel has ever had. This relation of plot and story tells us that we are dealing with a political novel of an unusual kind. The characters are of sufficient size for the plot; they are not large enough for the story – and that indeed is the point of the story.

This, in outline, is the plot: Adela Quested arrives in India under the chaperonage of the elderly Mrs Moore with whose son by a first marriage Adela has an 'understanding'. Both ladies are humane and Adela is liberal and they have an intense desire to 'know India'. This is a matter of some annoyance to Ronny, Mrs Moore's son and Adela's fiancé, and of amused condescension to the dull people at the station who try to satisfy the ladies with elephant rides – only very *new* people try to *know* India. Both Mrs Moore and Adela are chilled by Ronny; he has entirely

adopted the point of view of the ruling race and has become a
heavy-minded young judge with his dull dignity as his chief
recognized asset. But despite Ronny's fussy certainty about what
is and is not proper, Mrs Moore steps into a mosque one evening
and there makes the acquaintance of Aziz, a young Moslem
doctor. Aziz is hurt and miserable, for he has just been snubbed;
Mrs Moore's kindness and simplicity soothe him. Between the
two a friendship develops which politely includes Adela Quested.
At last, by knowing Indians, the travellers will know India, and
Aziz is even more delighted than they at the prospect of the
relationship. To express his feelings he organizes a fantastically
elaborate jaunt to the Marabar Caves. Fielding, the principal of
the local college, and Professor Godbole, a Hindu teacher, were
also to have been of the party but' they miss the train and Aziz
goes ahead with the ladies and his absurd retinue. In one of the
caves Mrs Moore has a disturbing psychic experience and sends
Aziz and Adela to continue the exploration without her. Adela,
not a very attractive girl, has had her doubts about her engagement to Ronny, not a very attractive man, and now she ventures
to speak of love to Aziz, quite abstractly but in a way both to
offend him and disturb herself. In the cave the strap of her field-
glasses is pulled and broken by someone in the darkness and she
rushes out in a frenzy of hallucination that Aziz has attempted to
rape her. The accusation makes the English of the station hysterical with noble rage. In every English mind there is the certainty
that Aziz is guilty and the verdict is foregone. Only Fielding and
Mrs Moore do not share this certainty. Fielding, because of his
liking for the young doctor, and Mrs Moore, because of an
intuition, are sure that the event could not have happened and
that Adela is the victim of illusion. Fielding, who openly declares
his partisanship, is ostracized, and Mrs Moore, who only hints
her opinion, is sent out of the country by her son; the journey
in the terrible heat of the Indian May exhausts her and she dies
on shipboard. At the trial Adela's illusion, fostered by the mass-
hysteria of the English, becomes suddenly dispelled, she recants,
Aziz is cleared, Fielding is vindicated and promoted, the Indians
are happy, the English furious.

Thus the plot. And no doubt it is too much a plot of event, too easily open and shut. Nevertheless it is an admirable if obvious device for organizing an enormous amount of observation of both English and native society; it brings to spectacular virulence the latent antagonisms between rulers and ruled.

Of the Anglo-Indian society it is perhaps enough to say that, 'more than it can hope to do in England', it lives by the beliefs of the English public school. It is arrogant, ignorant, insensitive – intelligent natives estimate that a year in India makes the pleasantest Englishman rude. And of all the English it is the women who insist most strongly on their superiority, who are the rawest and crudest in their manner. The men have a certain rough liking for the men of the subject race; for instance, Turton, Collector of the district, has 'a contemptuous affection for the pawns he had moved about for so many years; they must be worth his pains'. But the women, unchecked by any professional necessity or pride, think wholly in terms of the most elementary social prestige and Turton's wife lives for nóthing else. " 'After all," ' Turton thinks but never dares say, ' "it's our women who make everything more difficult out here." '

This is the result of the undeveloped heart. *A Passage To India* is not a radical novel; its data were gathered in 1912 and 1922, before the full spate of Indian nationalism; it is not concerned to show that the English should not be in India at all. Indeed, not until the end of the book is the question of the expulsion of the English mentioned, and the novel proceeds on an imperialistic premise – ironically, for it is not actually Forster's own – its chief point being that by reason of the undeveloped heart the English have thrown away the possibility of holding India. For want of a smile an Empire is to be lost.[1] Not even justice is enough. ' "Indians know whether they are liked or not," ' Fielding says, ' "– they cannot be fooled here. Justice never satisfies them, and that is why the British Empire rests on sand." ' Mrs Moore listens to Ronny defending the British attitude; 'his words without his voice might have impressed her, but when she heard the self-satisfied lilt of them, when she saw the mouth moving so complacently and competently beneath the little red nose, she felt, quite illogically, that this was not the last word on India. One touch of regret – not the canny substitute but the true regret – would have made him a different man, and the British Empire a different institution.'

Justice is not enough then, but in the end neither are liking and goodwill enough. For although Fielding and Aziz reach out to each other in friendship, a thousand little tricks of speech, a thousand different assumptions and different tempi keep them apart. They do not understand each other's *amounts* of emotion, let alone kinds of emotion. ' "Your emotions never seem in proportion to their objects, Aziz," ' Fielding says, and Aziz answers, ' "Is emotion a sack of potatoes, so much the pound, to be measured out?" '

The theme of separateness, of fences and barriers, the old theme of the Pauline epistles, which runs through all Forster's novels, is, in *A Passage To India*, hugely expanded and everywhere dominant. The separation of race from race, sex from sex, culture from culture, even of man from himself, is what underlies every relationship. The separation of the English from the Indians is merely the most dramatic of the chasms in this novel. Hindu and Moslem cannot really approach each other; Aziz, speaking in all friendliness to Professor Godbole, wishes that Hindus did not remind him of cow-dung and Professor Godbole thinks, ' "Some Moslems are very violent" ' – 'Between people of distant climes there is always the possibility of romance, but the various branches of Indians know too much about each other to surmount the unknowable easily.' Adela and Ronny cannot meet in sexuality, and when, after the trial, Adela and Fielding meet in an idea, 'a friendliness, as of dwarfs shaking hands, was in the air'. Fielding, when he marries Mrs Moore's daughter Stella, will soon find himself apart from his young wife. And Mrs Moore is separated from her son, from all people, from God, from the universe.

This sense of separateness broods over the book, pervasive, symbolic – at the end the very earth requires, and the sky approves, the parting of Aziz and Fielding – and perhaps accounts for the remoteness of the characters: they are so far from each other that they cannot reach us. But the isolation is not merely adumbrated; in certain of its aspects it is very precisely analyzed and some of the most brilliant and virtuose parts of the novel are devoted to the delineation of Aziz and his friends, to the investigation of the cultural differences that keep Indian and Englishman apart.

The mould for Aziz is Gino Carella of the first novel. It is the mould of unEnglishness, that is to say, of volatility, tenderness, sensibility, a hint of cruelty, much warmth, a love of pathos, the desire to please even at the cost of insincerity. Like Gino's, Aziz's nature is in many ways child-like, in many ways mature: it is mature in its acceptance of child-like inconsistency. Although eager to measure up to English standards of puritan rectitude, Aziz lives closer to the literal facts of his emotions; for good or bad, he is more human. He, like his friends, is not prompt, not efficient, not neat, not really convinced of Western ideas even in science – when he retires to a native state he slips back to mix a little magic with his medicine – and he, like them, is aware of his faults. He is hyper-sensitive, imagining slights even when there are none because there have actually been so many; he is full of humility and full of contempt and desperately wants to be liked. He is not heroic but his heroes are the great chivalrous emperors, Babur and Alamgir. In short, Aziz is a member of a subject race. A rising nationalism in India may by now have thrust him aside in favor of a more militant type; but we can be sure that if the new type has repudiated Aziz' emotional contra-dictions it has not resolved them.

Aziz and his friends are Moslems, and with Moslems of the business and professional class the plot of the novel deals almost entirely. But the story is suffused with Hinduism.[2] It is Mrs Moore who carries the Hindu theme; it is Mrs Moore, indeed, who is the story. The theme is first introduced by Mrs Moore observing a wasp.

Going to hang up her cloak she found that the tip of the peg was occupied by a small wasp. . . . There he clung, asleep, while jackals in the plain bayed their desires and mingled with the per-cussion of drums.

'Pretty dear,' said Mrs Moore to the wasp. He did not wake, but her voice floated out, to swell the night's uneasiness.

This wasp is to recur in Professor Godbole's consciousness when he has left Chandrapore and taken service as director of education in a Hindu native state. He stands, his school quite forgotten – turned into a granary, indeed – and celebrates the birth of Krishna in the great religious festival that dominates the third part of the novel. (The novel is divided: I Mosque, II Caves, III Temple. In his notes to the Everyman edition Forster points out that the three parts correspond to the three Indian seasons.) The wasp is mixed up in his mind – he does not know how it got there in the first place, nor do we – with a recollection of Mrs Moore.

He was a Brahman, she a Christian, but it made no difference, it made no difference whether she was a trick of his memory or a telepathic appeal. It was his duty, as it was his desire, to place himself in the position of the God and to love her, and to place himself in her position and say to the God: 'Come, come, come, come.' This was all he could do. How inadequate! But each according to his own capacities, and he knew that his own were small. 'One old Englishwoman and one little, little wasp,' he thought, as he stepped out of the temple into the grey of a pouring wet morning. 'It does not seem much, still it is more than I am myself.'

The presence of the wasp, first in Mrs Moore's consciousness, then in Godbole's, Mrs Moore's acceptance of the wasp, Godbole's acceptance of Mrs Moore – in some sybmolic fashion, this is the thread of the story of the novel as distinguished from its plot. For the story is essentially concerned with Mrs Moore's discovery that Christianity is not adequate. In a quiet way, Mrs Moore is a religious woman; at any rate, as she has grown older she has found it 'increasingly difficult to avoid' mentioning God's name 'as the greatest she knew'. Yet in India God's name becomes less and less efficacious – 'outside the arch there seemed always another arch, beyond the remotest echo a silence'.

And so, unwittingly, Mrs Moore has moved closer and closer to Indian ways of feeling. When Ronny and Adela go for an

automobile ride with the Nawab Bahadur and the chauffeur
swerves at something in the path and wrecks the car, Mrs Moore,
when she is told of the incident, remarks without thinking, ' "A
ghost!" ' And a ghost it was, or so the Nawab believed, for he
had run over and killed a drunken man at that spot nine years
before. 'None of the English knew of this, nor did the chauffeur;
it was a racial secret communicable more by blood than by speech.'
This 'racial secret' has somehow been acquired by Mrs Moore.
And the movement away from European feeling continues: 'She
felt increasingly (vision or nightmare?) that, though people are
important, the relations between them are not, and that in particular too much fuss has been made over marriage; centuries of
carnal embracement, yet man is no nearer to understanding man.'
The occasion of her visit to the Marabar Caves is merely the
climax of change, although a sufficiently terrible one.

What so frightened Mrs Moore in the cave was an echo. It is
but one echo in a book which is contrived of echoes. Not merely
does Adela Quested's delusion go in company with a disturbing
echo in her head which only ceases when she masters her delusion,
but the very texture of the story is a reticulation of echoes. Actions
and speeches return, sometimes in a better, sometimes in a worse
form, given back by the perplexing 'arch' of the Indian universe.
The recurrence of the wasp is a prime example, but there are
many more. If Aziz plays a scratch game of polo with a subaltern
who comes to think well of this particular anonymous native,
the same subaltern will be particularly virulent in his denuncia-
tion of Aziz the rapist, never knowing that the liked and the
detes_ed native are the same. If the natives talk about their
inability to catch trains, an Englishman's missing a train will
make all the trouble of the story. Mrs Moore will act with bad
temper to Adela and with surly indifference to Aziz, but her
action will somehow have a good echo; and her children will be
her further echo. However we may interpret Forster's intention
in this web of reverberation, it gives his book a cohesion and
intricacy usually only found in music. And of all the many
echoes, the dominant one is the echo that booms through the
Marabar cave.

A Marabar cave had been horrid as far as Mrs Moore was concerned, for she had nearly fainted in it, and had some difficulty in preventing herself from saying so as soon as she got into the air again. It was natural enough; she had always suffered from faintness, and the cave had become too full, because all their retinue followed them. Crammed with villagers and servants, the circular chamber began to smell. She lost Aziz and Adela in the dark, didn't know who touched her, couldn't breathe, and some vile naked thing struck her face and settled on her mouth like a pad. She tried to regain the entrance tunnel, but an influx of villagers swept her back. She hit her head. For an instant she went mad, hitting and gasping like a fanatic. For not only did the crush and stench alarm her; there was also a terrifying echo.

Professor Godbole had never mentioned an echo; it never impressed him, perhaps. There are some exquisite echoes in India ... The echo in a Marabar cave is not like these, it is entirely devoid of distinction. Whatever is said, the same monotonous noise replies, and quivers up and down the walls until it is absorbed into the roof. 'Boum' is the sound as far as the human alphabet can express it, or 'bou-oum', or 'ou-boum' – utterly dull. Hope, politeness, the blowing of a nose, the squeak of a boot, all produce 'boum'.

Panic and emptiness – Mrs Moore's panic had been at the emptiness of the universe. And one goes back beyond Helen Schlegel's experience of the Fifth Symphony in *Howards End*: the negating mess of the cave reminds us of and utterly denies the mess of that room in which Caroline Abbott saw Gino with his child. For then the mess had been the source of life and hope, and in it the little child had blossomed; Caroline had looked into it from the 'charnel chamber' of the reception room and the 'light in it was soft and large, as from some gracious, noble opening'. It is, one might say, a representation of the womb and a promise of life. There is also a child in the mess of the Marabar cave – for the 'vile, naked thing' that settles 'like a pad' on Mrs Moore's mouth is 'a poor little baby, astride its mother's hip'. The cave's opening is behind Mrs Moore, she is facing into the grave; light from the world does not enter, and the universe of death makes all things alike, even life and death, even good and evil.

... The echo began in some indescribable way to undermine her hold on life. .... It had managed to murmur: 'Pathos, piety, courage – they exist, but are identical, and so is filth. Everything exists, nothing has value.' If one had spoken vileness in that place, or quoted lofty poetry, the comment would have been the same – 'ou-boum'. If one had spoken with the tongues of angels and pleaded for all the unhappiness and misunderstanding in the world, past, present, and to come; for all the misery men must undergo whatever their opinion and position, and however much they dodge or bluff – it would amount to the same. .... Devils are of the North, and poems can be written about them, but no one could romanticize the Marabar because it robbed infinity and eternity of their vastness, the only quality that accommodates them to mankind. .... But suddenly, at the edge of her mind, religion appeared, poor little talkative Christianity, and she knew that all its divine words from 'Let there be Light' to 'It is finished' only amounted to 'boum'.

'Something snub-nosed, incapable of generosity' had spoken to her – 'the undying worm itself'. Converse with God, her children, Aziz, is repugnant to her. She wants attention for her sorrow and rejects it when given. Knowing Aziz to be innocent, she says nothing in his behalf except a few sour words that upset Adela's certainty, and though she knows that her testimony will be useful to Aziz, she allows Ronny to send her away. She has had the beginning of the Hindu vision of things and it has crushed her. What the Hindu vision is, is expressed by Professor Godbole to Fielding:

Good and evil are different, as their names imply. But, in my own humble opinion, they are both of them aspects of my Lord. He is present in the one, absent in the other, and the difference between presence and absence is great, as great as my feeble mind can grasp. Yet absence implies presence, absence is not non-existence, and we are therefore entitled to repeat: 'Come, come, come, come.'

Although Mrs Moore abandons everything, even moral duty, she dominates the subsequent action. As 'Esmiss Esmoor' she becomes, to the crowd around the courthouse, a Hindu goddess who was to save Aziz. And, we are vaguely given to understand, it is her influence that brings Adela to her senses and the truth. She recurs again, together with the wasp, in the mind of Professor Godbole in that wonderful scene of religious muddlement with which the book draws to its conclusion. She remains everlastingly in the mind of Aziz who hates – or tries to hate – all the other English. She continues into the future in her daughter Stella, who marries Fielding and returns to India, and in her son Ralph. Both Stella and Ralph 'like Hinduism, though they take no interest in its forms' and are shy of Fielding because he thinks they are mistaken. Despite the sullen disillusionment in which Mrs Moore died, she had been right when she had said to Ronny that there are many kinds of failure, some of which succeed. No thought, no deed in this book of echoes, is ever lost.

It is not easy to know what to make of the dominant Hinduism of the third section of the novel. The last part of the story is frankly a coda to the plot, a series of resolutions and separations which comment on what has gone before – in it Fielding and Aziz meet and part, this time forever; Aziz forgives Adela Quested and finds a friend in Ralph Moore; Fielding, we learn, is not really at one with his young wife; Hindu and Moslem, Brahman and non-Brahman are shown to be as far apart as Indian and English, yet English and Moslem meet in the flooded river, in a flow of Hindu religious fervor; and everything is encompassed in the spirit of Mrs Moore, mixed up with a vision of the ultimate nullity, with the birth of Krishna and with joy in the fertile rains.

Certainly it is not to be supposed that Forster finds in Hinduism an answer to the problem of India; and its dangers have been amply demonstrated in the case of Mrs Moore herself. But here at least is the vision in which the arbitrary human barriers sink before the extinction of all things. About seventy-five years before *A Passage To India*, Matthew Arnold's brother, William Delafield Arnold, went out to India as Director of Public Education of the Punjab. From his experiences he wrote a novel *Oakfield: Or Fellowship In The East*; it was a bitter work which denounced the English for making India a 'rupee mine' and it declared that the 'grand work' of civilizing India was all humbug.

William Arnold thought that perhaps socialism, but more likely the Church of England, could bring about some change. This good and pious man felt it 'grievous to live among men' – the Indians – 'and feel the idea of fraternity thwarted by facts'; he believed that 'we must not resign ourselves, without a struggle, to calling the Indians brutes'. To such a pass has Christianity come, we can suppose Forster to be saying. We must suffer a vision even as dreadful as Mrs Moore's if by it the separations can be wiped out. But meanwhile the separations exist and Aziz in an hysteria of affirmation declares to Fielding on their last ride that the British must go, even at the cost of internal strife, even if it means a Japanese conquest. Only with the British gone can he and Fielding be friends. Fielding offers friendship now: ' "It's what I want. It's what you want." ' But the horses, following the path the earth lays for them, swerve apart; earth and sky seem to say that the time for friendship has not come, and leave its possibility to events.

The disintegrating question, What, then, must be done? which many readers have raised is of course never answered – or not answered in the language in which the question has been asked. The book simply involves the question in ultimates. This, obviously, is no answer; still, it defines the scope of a possible answer, and thus restates the question. For the answer can never again temporize, because the question, after it has been involved in the moods and visions of the story, turns out to be the most enormous question that has ever been asked, requiring an answer of enormous magnanimity. Great as the problem of India is, Forster's book is not about India alone; it is about all of human life.

SOURCE: *E. M. Forster* (1943).

NOTES

1. H. N. Brailsford in his *Rebel India* (1931) deals at some length with the brutality with which demonstrations were put down in 1930. 'Here and there,' he says, 'mildness and good-temper disarmed the local agitation. I heard of one magistrate, very popular with the people,

who successfully treated the defiance of the Salt Monopoly as a joke. The local Congress leaders made salt openly in front of his bungalow. He came out: bought some of the contraband salt: laughed at its bad quality: chaffed the bystanders, and went quietly back to his house. The crowd melted away, and no second attempt was made to defy this genial bureaucrat. On the other hand, any exceptional severity, especially if physical brutality accompanied it, usually raised the temper of the local movement and roused it to fresh daring and further sacrifices' (p. 7 n).

2. The Indian masses appear only as crowds in the novel; they have no individualized representative except the silent, unthinking figure of the man who pulls the *punkah* in the courtroom scene. He is one of the 'untouchables' though he has the figure of a god, and in Adela's mind, just before the crisis of the trial, he raises doubts of the 'suburban Jehovah' who sanctifies her opinions, and he makes her think of Mrs Moore.

E. K. Brown

RHYTHM IN E. M. FORSTER'S
A PASSAGE TO INDIA (1950)

I

A NOVELIST may use many kinds of rhythm in one work. In this last discourse [the last of a series of lectures collected into book form] I propose to consider one work, to touch on the varied forms of the device, and to inquire briefly into the effect that comes from the combination of phrases, characters, and incidents, rhythmically arranged, with a profusion of expanding symbols, and with a complex evolution of themes. The one work is E. M. Forster's *A Passage to India*, and I may as well say now that I believe it to be a great novel. It is so unlike most great novels that for a long time I thought of it as remarkable rather than great. After many rereadings, always finding more in the work than I had before, I have changed my mind. One of the reasons why I set *A Passage to India* so high will, perhaps, appear in these pages: its greatness is intimately dependent on E. M. Forster's mastery of expanding symbols and thematic structure, and on that element in his spirit for which expanding symbols and thematic structure are appropriate language.

One of the first examples I gave of repetition with variation was from *Esther Waters*: the word-for-word repetition late in the book of the first paragraph, followed by the repetition with significant variation of the second paragraph. In *A Passage to India* there is something very like this, but subtle as well as emphatic.

In the second chapter of Forster's novel characters begin to appear. There is Aziz, the Mohammedan physician, engaged in friendly argument with Mohammedan friends: 'they were discussing as to whether or no it is possible to be friends with an Englishman'. The conclusion is that in India, at least, friendship

with the invader is impossible, unpermitted. Aziz is summoned
to his chief, the Civil Surgeon, Dr Callendar, and on the steps of
Callendar's bungalow suffers a slight from two Anglo-Indian
women. As they come out on the verandah he lifts his hat;
instinctively they turn away. They jump into the carriage he has
hired and are about to drive off without asking consent. Aziz says
'You are most welcome, ladies'; they do not think of replying.
The Civil Surgeon has left, and there is no message. Aziz takes
his injured feelings to the mosque, and in the night's coolness he
meditates upon the past of Islam. He recalls a Persian inscription
he had once seen on the tomb of a Deccan king, especially these
closing lines:

> But those who have secretly understood my heart –
> They will approach and visit the grave where I lie.

As he is repeating the words 'the secret understanding of the
heart' in the one place in Chandrapore where he was sure no
European would intrude, an Englishwoman steps into the moonlight. Aziz rages at her. But Mrs Moore has done the right thing,
has removed her shoes – says the right thing, 'God is here' – and
in a minute they are friends. They talk of their children, of
people round about, of India, of religion. 'The flame that not
even beauty can nourish' was springing up in Aziz, for this red-
faced old woman; and when she remarks 'I don't think I understand people very well. I only know whether I like or dislike
them,' Aziz declares: 'Then you are an Oriental.' He has learned
that one can be friends with an Englishman, even with an
Englishwoman, and in India. Two years later when the novel is
about to close, Aziz repeats the declaration. Not to Mrs Moore –
she is dead – but to her son, the young boy Ralph.

Aziz is no longer in British India. He has resolved to have no
more to do with the invader, and is physician to the rajah of a
Hindu state. Into a seclusion even deeper than that of the mosque
where he had met Mrs Moore, once more the English penetrate.
One of the intruders is Ralph who is stung by bees. So great is
Aziz' hatred of the English that he is sadistically happy to have
an English boy in his power. He will treat him with the savagery

the Civil Surgeon had used towards the young son of a Nawab. Ralph astonishes Aziz with a most unEnglish expression: 'Your hands are unkind.' The memory of Mrs Moore floods in, expelling all hatred. Aziz bids Ralph a gentle good-bye, and Ralph responds with equal gentleness. Aziz asks 'Can you always tell whether a stranger is your friend?' 'Yes,' Ralph replies simply. 'Then you are an Oriental' – the words are drawn out of Aziz, and he is appalled. 'He unclasped as he spoke, with a little shudder. Those words – he had said them to Mrs Moore in the mosque in the beginning of the cycle, from which, after so much suffering, he had got free.' Instead of the good-bye Aziz had planned, and the hurried escape from reinvolvement with the English, he talks with Ralph about Mrs Moore and in friendship takes the boy out on the water, as in friendship he had taken Mrs Moore to the Marabar Caves. What they say of Mrs Moore, and what befalls them on the water I am not yet ready to consider. But the cycle is clearly beginning again. The effect that George Moore sought in *Esther Waters*, and achieved, was of a closing in of the life in his tale; the effect in *A Passage to India* is of an opening out of life. It is as if at the point where one circle was completed, another and larger circle immediately began.

Ralph Moore serves in another kind of rhythmic process. I used the two daughters in *Le Père Goriot* and the two in *A Lear of the Steppes* as examples of a pair of characters radically alike in nature and in function. Balzac's daughters have only surface differences; with Turgenev's there is also gradation, a significant difference in the degree to which they are mastered by the same ruling passion, and a surprise. The likeness between Ralph Moore and his mother, profound, intimate, mysterious, is a gradation and a surprise of Turgenev's sort. Ralph is a prolongation of his mother. He is a simpler person because he lacks the shell of practical sense and adaptability which hid her essential nature from almost everyone until 'India brought her into the open'. It may be said of Ralph that he is what his mother is so far as she eternally matters. The repetition of Mrs Moore in the two children of her second marriage – for Ralph's sister Stella is of the same substance, although she remains a faint figure – hits the

reader more strongly since the child of the first marriage, the only
one of her children to appear in the early and middle parts of the
book, derives nothing from his mother. Ronnie Heaslop, bureaucrat, conventionalist, empire-builder, snob, is a thorough Wilcox.
He could have changed places with the younger Wilcox boy and
no one would have noticed the shift. Especially to one who reads
A Passage to India after reading *Howards End* the prolongation
of Mrs Moore in her youngest child is emotionally effective. It is
a vehicle for the mystery in which the meaning of *A Passage to
India* is so deeply engaged.

II

I mentioned the bee-stings which led to Ralph's encounter with
Aziz. They will take us to one of the expanding symbols.

Early in the novel, on the evening when she had met Aziz at
the mosque, Mrs Moore is undressing in her son's bungalow.
As she is about to hang up her cloak she notices that on the tip of
the peg is a wasp, a quite unEnglish wasp, an 'Indian Social Wasp'.

Perhaps he mistook the peg for a branch – no Indian animal has
any sense of an interior. Bats, rats, birds, insects will as soon nest
inside a house as out; it is to them a normal growth of the eternal
jungle, which alternately produces houses trees, houses trees.
There he clung, asleep, while jackals in the plain bayed their
desires and mingled with the percussion of drums.

'Pretty dear,' said Mrs Moore to the wasp. He did not wake,
but her voice floated out, to swell the night's uneasiness.

There the chapter ends. If you read these lines in the context they
take on certain precise meanings. Mrs Moore had divided her
evening between the English club (where no native was allowed)
and the mosque (where no English folk came). None of the sun-
dried Anglo-Indians would have called the wasp a pretty dear;
all of them would have been irritated by the wasp's inability to
discriminate a house from a tree, which is India's inability, India's
disinclination, to make the sharp tidy distinctions by which the
Western intelligence operates. At the club that evening the talk
had turned to religion. The Civil Surgeon's wife had said that the

kindest thing one could do for a native was to let him die. Mrs
Moore had inquired, with a 'crooked smile', what if he went to
heaven? A woman who had been a nurse in a native state was
ready for this with a razor-sharp distinction: 'I am all for Chap-
lains, but all against Missionaries.' The little incident with which
the evening closes epitomizes Mrs Moore's behaviour at the club
and at the mosque, her indifference to sharp distinctions, her
instinctive affection and consideration. But this, and other precise
meanings in her approach to the wasp, do not exhaust the force
or account for the charm of the passage. The disturbing noises
which accompany Mrs Moore's gesture of affection and consideration – the minatory baying of the jackals and percussion of the
drums offer an undertone of suggestion that, unexpectedly
beautiful and adequate as Mrs Moore's response to Aziz and to
the wasp had been, there are ordeals ahead to which even Mrs
Moore may be insufficient.

Late in the novel, long after her death, the wasp returns, or
rather it is now the idea of the wasp. The Brahman Godbole, at
the climactic moment in the book, is attempting union with the
divine. He does so in a ceremony that could satisfy no Western
person. It is a ceremony abounding in jumble, amorphousness.
Each of the noisy Corybantic worshippers is inviting the return
of the strongest, purest attachments in his experience. 'Thus
Godbole, though she was not important to him, remembered an
old woman he had met in Chandrapore days . . . she happened to
occur among the throng of soliciting images, a tiny splinter, and
he impelled her by his spiritual force to that place where completeness can be found.' Having impelled Mrs Moore triumphantly to her place, he tried again. 'His senses grew thinner, he
remembered a wasp seen he forgot where, perhaps on a stone. He
loved the wasp equally, he impelled it likewise, he was imitating
God.' There his triumph flared out. He found he could do
nothing with the stone, arbitrarily, superficially, cognitively
associated with the wasp. ' "One old Englishwoman and one
little, little wasp," he thought, as he stepped out of the temple
into the grey of a pouring wet morning. "It does not seem much,
still it is more than I am myself." '

Just what is achieved by the recurrence of the wasp? To have shown Godbole triumphantly impelling Mrs Moore would have established the effect that is most obviously needed: that of an affinity between Godbole and the old Englishwoman who has not come so far as he along the mystical path. In the novel they have but one important interchange – an interchange of spiritual ideas – and apart from this they scarcely see each other. They do not wish to, do not need to. Godbole's recollection of her at a spiritual moment crucial for him establishes that one interchange is enough. It tells us something that for E. M. Forster is most important about human relationships. All this, and more perhaps, can be achieved without the recurrence of the wasp.

The recurrence of the wasp does not point, as one of my students once suggested, to Professor Godbole's having taken an unrecorded walk by Mrs Moore's window when she was undressing. The recurrence of the wasp points to an identity in the objects to which the analogous characters were drawn. That each should have been powerfully attracted to something so apparently trivial as a wasp suggests that they were not only alike but mysteriously alike. Because of the wasp we appear to be in the presence of something so elusive that we cannot understand it, that we brood about it with a conviction that it contains some kernel of meaning we do not know how to extract. It can be said of the wasp as E. M. Forster said of Vinteuil's music that it has a life of its own, that it is almost an actor in the novel but not quite.

Between its two big moments the wasp is not wholly neglected. Not all the English in Forster's India adopt the prejudices of the official classes. The nurse from the native state was opposed to missionaries; but the missionaries in Chandrapore are more sensitive, more human, than the mass of their countrymen. In a review printed four years before the novel Forster wrote: 'It is the missionary rather than the Government official who is in touch with native opinion. The official need only learn how people can be governed. The missionary, since he wants to alter them, must learn what they are.' The missionaries never came to the club at Chandrapore, and on principle they used the third-class cars on the trains. The call to salvation, they knew and taught and lived, was addressed to all mankind. But what, their Indian friends would ask, of the animals? Were there mansions in heaven for the monkeys? The elder missionary thought not, but the younger was liberal, and 'saw no reason why monkeys should not have their collateral share of bliss'. As the conversation descended below the mammalian the younger missionary felt less at ease, and when the wasp was mentioned he was prone to change the subject. The call of the Western intelligence for a razor-sharp distinction became imperious. 'We must exclude someone from our gathering, or we shall be left with nothing.' The use of the wasp in this passage beautifully underlines by contrast the spiritual agreement between the Brahman and the contemplative Christian Mrs Moore: for them the divine call has no fixed exclusions – would not be divine if it had.

And then there are the bees with which I began. They live in the shrine of a Mohammedan saint, who had freed prisoners, and when the police intervened and cut off his head, 'ignored' this misadventure and slew as many of them as were about. The shrine is not a mosque, but there is a miniature mosque beside it. We are brought back to the encounter between Aziz and Mrs Moore at the beginning of the novel. The sudden rage of the bees against the intruders is like Aziz' sudden rage against her; and it ends as quickly. The rage of the bees seems to suggest that subhuman India is hostile to interracial friendships, a suggestion repeated with virtuosity throughout the book, and nowhere so forcibly as in the final paragraph. Aziz and the Englishman he has liked most, Cyril Fielding, are riding in the country. Aziz, in a sudden spurt of affection, pulls his horse so close to Fielding's that he can half kiss him; and Fielding responds by holding Aziz affectionately.

But the horses didn't want it – they swerved apart; the earth didn't want it, sending up rocks through which riders must pass single file; the temples, the tank, the jail, the palace, the birds, the carrion, the Guest House, that came into view as they issued from the gap and saw Mau beneath: they didn't want it, they said in their hundred voices, 'No, not yet,' and the sky said, 'No, not there.'

Clearly, the bees are divisive as the wasps are not. And yet the bees are not merely divisive – they were the occasion for the personal relation between Aziz and Ralph Moore, just as the wasp was, not indeed the occasion, but the evidence of mystery in the personal relation between Godbole and Mrs Moore.

The greatest of the expanding symbols in *A Passage to India* is the echo. The most lasting among the effects of the visit that Mrs Moore and Adela Quested made to the Marabar Caves as the guests of Aziz was the echo. Mrs Moore disliked the echo when she was in the one cave she entered; but after she had emerged and had had time to arrange her impressions she minded it much more. 'The echo began in some indescribable way to undermine her hold on life.' It blurred all distinctions, and even Mrs Moore had enough of the West in her to become uneasy. To the highest poetry and the coarsest obscenity the echo would have offered the same reply – 'ou-boum'. Other Indian echoes, Forster pauses to insist, are quite different; at Mandu long sentences will journey through the air and return to their speaker intact. At the Marabar the utterance is reduced to the dullness of one flat response mercilessly reiterated. Mrs Moore found that the echo voided of all meaning the past, present, and future of her life. The echo disturbed Adela Quested's steady balance. Love and marriage were on her mind as she moved towards the second cave, and she suffered the delusion that Aziz, who did not in fact care for her in any way except as an honoured guest, attempted to rape her.

The reader has been lured into pondering about echoes before they dominate the crucial scene at the caves. The Collector, the principal English official at Chandrapore, learning that Mrs Moore and Miss Quested wish to meet 'the Aryan Brother', gives what he calls a 'Bridge Party' for the leading local people of both colours. In vain do the two visitors from England try to bridge a gap, crossing from the side of the garden chosen by the pinko-greys, as Fielding calls them, to the side where India seems to promise revelations to anyone bold enough to seek. Mrs Moore and Miss Quested make special efforts with two Hindu women; but everything dies against 'the echoing walls of their civility'. At home the evening after the ineffectual party

Mrs Moore takes stock of what India has done for her in a few weeks. It has made her speak more often of God; but it has also moved the old spiritual landmarks, and God has seemed a less satisfactory formulation for the content of her belief. 'Outside the arch [and the arch is also a powerful expanding symbol with which I have not space to deal] there seemed always an arch, beyond the remotest echo a silence.'

As the narrative begins to move directly towards the Marabar Caves, sounds exercise a decisive effect on the two women who are to find the echoes in those caves so disturbing. The Brahman Godbole concludes a tea party at Fielding's by singing a song whose spiritual content is as bemusing as its form is at variance with Western conceptions of music. The Englishwomen are so affected by his song that in the days intervening between their hearing it and their starting for the caves they exist as if in cocoons. On the local train that takes them to the Marabar the dull repetitive sound of the wheels has an effect prefiguring the echo's on Mrs Moore. 'Pomper, pomper, pomper,' say the wheels and rob Adela Quested's sentences and ideas of any distinctness. On another line not far away the crack mail train that linked Calcutta with Lahore shot along with a shriek that meant business. That shriek Adela could have understood, it was of her world; but with 'pomper, pomper, pomper' she can do nothing. Unless one can do something, even do a great deal, with 'pomper, pomper, pomper,' one can do nothing with India. For the meanings of India are indistinct and repetitive. Until the Western visitor can make something of the indistinctness indefinitely repeated, he can neither comprehend any of the meanings of India nor begin to cope with them. India, says Forster, is not a promise, it is nothing so definite, it is only an appeal.

The indistinctness and repetitiveness, exasperating to a Western mind, are beautifully captured at the beginning of a notice that in 1919 Forster wrote for the *Athenaeum*. The book reviewed was *Hindu and Buddhist Monuments, Northern Circle*, published by the Mysore Archaeological Department.

'Ought we not to start? The elephants must be waiting.'
'There is no necessity. Elephants sometimes wait four hours.'

'But the temple is far.'

'Oh no, there are thirty of them.'

'Thirty temples! Are they far?'

'No, no, no, not at all – fifteen really, but much jungle; fifteen to come and fifteen to go.'

'Fifteen of what?'

'Fifteen all.'

After such preparations, and in such a spirit, the Temple used to be attacked; and came off victorious. Whether it was one, or fifteen or thirty, or thirty miles off, was never proved, because the elephant misunderstood, or plans changed, or tiffin was too delicious. Evening fell, and the pale blue dome of the sky was corniced with purple where it touched the trees. 'It will now be too late for the Temple.' So it keeps its secret in some stony gorge or field of tough grass, or, more triumphant still, in the land beyond either, where a mile and an elephant are identical and everything is nothing.

The Mysore Archaeological Department does not approach a monument in this instinctive fashion. It is as precise, as Western, as Aziz' plans for the expedition to the Marabar Caves. Aziz worked out a schedule that would honour the secretary of a national convention: transport, food, seating, even jokes, were minutely arranged. Lest he and his servants be late they spend the preceding night at the station. India is too much for them. Fielding and Godbole miss the train; and Mrs Moore and Miss Quested hate the caves – Mrs Moore will enter only one of them, Adela only two.

In the caves the indistinct meanings of India have agglomerated in a form of shocking intensity and explode at the visitors in the horrifying echo. Until she entered a cave Adela Quested had made nothing of these meanings. The most that can be said for her is that unlike the Anglo-Indians she has been aware of bafflement, conscious of a profound uneasiness. Mrs Moore was not quite so pitifully unprepared: she was spiritually active, moving blindly towards a more adequate formulation of the divine. She too was shattered by the echoes. For the length of many chapters after the scene at the caves, the echo leaves a disturbing residue in the minds of both Englishwomen. What the residue was I shall inquire when looking at the thematic structure of the novel.

After Mrs Moore's death and Adela's return to England, the echo begins to matter to Cyril Fielding. When, after the catastrophe, he entered a Marabar cave, the echo had no impact on him. In the hubbub of distorted rumour and opinion released in Chandrapore by Adela's charge against Aziz, Fielding kept his head, and was the only Englishman to do so. It was now his turn to exist within a cocoon – he was enclosed by his intuitive assurance that Aziz could not have done what he was charged with doing. No distorting, dispiriting echo could penetrate that cocoon. When Adela withdrew her charge the Anglo-Indian world at Chandrapore collapsed. But when a new crop of officials arrived they were, Fielding found, just like those who had been withdrawn. After he has met them at the club, Fielding muses: 'Everything echoes now; there's no stopping the echo. The original sound may be harmless, but the echo is always evil.' On this musing Forster comments: 'This reflection about an echo lay at the verge of Fielding's mind. He could never develop it. It belonged to the universe that he had missed or rejected.' Indistinct meanings were almost as alien to his fluid but yet Western mind as to the more rigid mind of Adela Quested. What he has, and she has not, is some grasp of the nature of personal relationships. He has shown again and again his appreciation of how attractive personalities falsify themselves and show at their worst when they suffer the impact of aggressive personalities that are antagonistic to them. At the close of his tea party he saw Aziz behaving in a repulsive way – 'impertinent' to Ronnie Heaslop, 'loud and jolly' to Godbole, 'greasily confidential' to Adela Quested – and instead of revising his opinion of Aziz, he merely concluded that something had happened to upset the nervous Mohammedan. Ronnie Heaslop had happened. And what is true of individuals, Fielding's political shrewdness tells him, is more painfully true of national groups and social classes. 'The original sound may be harmless, but the echo is always evil.'

As the novel approaches a close, Forster introduces perhaps the most moving of all his uses of the echo. In the courtroom scene at the middle of the *Passage*, when Mrs Moore's name is mentioned in testimony, the native crowd outside distorts it into 'Esmiss Esmoor', and chants these mysterious syllables as if they were the name of a goddess, or the means to salvation. Indeed they are. For it was after the crowd had chanted the distortion that Adela was freed from her delusion, and, changing her story, saved Aziz. When at the end Mrs Moore's younger children fall in with Aziz, the Hindus at their worship are repeating: 'Radhakrishna Radhakrishna Krishnaradha Radhakrishna'; and, suddenly in the interstices of the chant, Aziz 'heard, almost certainly, the syllables of salvation that had sounded during his trial at Chandrapore'.

The echo, like the bee-wasp symbol, is manifold in meaning. An echo distorts Mrs Moore's sense of the purport of life, but that distortion, we may shortly see, is not entirely ruinous. An echo distorts Adela's sense of what happened in the cave; but another echo restores her to the truth. Good and evil interweave in these expanding symbols, making them more mysterious; just as we shall see them interweave in the development of the themes.

III

A Passage to India is in three parts. Their titles – 'Mosque', 'Caves', 'Temple' – warn of a meaning which goes behind story, people, even setting. Each part has a curious and beautiful prefatory chapter, and each of these chapters abounds in symbols, abstractions, suggestions. Their full weight of meaning is slow in revealing itself; indeed I am not sure that any reader of the novel will ever possess all that has been flung into these chapters.

It is obvious that they are in balance. They also interweave. The first chapter in the part called 'Mosque' begins: 'Except for the Marabar Caves,' and ends: 'These fists and fingers are the Marabar Hills, containing the extraordinary caves.' There is a reference to temples tucked away in a detailed catalogue of the topography of Chandrapore. To mosques the only reference is in the title for this part of the novel, standing at the top of the opening page and then used as a running head. The first chapter of the part called 'Caves' has no backward glance towards the mosque or any element of the Moslem faith; but it is packed with suggestive remarks that point forward to the temple and the Hindu faith; and these are sharply in contrast with the chief substance of the chapter, the account of an India far older than Moslem or Hindu, whose faith has left a mysterious residue in the primitive Marabar Caves. The first chapter of the part called 'Temple' opens as the first chapter of 'Mosque' opened, with a reference to the caves; and the Moslem element is gathered in by the importance to the action in the chapter of the chief Moslem person in the novel, Aziz. In the interweaving of elements in these prefatory chapters there is increasing complication but no petty mechanical balancing, no sterile exactness of repetition. Vitality is not sacrificed to pattern.

It is useful to look at the prefatory chapters as a group; seen in this way they offer an initiation into the kind of approach the three parts of the novel will best respond to. What has appeared in the chapters will be recognized, although not so readily, in the three big blocks that compose *A Passage to India*.

In the first of these blocks we are brought to a mosque; in the second to the caves; in the third to a temple. Each visit has consequences which linger through the rest of the novel. The novel thus becomes progressively more complex. In the first block not only is the Moslem element dominant – it far outweighs the caves and the temple; all that we get about caves and temple is preparatory. At the other extreme, in the third block, where the Hindu element is dominant, the persistence of the Moslem and of that more primitive and elusive element represented by the caves is multiform and of a kind to command a great part of the reader's attention and emotion.

In her visit to the mosque at Chandrapore Mrs Moore enters with a happy and intuitive adequacy into an understanding of the Moslem element. She leaves the stifling club late in the evening and approaches the mosque alone. We have seen how easily she enters into a personal understanding of Aziz. The understanding so quickly and strangely established endures throughout the novel. She never doubts that Aziz is innocent of the charge Adela brings against him. In the next to last chapter Aziz tells Ralph Moore: 'Yes, your mother was my best friend in all the world.' 'He was silent,' the passage continues, 'puzzled by his own great gratitude. What did this eternal goodness of Mrs Moore amount to? To nothing, if brought to the test of thought. She had not borne witness in his favour [Adela had done that], nor visited him in the prison [Fielding had done that], yet she had stolen to the depths of his heart, and he always adored her.' To return to the images in Helen Schlegel's interpretation of the Fifth Symphony, the goblins have no power whatever over the relation between Mrs Moore and Aziz. When he first saw her white form in the darkness of the mosque, he had been repeating to himself in Persian 'the secret understanding of the heart'. So far as the main meaning of the first block in the novel admits of formulation, there is the formula.

Before the second part of the novel has begun, at Fielding's tea party (an indirect outcome of the meeting at the mosque) the Marabar Caves begin to threaten. Aziz has never seen them, nor has he any knowledge of them beyond common report. But when the English visitors express a wish to see more of India, and see more deeply, he proposes an expedition to the caves. He asks the Brahman Godbole to describe them. Godbole confines himself to brief negatives. The caves contain no sculpture, no ornament of any kind; nor are they especially holy. To every effort Aziz makes to discover why the caves are worth seeing, Godbole is impenetrable. The comparatively simple mind of the Mohammedan, we are told, 'was encountering Ancient Night'. It is an ominous and mysterious overture. Godbole is invited to join the expedition, and agrees; but when the time comes he prolongs his prayers, innocently misses the train, and makes Fielding miss it too. The visitors from England approach the caves under the guidance of Aziz, the blind led by the blind.

The caves are in an outpost of the high places of Dravidia, which were land when the oceans covered the holy places of Hindustan, before there was a Ganges, before there were Himalayas. Forster has moved them some hundreds of miles, as he tells us in a note to the Everyman edition, doubtless to bring them within reach of the Ganges where for many reasons he prefers to situate the early and middle parts of his story. The hills in which they lie were flesh of the sun's flesh, their contours never softened by the flow of water, and some of the edges and masses they had when they belonged to the sun they still preserve. The hills, like so many of the aspects of India, strike Forster as violating the beauties of proportion and thus certain to confuse and depress a European. When Cyril Fielding returns to Europe at the end of the second block of the novel he lands at Venice after a stay in Egypt and a sight of Crete. 'The buildings of Venice,' he noted, 'like the mountains of Crete and the fields of Egypt, stood in the right place, whereas in poor India everything was placed wrong. He had forgotten the beauty of form among idol temples and lumpy hills.' The Marabar Hills are lumpy; they rise 'abruptly, insanely, without the proportion that is kept by the wildest hills elsewhere'. Mrs Moore and Miss Quested did not find them attractive or interesting; they could not see why these hills should have a reputation and draw people to look on them. They did not understand that to lack form is not simply a negation: that the vacuum left is filled by something else, elusive but perhaps of equal importance.

What Forster is doing in the description of the hills, and later of the caves, is easy to formulate if one is content with general terms. He is taking his characters beyond their depth; the minds of Mrs Moore and Miss Quested, Western, modern, complex, cannot operate on the level of primitivism which the hills and the caves exemplify. Mrs Moore is not so much at a loss as Miss Quested, even momentarily, for she is less Western, less modern, even less complex. Miss Quested's mind goes wild and she makes the absurd charge against Aziz; Mrs Moore's mind goes dead – she is aware of its incompetence, aware that in the circumstances of the caves and hills it cannot operate at all. The secret understanding of the heart is no longer enough.

The echo in a Marabar cave is almost exactly like the utterance of the goblins in the Fifth Symphony, a denial of human values, in this case by way of a denial of all distinctions. 'Pathos, piety, courage – they exist, but are identical, and so is filth,' the echo

persuades Mrs Moore. 'Everything exists, nothing has value.'
Panic and emptiness were what the goblins infused into Helen
Schlegel listening to Beethoven in the Queen's Hall; and the
echo infuses them into Mrs Moore. Emptiness. The relations that
have made hers a full life – her affection for her children, her
devotion to God – have suddenly snapped. She could not – and
this happens in a moment – interest herself in the fortunes of her
children, either in those of the son at Chandrapore or in those of
the youngest two in England. The Christian God, whom she had
worshipped with so much fervour in her parish in the Northamp-
tonshire countryside, and who was once the source of her greatest
happiness, ceased, also in a moment, to have any meaning. Panic.
'She was terrified over an area larger than usual; the universe,
never comprehensible to her intellect, offered no respose to her
soul.'

For Mrs Moore there is no re-establishment from what befell
her on the Marabar. Soon afterwards she leaves India. By her own
estimate her passage to that land has been a failure. As she crosses
the country by train to go aboard at Bombay she thinks 'I have
not seen the right places.' The voice of the Marabar Caves was
not the voice of India, only one of the voices; but it had prevented
her hearing the others. The voice of Asirgarh, for instance, a
fortress among wooded hills passed at sunset. She at once forgets
Asirgarh; but ten minutes later Asirgarh reappears – the train has
made a semicircle. 'What could she connect it with, except its
own name? Nothing; she knew no one who lived there. But it had
looked at her twice and seemed to say: "I do not vanish." ' On
the passage home, she dies, and her body is committed to the
Indian Ocean. She will never hear the voice of Asirgarh again;
but Asirgarh will hear hers.

The goblins are powerful in this novel, but before the dark
second part ends Forster begins to put them to rout. It is true
that Mrs Moore could not cope with what the caves had spoken
to her. But, like Mrs Wilcox, she is a redemptive character; unable to save herself, she did miraculous things for others. She
did them by being the sort of person she was. She continued to
do them after her ordeal at the Marabar. Whenever Adela

Quested is in her company, and only then, Adela is relieved of the echo, and becomes not her usual self, but at times a better self than she has ever been. The mention of Mrs Moore's name at the trial clears the confusion from Adela's brain, and in this way Aziz is saved. A little later the mention of her name to Aziz persuades him to be generous with Adela and give over an action for damages. And the beneficent influence of Mrs Moore flowing out of the secret understanding of the heart will swell throughout the third part until it becomes next to the main determinant in the final scenes of the novel.

Even in the second part, the dark part of the novel, the goblins encounter another powerful enemy in the Brahman Godbole. He is asked by Fielding for his opinion of what occurred in the cave. The breadth of his conception brings a quietude that reassures the reader if it leaves Fielding exasperated. What happened, says Godbole, was an evil thing. But the precise nature of the evil is not of any real account: nothing is to be achieved through the law courts, by ascertaining whether Aziz attacked Adela Quested, or whether someone else, the guide or a wandering Pathan, attacked her, or whether she was attacked by her own poisoned imagination. What concerns Godbole is why she was attacked. Evil had the power to attack her because of the shortcomings of the universe, because, to take an example of the shortcomings – this is my example, not Godbole's – of the warped society in which Adela and Aziz are living. Perhaps if the cave had been in Wiltshire or in Greece, Aziz and Adela might have left it unscathed. 'When evil occurs,' says Godbole, 'it expresses the whole of the universe.' But if all have a responsibility for letting the goblins loose, the power of the goblins is no proper reason for despair. Evil is not unrelated to good: it is the absence of good, and thus has a subtle unbreakable bond with the good. The presence of evil does not imply that good has been vanquished, only that it has receded. Godbole is also concerned with what should be done; not at the trial of Aziz, which, like Mrs Moore, he will not take seriously, but in the effort to make good return. It is right, Godbole thinks, indeed it is imperative, that we continue our plea to God that He 'come', that good may return and

evil recede before it. Even so intimate a friend of the author as
Lowes Dickinson was impatient to know what did occur in the
cave; Forster never offers even a hint, and we must thus conclude
that like Godbole and Mrs Moore he is concerned, and wants us
to be concerned, not with what happened, but only with why it
happened and with what could and should be done to assure and
speed the recession of evil and the return of good.

The third part of the novel is Godbole's until it becomes also
Mrs Moore's. Godbole leads the mysterious ceremony of Hindu
worship with which this last part opens. The temple where he
dances and prays, smears his forehead with butter and tries to
swallow the butter as it trickles down his face and the faces of his
friends, is not in Chandrapore; it lies outside the strains of British
India, in a small native state a few miles only from the fortress of
Asirgarh. If the ceremony violates all Western feelings about
proportion and religious decorum, we are brought to understand
that the violation of proportion and religious decorum is the
very circumstance that enables the ceremony to intensify the
spiritual being of the worshippers. Godbole achieves union with
the divine, he propels Mrs Moore and the wasp into this union,
he routs the goblins, because in his worship he makes no fixed
exclusions, he does not exclude humour, he does not exclude
ugliness. Everything but evil becomes the ally of good. So powerful is the effect of this worship that even the non-Hindus in the
native state find their spiritual being intensified.

The next scene is theirs. Aziz takes Ralph Moore on the water
to witness the last stage in the Hindu ceremony. Fielding and
Stella Moore, his wife, are in another boat. The four non-Hindus
are intent on the ceremony unrolling by the shore. A raft is
launched bearing a clay god, who is to melt in the water. Suddenly
the two boats are very close to the raft and to each other. From
the Hindus lining the shore comes a howl, whether of wrath or of
joy no one else can tell, but it is reassuring that Godbole is there.
Stella leans first towards her husband, then with an instinctive
recognition of affinity that is among the most delicate and moving
touches in the novel, she leans towards Aziz. The strange and
unexpected gesture leads the two boats to overturn in the shallow

water, after colliding with the raft. The god and his earthen retinue are involved in the confusion and the clay melts into mud. Meanwhile with a volume and complexity that reminds one of Forster's description of the close of the Fifth Symphony, guns roar, elephants trumpet, and like a mallet beating on a dome comes one crack of thunder loud enough to drown all else. A part of the god's retinue, now turned to mud, is swept back to shore and Godbole happily smears it on his forehead. The goblins are routed. All are one. The spirit of the ceremony with which this third part began reappears, to affect all the personages. Even a letter from Adela Quested, and another from Ronnie Heaslop, which had confirmed Aziz in his suspicions, float in the water with the sacred clay. The passage to India is over, and it has not been a failure. One of the voices of India that Mrs Moore had not heard has spoken with trenchant power, and strangely her own voice has spoken in unison with it.

But no, the passage is not quite over. In Helen Schlegel's elucidation of the Fifth Symphony it was said that the goblins were still there. 'They could return. He had said so bravely, and that is why one can trust Beethoven when he says other things.' Forster too will say bravely that the goblins could return. The last ride together of the two friends Aziz and Fielding is a proof of the force and the fineness of the revived friendship; but it also shows how precarious their personal understanding was, how impotent they were to maintain it equably, how dependent it was on aid drawn from above themselves from the Brahman Godbole, from Mrs Moore.

Three big blocks of sound – that was Forster's account of rhythm in the Fifth Symphony. Three big blocks of sound – that is what *A Passage to India* consists of. A first block in which evil creeps about weakly, and the secret understanding of the heart is easily dominant. A second block very long, and very dark, in which evil streams forth from the caves and lays waste almost everything about, but yet meets an opposition, indecisive in some ways, but unyielding, in the contemplative insight of Professor Godbole, and the intuitive fidelity of Mrs Moore. A third block in which evil is forced to recede, summarily, and spectacularly, not by the secret understanding of the heart, but by the strength on which the secret understanding of the heart depends, contemplative insight, intuitive fidelity. Then the final reminder, that good has merely obliged evil to recede as good receded before evil a little before.

Reduced to the barest terms, the structure of *A Passage to India* has the 'rhythmic rise-fall-rise' that Forster found in what has been for him, early and late, the greatest of novels, *War and Peace*.

IV

It is time, and perhaps rather more than time, to ask how the varied kinds of repetition with variation that abound in *A Passage to India* aid that book in producing its effect. A question that is difficult, perhaps impossible, but it must be asked. It is so difficult because the effect of *A Passage to India* is not a simple one, as the effect of *The Old Wives' Tale* or *Vanity Fair* is simple. Forster's imaginative sympathies have outrun his intellectual commitments, and when this happens to a novelist the result is either a confusion or a fine complexity. Forster's intellectual commitments are clearly set out in his pamphlet *What I Believe*. 'My law givers are Erasmus and Montaigne, not Moses and St Paul.' And again: 'Tolerance, good temper and sympathy – they are what matter really.' The person in *A Passage to India* who has the best combination of tolerance, good temper, and sympathy, who would be most likely to take Erasmus and Montaigne as law givers, is Cyril Fielding. But *A Passage to India* is not conceived according to Fielding's liberal, sceptical, humanist values. It is conceived according to values much better apprehended by Mrs Moore, who is irritable, of uncertain sympathies, in her time of crisis acridly intolerant, and who quotes only one author – St Paul. It should not be too much of a disturbance in interpreting a novel to find the artist's imaginative sympathies outrunning his intellectual commitments – even so temperate an artist as Turgenev had it happen to him in rendering Bazarov in *Fathers and Sons*.

The main effect in *A Passage to India* is, I believe, of order in the universe, but order that can be merely glimpsed, never seized for sure. In the poem from which the title comes, Whitman ends by bidding us

> steer for the deep waters only,
> Reckless O soul, exploring, I with thee, and thou with me,
> For we are bound where mariner has not yet dared to go,
> And we will risk the ship, ourselves and all.
>
> O my brave soul!
> O farther farther sail!
> O daring joy, but safe! are they not all the seas of God?
> O farther, farther, farther sail.

It is because they are exploring in the seas of God that Mrs Moore is not deluded in respecting the admonition of Asirgarh 'I do not vanish'; that Godbole is not deluded when among the circling images he is led to propel Mrs Moore and the wasp towards the divine. They move in mystery, but the mystery is not a muddle. It is an order.

To express what is both an order and a mystery, rhythmic processes, repetitions with intricate variations, are the most appropriate of idioms. Repetition is the strongest assurance an author can give of order; the extraordinary complexity of the variations is the reminder that the order is so involute that it must remain a mystery. *A Passage to India* is a prophetic novel, a singing in the halls of fiction: the infinite resourcefulness of Forster has given it a rhythmic form that enables us to respond to it as prophecy and song; to pass beyond character, story, and setting, and attend, delightedly, to the grouping and ungrouping of ideas and emotions; to feel that numinous element so constantly present in the experience of the great man whom in these discourses I have wished to honour.

SOURCE: *Rhythm in the Novel* (1950).

Reuben A. Brower

THE TWILIGHT OF THE DOUBLE VISION: SYMBOL AND IRONY IN *A PASSAGE TO INDIA* (1951)

> ... the twilight of the double vision ...
> (*A Passage to India*)

IN *A Passage to India*, as in all of E. M. Forster's novels, there are admirable scenes of social comedy that remind us of the sunny repose of Jane Austen. We can enjoy the behavior of Mrs Turton, the great lady of a British civil station, with the same satisfaction with which we view the absurdities of Mrs Bennet and Lady Catherine de Bourgh. Here is Mrs Turton commenting on her Indian guests at the Bridge Party given for Adela Quested and Mrs Moore soon after their arrival in India:

> 'They ought never to have been allowed to drive in; it's so bad for them,' said Mrs Turton, who had at last begun her progress to the summer-house accompanied by Mrs Moore, Miss Quested, and a terrier. 'Why they come at all I don't know. They hate it as much as we do. Talk to Mrs McBryde. Her husband made her give purdah parties until she struck.'
> 'This isn't a purdah party,' corrected Miss Quested.
> 'Oh, really,' was the haughty rejoinder.
> 'Do kindly tell us who these ladies are,' asked Mrs Moore.
> 'You're superior to them, anyway. Don't forget that. You're superior to everyone in India except one or two of the Ranis, and they're on an equality.'
> Advancing, she shook hands with the group and said a few words of welcome in Urdu. She had learnt the lingo, but only to speak to her servants, so she knew none of the politer forms and of the verbs only the imperative mood. As soon as her speech was over, she enquired of her companions, 'Is that what you wanted?'

'Please tell these ladies that I wish we could speak their language, but we have only just come to their country.'

'Perhaps we speak yours a little,' one of the ladies said.

'Why, fancy, she understands!' said Mrs Turton.

'Eastbourne, Piccadilly, High Park Corner,' said another of the ladies.

'Oh yes, they're English-speaking.'

'But now we can talk: how delightful!' cried Adela, her face lighting up.

'She knows Paris also,' called one of the onlookers.

'They pass Páris on the way, no doubt,' said Mrs Turton, as if she was describing the movements of migratory birds. Her manner had grown more distant since she had discovered that some of the group was Westernized, and might apply her own standards to her.

From a politically liberal, cosmopolitan point of view we may be amused at Mrs Turton's having 'learnt the lingo' or at the charming rudeness of her grammar. But we shall not be able to maintain this comfortable frame of mind for long. Or if we suppose so, like Adela we have been taken in by a surface simplicity and by our own excellent principles. Reading a little further, we realize that our enlightened point of view has itself been undermined:

Miss Quested now had her desired opportunity; friendly Indians were before her, and she tried to make them talk, but she failed, she strove in vain against the echoing walls of their civility. Whatever she said produced a murmur of deprecation, varying into a murmur of concern when she dropped her pocket-handkerchief. She tried doing nothing, to see what that produced, and they too did nothing.

The scene leaves us in a most discomforting state of mind. The essence of its irony is expressed in a metaphor, 'the echoing walls of their civility': friendly conversational gestures are so perfectly reproduced as to prove that nothing whatever has been communicated. But the phrase sends out tentacles of connection well beyond the immediate context. We are reminded of the more sinister echoes of a Marabar cave or of the image that came to

Mrs Moore after telling her son that the British must love the
Indians because it 'satisfies God':

> Mrs Moore felt that she had made a mistake in mentioning
> God . . . She must needs pronounce his name frequently, as the
> greatest she knew, yet she had never found it less efficacious.
> Outside the arch there seemed always an arch, beyond the re-
> motest echo a silence.

'The echoing walls' adds a new level of irony to the dialogue of
the Bridge Party and at the same time introduces one of the major
symbols of *A Passage to India*.

It is a characteristic of *A Passage to India*, as it is utterly un-
characteristic of *Pride and Prejudice*, that the irony should be
expressed through metaphor and that the meaning of an ironic
expression can be appreciated only in relation to other expressions
that are clearly symbolic. The central design of Forster's novel is
composed of a group of symbolic metaphors, and his irony is in-
herent in the meaning of his symbols. By interpreting them and
seeing how they unify the experience of the novel, we can also
understand the peculiar character of Forster's irony, how like
and how unlike it is to that of Jane Austen.

The main symbols of *A Passage to India* are named in the titles
to the three Parts of the novel: Mosque, Caves, and Temple. Each
is more or less closely related to a corresponding variant: Arch,
Echo, and Sky. To anyone familiar with the book the three title
words* are immediately and richly expressive. Each conveys a
generalized impression of a salient object or event in the narrative, an impression that stands for and is inseparably connected
with various large meanings. To get a sense of Forster's total
design it is necessary to see how the meanings of these symbols

* It would be hard to find purer examples of symbolic expressions.
They are obviously 'iconic'; the reader is to think of something (the
subject) in terms of the Mosque or the Caves or the Temple (i.e. the
generalized impressions). And the 'subject' is not otherwise stated.
Throughout this chapter expressions of the type, 'the Mosque', 'the
Caves', et cetera, refer to the iconic half of the metaphor. The terms
without the article, Mosque, Caves, et cetera, refer to the symbol as
a complete metaphor.

are built up through the dramatic structure. What follows is an attempt to display the kind of design – symbolic, ironic, and dramatic – peculiar to *A Passage to India*. (I shall also indicate where and why the design seems to break down.)

The most general meaning of the Mosque symbol is perhaps best expressed in the scene between Mrs Moore and Aziz, the young Indian doctor whom she meets in a mosque near the civil station. In a dialogue which is a blend of minor mistakes and underlying sympathy Mrs Moore and Aziz reach a surprisingly intimate relationship, Aziz declaring that the Englishwoman is 'an Oriental'. Although in a later scene Mrs Moore calls him her friend, there is something precarious about their intimacy. In spite of his affectionate declarations Aziz quickly forgets that he has promised to take Mrs Moore and Adela to visit the Marabar Caves. From the scene in the mosque and from similar episodes, the Mosque comes to symbolize the possibility of communication between Britons and Indians, and more generally the possibility of understanding relationships between any two persons. And in every instance this larger meaning always implies its opposite or near-opposite, an ambivalence finely suggested by the first description of the mosque. Aziz is especially pleased by the dualism of 'black and white' in the frieze above the arches, and he appreciates the stillness and beauty of the building in contrast with 'the complex appeal' of the night. At the end of the scene,

As he strolled downhill beneath the lovely moon, and again saw the lovely mosque, he seemed to own the land as much as anyone owned it. What did it matter if a few flabby Hindus had preceded him there, and a few chilly English succeeded?

In relation to this and various other points in the narrative, the Mosque represents the ambiguous triumph of Islam, the belief Aziz shares with his Moslem friends 'that India was one; Moslem; always had been; an assurance that lasted until they looked out of the door'.

The Mosque also expresses Fielding's friendship with Aziz and more generally Fielding's conviction that 'The world . . . is a globe of men who are trying to reach one another and can best

do so by the help of good will plus culture and intelligence . . .'
But this Anglo-Indian relationship is a precarious one, too, its
instability being finely expressed in the crisscross of the conversation when Fielding visits Aziz during his illness. After his friend
leaves, the Indian goes to sleep, dreaming happily of 'good
Fielding', in a Moslem paradise with domes 'whereunder were
were inscribed, black against white, the ninety-nine attributes of
God'. The ironic dualism of color echoes the halfhearted comment on his *rapprochement* with Fielding: '. . . affection had triumphed for once in a way'.

Miss Quested's blundering attempts to 'know' Indians and her
shifting relationship with her fiancé, Mrs Moore's son, Ronny
reinforce the negative meanings of the symbol. She naïvely imagines that Mrs Moore in meeting Aziz at the mosque had seen 'the
real India', a remark that imparts to the symbol still another ironic
connotation. Ronny, who interprets the same episode as a piece
of native insolence, reveals as always the reduction of human
intercourse to the automatic responses of a governing class.

The opening section of the novel is thus composed as a series
of dramatic variations on Mosque themes. While the connection
between the narratives and the symbol is always clear, there is
hardly ever a point where, as in *The Longest Journey*, we feel the
cold hand of allegory. Our attention is always more engaged by
what is happening than by any generalized significance. The dialogue is always sufficiently confusing; it mirrors the complex play
of interests, amusements, and mistakes that is fairly typical of
social intercourse. There is also in the Mosque section complexity
of a sort that is more important in the structure of the whole
novel. Through the oddly interrupted episodes run lines of
symbolic meaning that point to the scene in the Marabar Caves.

By focusing attention on this episode, particularly on Mrs
Moore's curious 'vision', we can see how admirably Forster has
prepared us for a moment of dramatic change through building
up meanings of various major symbols. What does the experience
of hearing the echo mean for Mrs Moore? The sentence that best
sums up her situation and its significance is one describing her
state of mind as she 'surrenders to her vision':

Then she was terrified over an area larger than usual; the universe, never comprehensible to her intellect, offered no respose to her soul, the mood of the last two months took definite form at last, and she realized that she didn't want to write to her children, didn't want to communicate with anyone, not even with God.

The change in Mrs Moore's relation to her family and friends is the most obvious effect of her jarring experience. She 'loses all interest, even in Aziz', and in her later conversations with Adela and Ronny she exhibits the most snappish and capricious irritability and a complete indifference concerning the 'unspeakable attempt' in the cave, an attitude that extends to marriage and love in general:

'Why all this marriage, marriage? ... The human race would have become a single person centuries ago if marriage was any use. And all this rubbish about love, love in a church, love in a cave, as if there is the least difference, and I held up from my business over such trifles!'

All distinctions of feeling and of moral value have become confused and meaningless:

... the echo began in some indescribable way to undermine her hold on life. Coming at a moment when she chanced to be fatigued, it had managed to murmur, 'Pathos, piety, courage – they exist, but are identical, and so is filth. Everything exists, nothing has value.'

The doctrines of Western religious faith become equally empty:

But suddenly, at the edge of her mind, Religion appeared, poor little talkative Christianity, and she knew that all its divine words from 'Let there be Light' to 'It is finished' only amounted to 'boum'.

Finally, the comforting belief in a universe or in some eternal setting for human life is shaken; and at the same time serene acceptance of this world as an end in itself is impossible:

She had come to that state where the horror of the universe and its smallness are both visible at the same time – the twilight of the double vision in which so many elderly people are involved.

If this world is not to our taste, well, at all events there is Heaven, Hell, Annihilation – one or other of those large things, that huge scenic background of stars, fires, blue or black air. All heroic endeavour, and all that is known as art, assumes that there is such a background, just as all practical endeavour, when the world is to our taste, assumes that the world is all. But in the twilight of the double vision, a spiritual muddledom is set up for which no high-sounding words can be found; we can neither act nor refrain from action, we can neither ignore nor respect Infinity.

Mrs Moore has had a somewhat more than adequate glimpse of complete muddle, an exposure to chaos in personal relations and in the universe.

These are certainly large and varied meanings for a novelist to press from the story of an old woman's visit to some not so 'extraordinary' Indian caves. Forster's surprising success in bringing us to accept the strange and wonderful significance of the event depends on his earlier building up of symbolic meanings of Cave, Sky, and Echo. Throughout the preceding narrative, beginning with the opening sentence of the novel, he has imparted to the caves a twofold significance, suggestions of mystery and order that are constantly countered by suggestions of disillusionment and muddle. At the moment of climax the more unpleasant alternatives emerge with the force of truths already experienced and half acknowledged.

The preparation begins in the Mosque symbolism, through which hints of communication between persons and peoples have been accompanied by 'clinging forms' of uncertainty. The Cave symbol is not (as I once supposed) simply the antithesis of the Mosque, but in part a parallel symbol repeating the same oppositions. When at Fielding's tea party Aziz first proposes a trip to the Marabar, it seems that the expedition will be a triumph of Anglo-Indian friendship. And during the ecstatic moments of the later tea party outside the caves, this possibility is apparently about to be realized. Once the horrid tour has taken place, the Caves symbolize the failure of all communication, the collapse of human relationships ironically foreshadowed in the less pleasant meaning of the Mosque symbol.

That the Caves should symbolize 'mystery' as well as 'muddle' depends on preparations that are fairly subtle, particularly in relation to Mrs Moore. From her first appearance in the novel Mrs Moore has been presented as ready for 'a mystery', for some revelation of unity. Shortly after meeting Aziz in the mosque, she has a minor mystical vision:

She watched the moon, whose radiance stained with primrose the purple of the surrounding sky. In England the moon had seemed dead and alien; here she was caught in the shawl of night together with earth and all the other stars. A sudden sense of unity, of kinship with the heavenly bodies, passed into the old woman and out, like water through a tank, leaving a strange freshness behind.

This mood is recalled much later, when Mrs Moore is caught 'in the twilight of the double vision' and able neither to 'ignore nor respect Infinity':

Mrs Moore had always inclined to resignation. As soon as she landed in India it seemed to her good, and when she saw the water flowing through the mosque-tank, or the Ganges, or the moon, caught in the shawl of night with all the other stars, it seemed a beautiful goal and an easy one. To be one with the universe! So dignified and simple. But there was always some little duty to be performed first, some new card to be turned up from the diminishing pack and placed, and while she was pottering about, the Marabar struck its gong.

The Sky (or the 'heavenly bodies') as a symbol of the universe and of infinity had also been introduced in other, nondramatic contexts: in the picture of the 'overarching sky' at the very beginning of the novel,

. . . the stars hang like lamps from the immense vault. The distance between the vault and them is as nothing to the distance behind them, and that farther distance, though beyond colour, last freed itself from blue . . .

and in the ironic setting for the Bridge Party:

Some kites hovered overhead, impartial, over the kites passed the mass of a vulture, and with an impartiality exceeding all, the sky, not deeply coloured but translucent, poured light from its whole circumference. It seemed unlikely that the series stopped here. Beyond the sky must not there be something that over-arches all the skies, more impartial even than they? Beyond which again . . .

But in Mrs Moore's reflections on God and love the infinite series of arches had also been associated with an echo, an association that anticipates the later link between Sky and Caves. God, the traditional Christian order that had sheltered and contained her world, oddly recedes in her thoughts like a fading echo. (The Sky, like the other symbols, has its antithetical and ironic con-notations.) Imagery used in various descriptions of the caves also tends to link the two symbols. They are circular, perhaps num-berless, and 'when a match is struck' and reflected in the 'mar-vellously polished walls . . . two flames approach and strive to unite' in something like an ecstasy of love. The caves take on some of the mysterious qualities of the night sky, and the reader is not altogether surprised that Mrs Moore finds cosmic signifi-cance in making a visit to them. It is quite appropriate that she should have a vision of infinity, though it turns out to be less acceptable than she had imagined.

The preparation for the caves episode as a revelation of 'muddle' extends through nearly every phase of the narrative up to the moment of Mrs Moore's panic. All of the kinds of muddledom that she consequently experiences are anticipated and connected more or less subtly with the Marabar. The con-versation in which she first hears that 'India's a muddle' is a nice example of this twofold preparation. Miss Quested has been describing a tiny social muddle that began at the Bridge Party in a 'shapeless discussion' with two Hindus, Mr and Mrs Bhatta-charya. The 'couple with the unpronounceable name' (a signifi-cant comment) change their plans in order to have Mrs Moore and Adela visit them, and then on the appointed day fail to send their carriage for their guests. Adela wants Fielding to help her clear the matter up:

'I do so hate mysteries,' Adela announced.
'We English do.'

'I dislike them not because I'm English, but from my own personal point of view,' she corrected.

'I like mysteries but I rather dislike muddles,' said Mrs Moore.

'A mystery is a muddle.'

'Oh, do you think so, Mr Fielding?'

'A mystery is only a high-sounding term for a muddle. No advantage in stirring it up, in either case. Aziz and I know well that India's a muddle.'

'India's – Oh, what an alarming idea!'

'There'll be no muddle when you come to see me,' said Aziz, rather out of his depth. 'Mrs Moore and everyone – I invite you all – oh, please.'

The old lady accepted: she still thought the young doctor excessively nice; moreover, a new feeling, half languor, half excitement, bade her turn down any fresh path.

In a few moments Aziz shows that he is as unstable as the Hindus. Having issued his invitation, he thinks with horror of his detestable bungalow and changes the place to the Marabar Caves.

Another symbolic connection is anticipated a little later in a conversation that takes place between Aziz and Professor Godbole, the 'Deccani Brahman'. The echo, we recall, produced in Mrs Moore a curious spiritual confusion. What she had known as religion became meaningless, and yet she had had an experience that was somehow religious, a glimpse of evil, of 'the undying worm itself'. The Caves, it appears, stand for a type of religious experience accessible only to a peculiar type of Oriental intelligence. When Aziz questions Godbole about the Marabar Caves, he gets nowhere. But it is perfectly clear that the Hindu was 'concealing something'. Adela, who listens without understanding, does 'not know that the comparatively simple mind of the Mohammedan was encountering Ancient Night'. Just after the caves are mentioned again Godbole sings a Hindu song, the effect of which is described in imagery that suggests the baffling caves and their echoes:

His thin voice rose, and gave out one sound after another. At times there seemed rhythm, at times there was the illusion of a Western melody. But the ear, baffled repeatedly, soon lost

any clue, and wandered in a maze of noises, none harsh or unpleasant, none intelligible. It was the song of an unknown bird.

Somehow – and the 'how' cannot be very well defined – we are
made to feel that the Marabar may be the scene of a revelation,
perhaps confused and murky, but comprehensible to the Hindu
mind.

Mrs Moore's indifference to values and her moral confusion
focused in her loss of faith in Christian marriage. The dramatic
appropriateness of this is obvious, especially in relation to Adela's
discovery on entering the second cave, that she has left out love
in deciding to marry Ronny. Mrs Moore has observed the un-
steady course of her 'young people's' relations with growing
signs of irritation and disillusionment. She hears the word of
their engagement with no joy: '. . . though it was all right now
she could not speak as enthusiastically of wedlock or of anything
as she should have done.' The connection between the caves and
the unsatisfactoriness of marriage is made at various points in the
narrative of Adela's and Ronny's engagement. They quarrel
rather bitterly over Aziz's invitation, while Mrs Moore listens to
them with extreme annoyance:

'I've never heard of these caves, I don't know what or where
they are,' said Mrs Moore, 'but I really can't have' – she tapped
the cushion beside her – 'so much quarrelling and tiresomeness!'

Adela, declaring (with unconscious irony) that what she has to
say has 'nothing to do with the caves', proceeds to tell Ronny
that she will not marry him. It is symbolically a little too neat
that they get re-engaged during an accident while driving at night
on the Marabar Road. The car in which they were riding hits a
hyena or a ghost or . . . ?

But the most subtle preparation for Mrs Moore's disillusioning
vision of marriage comes in the superb account of the approach
to the caves. Here the main symbols – Mosque, Caves, and Sky –
all appear, unobtrusively woven into a narrative that has a pre-
dominant tone of dullness and nightmarish confusion. The party
itself is made up of an incredible jumble of persons whom Aziz
barely succeeds in holding together; in fact Fielding and Godbole

arrive only when Adela is rushing away in panic. As the 'train half asleep' moves along in a scene of 'timeless twilight', Mrs Moore and Adela apathetically discuss plans for Adela's married life. Mrs Moore's reflections indicate an approaching crisis in her uncertainty about marriage:

She felt increasingly (vision or nightmare?) that, though people are important, the relations between them are not, and that in particular too much fuss has been made over marriage; centuries of carnal embracement, yet man is no nearer to understanding man. And to-day she felt this with such force that it seemed itself a relationship, itself a person who was trying to take hold of her hand.

The sky, with appropriate irony, brightens up as if for a 'miracle', but there is no sunrise, only a 'false dawn'. There is '. . . a spiritual silence which invaded more senses than the ear. Life went on as usual, but had no consequences, that is to say, sounds did not echo or thoughts develop.' There was, for example, '. . . a confusion about a snake which was never cleared up'. (The echoes are later described as serpent-like in their coiling movement.) It is again suggested that the mystery of the Marabar could be understood only by a Hindu:

. . . he [Aziz] had no notion how to treat this particular aspect of India; he was lost in it without Professor Godbole, like themselves.

For a few minutes before entering the caves, the happy Mosque relationship between Mrs Moore and Aziz is revived, and understanding between individuals and even peoples seems possible. But Aziz warns Adela of the deceptions of 'Akbar's universal religion': 'Nothing embraces the whole of India,' he tells her, 'nothing, nothing, and that was Akbar's mistake.' As the oddly assorted members of the party go into the first cave, we get a final and tremendous impression of annihilation of human relationships and distinctions:

The small back hole gaped where their varied forms and colours had momentarily functioned. They were sucked in like water

down a drain. Bland and bald rose the precipices; bland and
glutinous the sky that connected the precipices; solid and white,
a Brahminy kite flapped between the rocks with a clumsiness that
seemed intentional. Before man, with his itch for the seemly, had
been born, the planet must have looked thus. The kite flapped
away. . . Before birds, perhaps. . . And then the hole belched and
humanity returned.

The pressure felt behind each of the details in this narrative,
their power of evoking at once a sequence of dramatic relationships and a rich variety of feelings, is due to the kind of far-
reaching preparation we have been tracing. When the echo
comes, it seems to the reader as to Mrs Moore that this is what
he has been waiting for all along. As the 'echoes generate echoes',
the layers of meaninglessness unfold and the whole range of
'muddles', in personal relationships, in moral and religious values,
and in concepts of the universe, is revealed. The symbolic values
of Caves, Mosque, and Sky were being built up for this moment,
the perfect aptness of their ironic character now being clear.

The Echo, though less ambiguous than the other symbols, has
a dual value for the reader. As an image linked with the receding
arches of the sky and with Mrs Moore's glimpses of infinity it
recalls the possibility of a revelation. But through its monotonous
meaningless 'bou-oum' the echo brings to the surface uglier levels
of experience already associated with the Marabar and hinted at in
the less sinister symbols of Mosque and Sky. The vision turns out
to be a nightmare. Forster's success in making it so convincing
and so meaningful arises from his handling of a complex design
which is at once dramatic, symbolic, and ironic. As an artist he
has earned the right to attribute large and various meanings to
Mrs Moore's curious experience and to express a significance that
goes well beyond the immediate dramatic moment. While presenting a seemingly personal crisis Forster has expressed the
vision perhaps most characteristic of the twentieth century, the
discovery that the universe may not be a unity but chaos, that
older philosophic and religious orders with the values they
guaranteed have dissolved. The vision of *A Passage to India* has
its counterparts in *The Education of Henry Adams* and in 'Geron-

tion' and 'The Waste Land'. All these visions are – with differing emphases – the result of various kinds of over-exposure, to too many civilizations (which seem to make nonsense of one another), to too many observations of complexity in the mind and in the physical world –

After such knowledge, what forgiveness?

We are not concerned here with the proper action after such a vision, but with Forster's novel and with how he completes the structure which he began with such art. I think there can be few readers who will say that the concluding Temple section of *A Passage to India* gives them no pause. Is this section of the novel merely a *tour de force*, or does it have an integrity of design comparable to that of the earlier sections? Is its structure complementary to the design we have been tracing? We can answer these questions best by asking and answering a question of the sort we have put to each of the other symbols: what does the Temple symbol mean in dramatic terms?

It signifies most clearly Hinduism, the religion of Godbole, who presides over the ceremony at Mau in which the worshippers 'love all men, the whole universe' and in which 'the Lord of the Universe' is born. But from a Western point of view, the narrator observes, 'this ... triumph of India was a muddle ... a frustration of reason and form'. Forster's account of the ceremony is shot through with comic, sometimes farcical touches, with the result that of all the symbols the Temple seems the most crudely ironic. Its twofold meaning is expressed very well in the final picture of Fielding's and Aziz's relationship. For a brief time, after being reconciled during the jumble of the Hindu ceremony, they are friends; but their friendship, like the unity of India, is unstable. In the concluding words of the novel we are told that that the 'temples' as well as 'the tank' (i.e. the Mosque), and 'the sky' do not want them to be friends. This, we may say, is a finely poised irresolution, the only possible conclusion for a novel of irony. The Temple is a symbol of Hindu unity in love which is no unity.

But if we try to interpret the Temple symbol in terms of the dramatized experiences of Mrs Moore and of her children, we get into difficulties. We find 'muddle' in the relations between symbolic and dramatic designs and at some points a kind of dramatic vacuum. For example, the temple ceremony has an odd meaning in the account of what has happened to Fielding's wife and her brother, Ralph. Fielding tells Aziz that his wife now 'believes that the Marabar is wiped out', and after adding that Ralph 'rides a little behind her, though with her', he says:

'From her point of view, Mau has been a success. It calmed her – both of them suffer from restlessness. She found something soothing, some solution of her queer troubles here.'

Though there is a notable lack of irony in Fielding's remarks, it is not wholly out of character for him to describe such changes as conceivable, for he has several times shown tolerance for religious experiences that he cannot himself share. For example, he has asked Aziz to sing of 'something in religion . . . that the Hindus have perhaps found'. But for some reason we are embarrassed by the injection of such vague and solemn mysticism at this point in the novel. We are embarrassed not because the possibility of mystical experience is to be rejected, but because we cannot believe in it here as a part of the fictional experience. Something has gone wrong, or perhaps something is wanting, in the literary structure. The test again is to ask what the metaphors mean in the dramatic context. How has 'Mau' (the temple ceremony) 'calmed' Fielding's wife, and what is this 'wiping out of the Marabar'? If 'the Marabar' was 'muddle' and panic, the 'calming' is apparently an experience of unity and peace, a Hindu vision in which chaos is reduced to order. But once we refer these mystical effects to the narrative of the Mau celebration and recall the glorious muddle of Godbole's 'vision', we can no longer solemnly accept 'Mau' as a symbol of a soothing revelation of unity.

The 'peace of Mau' also seems to be induced through some queer telepathic influence of Mrs Moore and her children, who have apparently inherited something more marvelous than their mother's 'restlessness'. In the operatic scene in which Aziz and

Ralph hear the chant of 'Radhakrishna Radhakrishna', Aziz forgets the wrong done him at Marabar and 'focusing his heart on something more distant than the caves, something beautiful', he becomes reconciled with Mrs Moore's son and discovers that he, like his mother, is 'an Oriental'. The imagery reminds us of the 'distant' sky, of the ultimate unity, but the dramatic preparation for the mystical effect of Mrs Moore's influence is lacking or unconvincing. More than once after the caves episode we hear that Mrs Moore 'knew something' inaccessible to Fielding and Adela. The queer girl also believes that 'only Mrs Moore could drive' the sound of the echo 'back to its source and seal the broken reservoir. Evil was loose . . .' Mrs Moore can somehow restore the broken unity and give peace to those who, like her children and Aziz, are in communication with her as Esmiss Moore, a sort of Hindu demigoddess. The impression created before the Marabar visit, that the caves were comprehensible only to a Hindu, prepared us for Mrs Moore's bafflement but hardly for her 'reincarnation'. When we recall in contrast with such fragmentary hints what has been so completely and wonderfully presented, the cave nightmare, we can hardly accept this about-face in Mrs Moore's role and its symbolic value. We cannot at the end of the novel regard Mrs Moore as in tune with the infinite and conveniently forget the mocking denial of her echo. 'To be at one with the universe! So dignified and simple.' The exquisite irony of that comment has been too vividly realized in 'the muddle' of the Caves.

Put crudely, there is little dramatic evidence that Mrs Moore or her children ever had any experience of cosmic unity and the peace that passeth understanding. There are some marvelously clever bits of sleight of hand, oblique allusions to being 'calmed' and to 'knowing something', but not much more. It can be said that Forster, like his characters, was up against the inexpressible: visions of unity are not to be dramatized. Or perhaps they are not easily presented in fiction. They lend themselves better to self-dramatization, as in the poetry of Wordsworth or Vaughan or St John of the Cross. But it is always unwise to say what cannot be done in literature; in the present instance it is better to say that

Forster did not succeed in giving dramatic meaning to the Temple as a symbol of unity. By contrast, the positive meaning of the Mosque – the attainment of closer understanding – is portrayed with sharp particularity as in the scenes between Aziz and Mrs Moore or between Aziz and Fielding. As Forster's other novels triumphantly prove, he commands this area of experience: he is above all the novelist of personal relations.

It is fortunate that Forster did not succeed in recovering for Temple and Sky single meanings of peace and unity, for the total design of his novel moves toward no such clear resolution. Whenever he emphasizes these simply serious connotations, he is in effect attempting to transcend the limits of his own ironic vision. (Sweet are the uses of ambiguity to the ironist, especially to one who presents experience through richly ambiguous symbols.) In the best of *A Passage to India* Forster enjoys to the full the freedom of giving varied and even opposite meanings to his symbolic metaphors. In the Mosque-Cave sequences the narrative precisely and fully defines the double meanings of the symbols, and there is complete harmony between symbolic and dramatic designs: we saw how beautifully Forster built up the unpleasant implications of Mosque, Caves, and Sky to prepare for the climactic moment when their full force was realized.

The contrast between his ironic-fictional design and Jane Austen's is now clear. Her balancing of possible interpretations, since it depended on well-defined beliefs, led inevitably to a choice and a resolution. Hers was the irony that moves toward the cancellation of irony. Forster's pattern leads to no such resolution. Playing, sometimes capriciously, with every possible meaning of an experience, he cannot reach conclusions. For his basic assumption, best expressed through Fielding, is that anything may be true, that the unreasonable explanation may be as valid as the reasonable one. Only one allegiance remains unshaken throughout the novel, a belief in the possibility and value of communication between individuals, a belief accompanied by the reservation that human relationships are always on the verge of breakdown. The hope of communication is generous, but skeptical, and hints of unity among all men or all nations or all things can hardly be accepted without an ironic smile. The design of Forster's fiction suffers only when he deviates into solemnity.

SOURCE: *The Fields of Light* (1951).

Gertrude M. White

A PASSAGE TO INDIA:
ANALYSIS AND REVALUATION
(1953)

I

A Passage to India, apparently the last, and certainly the best of
E. M. Forster's novels, was published twenty-nine years ago, in
1924. It was accorded instant recognition, as a fine novel and as a
perceptive and sympathetic treatment of the problem of 'Anglo-
India'. The years that followed saw the book established as a
modern classic. It has reached a wide audience in the Everyman,
Modern Library, and Penguin editions, and has challenged as
well the attention of able critics. But, though the novel has
received its just dues in many ways, there remains one aspect –
and, I think, a fundamental one – still unexplored. It is acknowledged on all sides that thought is the most important element in
Forster's novels, yet the dialectical pattern of *A Passage to India*
has never, to my knowledge, been fully and specifically recognized. This omission has resulted not only in a certain incompleteness in critical accounts of the book, but in not a little
confusion and obscurity as well.

A score or more of penetrating studies have analyzed *A Passage* as a social document: 'a book which no student of the Indian
question can disregard' (Peter Burra). Its plot, style, character-
drawing, particular ideas and attitudes have likewise been ex-
haustively discussed, evaluated, and related to the body of
Forster's work and to modern literature generally. Its author
has been hailed as 'the last survivor of a cultured liberal tradition'
(Rex Warner, *E. M. Forster*, 1950) and 'the only living novelist
who can be read again and again' (Lionel Trilling, *E. M. Forster*,
1943).

Even those who have written of him with most appreciation, however, have apparently failed to grasp fully the meaning and importance of the novel's theme, and thus have given only partial accounts of it. Penetrating and provocative as they are, such treatments as those of Burra, Trilling, Brown, Zabel, and Hoare – to name a few of the best[1] – still tend to be over-general, and to put a somewhat undue emphasis on the 'mystery' of the novel. Burra seems to speak for all of them when he tells us that its 'thought, like music's, cannot be fixed, nor its meaning defined'. Though this is, no doubt, true in a sense, I feel that the mistiness of the book has been exaggerated.

This same failure to apprehend clearly the framework of thought in the novel has led other critics into undue censure or misunderstanding. For example, we hear that, 'He beats the bush with admirable dexterity, but nothing appears. No wonder his book leaves on our minds an impression of waste.' Or we are told, 'In his comedy . . . he shows himself the born novelist; but he aims also at making a poetic communication about life, and here he is, by contrast, almost unbelievably crude and weak.'[2] These are severe judgments indeed. And there are those who openly confess themselves at a loss: 'One can re-read a dozen times and be no nearer a solution.'[3]

Any attentive reader of *A Passage* has certainly realized that Forster indeed suggests more than can be explained; and to translate suggestive and poetic language into explicit statement is always to risk destroying one kind of reality without furnishing another. It is my belief, however, that there exists in *A Passage* a dialectical pattern, strong and subtle, by which the author attempts to bind social, psychological, and philosophical levels into a harmony and to relate the characters and events of the novel to each other and to the informing idea of the whole. Further, I believe that incompleteness and misunderstanding alike can best be avoided by a grasp of this design, and that a clear understanding of it will contribute materially to a revaluation of the novel. It is my purpose in this paper to analyze the basic thought of the book as closely as possible. But an acknowledgment and a warning is first of all in order.

'To summarize any good, developed idea is to betray it' (Trilling, p. 51). It cannot be too strongly emphasized that the *schema* of the novel that follows is not the novel itself, which, in richness and complexity, far transcends it. The importance of *A Passage* lies in the way Forster has given life and force to the philosophical pattern, and they are right who seek its chief meaning in character, idea, attitude, and atmosphere: in all the multitudinous richness of texture and substance which the book offers. My excuse must be, not that the theme is the *major* thing in the book, but that it is the *basic* thing; and that its neglect causes even the most gifted reader to fail, at least partially, in appreciation and understanding.

It is generally agreed that Forster is a writer of the 'contemplative' novel; and further, that all his novels tend to be illustrations of a single idea. This single theme is, in the critics' various terms, 'the chasm between the world of actions and the world of being' (Brown, p. 352); 'the search for the *wholeness* of truth,' and the harmonizing of 'the tragic antitheses of mankind' (Zabel, pp. 413, 416); the antithesis 'between Real and not-Real, true and false, being and not-being' (Rose Macaulay, *The Writings of E. M. Forster*, 1938). Each book develops this single theme in somewhat different terms, and on many levels. The dominant idea of *A Passage* is best expressed by the Whitman poem from which the novel takes its title:

Passage to India!
Lo, soul, sees't thou not God's purpose from the first?
The earth to be spanned, connected by network,
The races, neighbors, to marry and be given in marriage,
The oceans to be crossed, the distant brought near,
The lands to be welded together.

Then not your deeds only O voyagers, O scientists and
    inventors, shall be justified,
All these hearts as of fretted children shall be soothed,
All affection shall be fully responded to, the secret shall be
    told,
All these separations and gaps shall be taken up and hook'd
    and link'd together,

The whole earth, this cold, impassive, voiceless earth, shall be
  completely justified,

Nature and Man shall be disjoined and diffused no more,
The true son of God shall absolutely fuse them.

(O pensive soul of me – O thirst unsatisfied – waitest not there?
  Waitest not haply for us somewhere there the Comrade per-
    fect?)[4]

It is the theme of fission and fusion; of separateness and of desired union. The threefold division of the book, 'Mosque',
'Caves', and 'Temple', which Forster himself tells us represent
the divisions of the Indian year, the Cold Weather, the Hot
Weather, and the Rains, represent also a kind of Hegelian Thesis
– Antithesis – Synthesis; or, more properly perhaps, the statement of the problem, and two opposite resolutions.

In part I, 'Mosque', the central problem, 'all these separations
and gaps', is set up and explored on many different levels. The
most obvious gap, at first, is that between Indian and English.
Chandrapore is two towns, the native section and the English
civil station, from which the town 'appears to be a totally different place' (p. 8).[5] The separation is complete: the civil station
'shares nothing with the city except the overarching sky' (p. 8),
the first hint of a division more fundamental than any human
differences. The universe itself is to be a protagonist in the drama
of the many and the one.

But these broad divisions are themselves divided. India is not
one but a hundred, of which Moslem and Hindu are only the
most noticeable. India is a muddle; nothing embraces the whole
of it; no one race or creed or person can sum it up or know all of it;
nor are differences clear cut: 'Nothing in India is identifiable, the
mere asking of a question causes it to disappear or to merge in something else' (p. 86). India, in fact, is presented to us throughout as
the very place of division; the unhappy continent where separations are felt more profoundly than in other places; and later we
shall learn that Aziz's picnic fails 'because he had challenged the
spirit of the Indian earth, which tries to keep men in compartments' (p. 127).

If the continent and its conquered inhabitants are not united, neither are the conquerors. The English, in their club from which all Indians are excluded, are divided among themselves by the same barriers. Those who have been for some time in India are different in outlook from the newcomers, who have not yet retreated behind the defenses of tradition, race, caste, and position. Major official looks down upon minor official; wives of major officials look down upon their inferior sisters. The soldier's attitude differs from the civilian's. And though the English-woman does not live in purdah, as does the Indian lady, there is an antagonism between the sexes which raises a more subtle but as effective barrier between them: the women think their men 'weak' in dealing with natives; the men believe, in their secret hearts, that it is their women who complicate matters.

The gaps and separations between human beings are not the only ones. Men themselves are separate from the rest of creation. Young Mr Sorley, a missionary with advanced ideas, sees no reason why the mercy of God should not embrace all mammals; but he becomes uneasy if the conversation descends to wasps, and is totally unable to admit into the Divine unity 'oranges, cactuses, crystals, and mud' (p. 38). Yet men are only a small part of creation: 'It matters so little to the majority of living beings what the minority, that calls itself human, desires or decides' (p. 114). And the universe itself, powerful, indifferent, is apart from or even hostile to the concerns of all sentient creatures.

If multiplicity is the fact, unity of some sort is the desire. Separated from each other by race, caste, religion, sex, age, occupation, and the hundred barriers of life, men still must strive to unite with each other and to achieve some harmonious resolution of their differences. And they desire as well, though some of them may not know it, to find that unity that shall embrace the whole scheme of things, from which nothing shall be excluded. 'Mosque' is therefore not only a symphony of differences but of attempts at oneness. But this unity which is sought is of two different kinds, which must be carefully distinguished. One is the unity of negation, the other of affirmation; one of exclusion, the other of inclusion. The one emphasizes differences and separations; the other reconciles them in a larger synthesis. The one merely breeds misunderstanding, violence, and hatred; the other seeks peaceful resolution.

The first, of course, is the more easily come by. The Indians are united among themselves only by hatred and suspicion of the English, the one force strong enough to bind together the different races and creeds. Within separate groups, such as Moslem and Hindu, they are united by their traditions, their history, their religion, and their art. Aziz and his friends, quoting the poetry of Islam, feel that India is one and their own; Aziz, visiting his mosque, finds the home of his spirit in that faith. And these forces, which bind together members of the same group, by the same token set them apart from those of other groups. Aziz, embracing a Hindu friend, thinks, 'I wish they did not remind me of cowdung,' at the same moment that his friend is thinking, 'Some Moslems are very violent' (p. 267). The English, too, find the unity of exclusion, of suspicion, and of hatred. The anthem of the Army of Occupation reminds every member of the club that he is British and in exile, enabling them for the moment to sink their personal prejudices. Unity of this kind is achieved not *with* but *against*; it is essentially hostile and evil in nature, and the breeder of more hostility and more evil.

As the first kind of oneness affirms and ratifies the differences and separations natural to life, the second attempts to embrace and to reconcile them by good will, sympathy, kindness, and love. The effort may be on either a purely secular level, or on a religious basis. Fielding, the 'holy man minus the holiness' (p. 121), believes that the world 'is a globe of men who are trying to reach one another and can best do so by the help of good will plus culture and intelligence' (p. 62). Adela desires to 'see the real India' (p. 24); to learn and to understand. But though she has true good-will, she is deficient in emotional response; in 'the secret understanding of the heart' (p. 20). From this deficiency all her future troubles will stem. Mrs Moore, on the other hand, a Christian mystic, is made up of intuitive understanding and sympathy, of an all-embracing charity. It is she who reminds her

son Ronny of the necessity for love in all relationships, the
political as well as the personal; that God is Love.

In this first section, every event, every character, every detail
is a variation on the same theme. The gulf between English and
Indians is shown from both points of view: at the dinner in
Hamidullah's home, in the English club, at the farcical 'Bridge
Party'. But what a different story when Aziz, the Indian, meets
the newcomers, who wish to communicate, to bridge the gap,
who offer genuine good-will, kindness, even love. Instantly he
responds to Mrs Moore's understanding on their meeting in the
mosque; instantly he makes friends with Fielding; he accepts,
though he does not really like, Adela; and generously and at
infinite pains he makes plans for the visit of the ladies to the
Marabar Caves.

At the end of the section, it seems that brotherhood is about to
triumph. The omens are auspicious: East and West have met and
embraced; friendship and love are in the ascendant. Islam, whose
symbol the mosque gives the section its title, preaches the eternal
oneness of God. Christianity, the religion of the English, teaches
the oneness of all men in the Divine love. The season of the year
is the Cold Weather, most suitable to human life and activity; the
climate in which men can live and grow. But 'April, herald of
horrors' (p. 115) is at hand: the Hot Weather, dangerous and
oppressive to all life. Professor Godbole, the Hindu, has sung
his haunting song of invitation to Shri Krishna, Lord of the
Universe: 'Come, come, come, come, come, come' (p. 80). But
the god refuses to come. And his refusal poses the problem for
the next section.

II

If part I has been Thesis, the problem of separation and attempts
at bridging the gulfs, part II is Antithesis; for in 'Caves' we see
the utter rout of the forces of reconciliation, the complete triumph
of hostility, evil, and negation.

The central episode of this section, and of the entire novel, is
the experience of the two Englishwomen, Adela Quested and

Mrs Moore, in the Marabar Caves. It is a shattering experience, calamitous to everyone: it destroys Mrs Moore both spiritually and physically; it drives Adela to the brink of madness; it threatens ruin to Aziz, and actually alters his entire future; it imperils all relations between English and Indians; and it destroys all constructive relationships between individuals. Yet it is never satisfactorily explained by the author. The nature and meaning of Adela's and Mrs Moore's experience is left in darkness, dealt with only in highly oblique and allusive language. What was the voice of the Marabar?

The Marabar Caves are the very voice of that union which is the opposite of divine; the voice of evil and negation; of that universe which is 'older than all spirit' (p. 124). They are the voice of Chaos and Old Night, when 'the earth was without form, and void, and darkness was upon the face of the deep'; long before the Spirit of God moved upon the waters and said, 'Let there be Light.' The answer they give to the problem of oneness is an answer of horror and despair, whether on the human or on the universal level.

To each lady, the voice of the Marabar speaks of a kind of one-ness, but in different terms; terms appropriate to character, age, and situation. To the elder, the religious mystic who wishes to communicate with God, to become one with the universe, in the conviction that such union is beautiful and full of meaning, the echo speaks of a universe in which all differences have been annihilated, an infinity of Nothing. Good and evil are identical: 'Everything exists, nothing has value' (p. 149). All has become one; but the one is Nothing. Here is unity with a vengeance! To the younger Adela, who has wished to understand but not to love India and the Indians, who has become engaged to a man she does not love, who is not convinced that love is necessary to a successful union, the meaning of the echo presents itself in different terms. To her, it speaks of the last horror of union by force and fear, without love. She believes that Aziz has attempted to assault her, goes nearly mad with horror, and sets in motion the machinery that shall prosecute and punish him. For the Marabar has revealed to her what such union is: Rape.

Upon Mrs Moore, who had told her son that God is Love, the effect of the Marabar is immediate and profound despair. We have had hints of India's impact upon her previously. 'God . . . had been constantly in her thoughts since she entered India, though oddly enough he satisfied her less. She must needs pronounce his name frequently, as the greatest she knew, yet she had never found it less efficacious. Outside the arch there seemed always an arch, beyond the remotest echo a silence' (p. 52). Since Professor Godbole had sung his queer song at Fielding's tea party, she had been apathetic. Already disillusionment is upon her, a sense of the futility of all attempts at union. 'She felt increasingly (vision or nightmare?) that, though people are important, the relations between them are not, and that in particular too much fuss has been made over marriage; centuries of carnal embracement, yet man is no nearer to understanding man. And today she felt this with such force that it seemed itself a relationship, itself a person who was trying to take hold of her hand' (p. 135).

In this state of mind she enters the Marabar, and hears the echo of that oneness which is nothingness. 'The mood of the last two months took definite form at last, and she realized that she didn't want to write to her children, didn't want to communicate with anyone, not even with God' (p. 150). From this moment, she takes no more interest in anything. She dismisses Adela's experience: 'all this rubbish about love, love in a church, love in a cave, as if there is the least difference' (p. 202). Knowing Aziz to be innocent, she neither speaks nor stays to testify at his trial. She departs, in this season of the Hot Weather when travel is dangerous, and dies at sea. The echo has ended everything for her. To the Christian mystic the Marabar has said that the universe is muddle rather than mystery; the answer to its riddle is Nothingness.

To Adela the meaning of the echo has presented itself in terms very different, though nearly as disastrous. The keynote of her character, from the beginning, has been an honest but arid intellectualism. Unlike Mrs Moore, with her intuitive sympathies and responses, Adela approaches the problems of life by means of the rational intellect. Her good will, her kindness, come not from the heart but from the head. Fielding is to point out to her that she fails because she has no real affection for Aziz or for Indians generally; she herself confesses to him that her instincts never help her.

Adela's engagement to Ronny has taken place only because of the accident to the Nawab Bahadur's car. Previously, she has refused to marry him; but the accident has linked her to him in a spurious union. The same forces that unite the English against outsiders have united the young man and woman. She does not love him; but until the day of the expedition this question has not even occurred to her. But now, as she goes with Aziz alone to explore a cave, she thinks for the first time, ·'What about love?' (p. 152), a question in some way suggested to her by a pattern in the rock similar to that traced in the dust by the wheels of the Nawab Bahadur's car. For the first time, she realizes that she and Ronny do not love each other. 'The discovery had come so suddenly that she felt like a mountaineer whose rope had broken. Not to love the man one's going to marry! Not to find it out till this moment! Not even to have asked oneself the question until now! . . . There was esteem and animal contact at dusk, but the emotion that links them was absent' (p. 152).

But Adela, being the person she was, 'wasn't convinced that love is necessary to a successful union' (p. 152). Recovering herself, she drives Aziz from her side in embarrassment by her question, 'Have you one wife or more than one?' and goes alone into the cave, there to undergo the ordeal, as she thinks, of his attempted rape.

The analogy here between the personal situation of Adela and Ronny, and the political situation between India and England is clear. It is almost as if she has felt about their personal relationship what Ronny feels about the union of India and England politically. He had told his mother that the English were not in India to be pleasant but 'to hold this wretched country by force' (p. 50). Mrs Moore had thought at that time that, 'One touch of regret – not the canny substitute but the true regret from the heart – would have made him a different man, and the British

Empire a different institution' (p. 51). The English are, for the most part, honest, sincere, incorruptible, earnestly attempting to do justice in administering India. But, as Mrs Moore reminds her son, 'Though I speak with the tongues of men and angels, and have not love . . .' (p. 52), it profits nothing. Aziz, in his illness, has told Fielding that what India needs is 'Kindness, more kindness, and even after that more kindness. I assure you it is the only hope. . . . We can't build up India except on what we feel' (p. 117). Instead, the English are holding India by fear and force, without kindness or love. 'Mosque' has been full of this sort of union: hostile, evil, and negative. Now Adela, joined to Ronny without love, by the same forces which operate to link together the English in India against native and outsider, experiences symbolically the utmost degradation of such union.

The effect of their experience in the Marabar is to quench every little flame of kindness and good will in those around them. The bridges thrown across the gulfs crumble; the abysses widen and deepen. Evil and negative unity alone is left. The English draw together more firmly than ever against natives, in a union that annihilates all reason, all justice, and all mercy. Fear and hate unite the Indians in Aziz's defense. Fielding, throwing in his lot with them, realizes at that moment the profundity of the gulf that divides him from them. The evil spreads and propagates; the spirit of violence stalks abroad; the echo of the Marabar, spouting from its cave, has spread until it threatens to engulf the lives of everyone.

Adela, recovering from her ordeal, is troubled by the echo, which still sounds in her ears. She feels in some vague way, contrary to what her intellect tells her, that she has committed a crime, is leaving the world worse than she found it. Attempting to understand what has happened, she is puzzled by the difference between what she *feels* and what she *knows*, and says incoherently, 'I shouldn't mind if it had happened anywhere else; at least I really don't know where it did happen' (p. 199). For it has not happened to her, in the Marabar; it has happened everywhere in India, it has happened in all places and at all times when men attempted union without love.

Mrs Moore, engulfed in her own failure and her own despair, refuses help. Nevertheless, her mere presence helps Adela's echo, and suggests the possibility of a mistake. The machinery she has set in motion grinds on; and after Mrs Moore's departure, though the question of an error still occurs to her intellect, it ceases to trouble her conscience. But at the trial, it is the name of Mrs Moore, chanted like an incantation by Indians who do not know what the syllables mean, that shows Adela the truth, as in a vision: that nothing 'in reality' had happened to her in the Marabar. The charge is withdrawn and Aziz saved. Adela's echo vanishes. Aziz, consulting Mrs Moore's spirit, renounces the compensation that would have ruined his enemy. And Fielding and Adela, attempting to understand the whole muddle, have to give it up. 'She was at the end of her spiritual tether, and so was he. . . . Perhaps life is a mystery, not a muddle; they could not tell. Perhaps the hundred Indias which fuss and squabble so tiresomely are one, and the universe they mirror is one. They had not the apparatus for judging' (p. 263).

Though the spirit of Mrs Moore has averted the ultimate disaster, nothing good is left: the Marabar has brought nothing but evil. Political relationships have been imperiled; personal ones fare no better. Adela is rejected by the English community; Ronny breaks his engagement. Fielding, also cast out by his compatriots, is misunderstood by the Indians, his friendship with Aziz wrecked by the latter's suspicion of treachery. Kindness and good will have failed; of all the hopes and tentative gestures of union in part I, nothing is left but hatred, force, and fear. The Marabar has triumphed.

'Mosque', symbol of Islam; of human desire for that unity which is the indubitable attribute of God; of the Cold Weather, favorable to human lives and hopes: the problem in its multifarious forms. 'Caves' is one answer; the voice of chaos, of a universe of evil and annihilation, and of the Hot Weather, that climate in which men cannot live. But the caves are only one part of India. As Mrs Moore's ship sails from Bombay, 'thousands of coco-nut palms appeared all round the anchorage and climbed the hills to wave her farewell. "So you thought an echo was India;

you took the Marabar caves as final?" they laughed. "What have
we in common with them, or they with Asirgarh?" ' (p. 210). It
may be that the voice of the chaos older than all spirit is not the
final one. 'Temple', title of the third section of the novel, is the
symbol of the Hindu religion; of a possible reconciliation of
differences not in negation but in a larger synthesis; of a universe
which is perhaps a mystery rather than a muddle, a riddle to
which an answer exists; and of the Rains, token of renewed life,
of regeneration, and of hope.

III

'Temple' opens with the enigmatic figure of the Hindu, Professor
Godbole, who has appeared briefly in the first two sections. It is
he who has invoked the god, at Fielding's tea party, in his song;
he who has refused to answer Aziz's questions about the Marabar
at that same time; and he with whom Fielding has had a curious
and inconclusive conversation about good and evil at the time of
the trial. Godbole, a Hindu mystic, is utterly immersed in the life
of the spirit; so much so, indeed, as to be completely unfitted for
practical action or decision. He dwells entirely in the world of
being, and men of action, like the English generally and Fielding
in particular after the Marabar expedition, find him madden-
ing.
     Godbole thus represents in his person the life of the spirit
developed to its uttermost degree: he stands at the opposite pole
from Ronny and the English in general, who excel at the practical
life but are lost in the spiritual. Philosophically, he stands for
that universality characteristic of Hinduism. Unlike Islam and
Christianity, Hinduism makes no distinctions between humanity
and the rest of the creation; its creed teaches that each particular
part is a member of all other parts, and that all is one in the
Divine. In his talk with Fielding, Godbole expresses the belief
that nothing can be performed in isolation; that all perform a good
action when one is performed, and when an evil action is performed, all perform it. Evil and good alike express the whole of
the universe. Further, good and evil are both aspects of God. He

is present in the one, absent in the other. 'Yet absence implies presence, absence is not non-existence, and we are therefore entitled to repeat, "Come, come, come, come" ' (p. 178). Godbole, then, stands for the union in reality of all men, whether they will or no, and for a universe in which God exists, though he may at a particular time and place not be present; for a universe which may be a mystery but is not a muddle.

In the festival which opens the 'Temple' section, the celebration of the birth of Shri Krishna, universality is the theme. At the birth of the god, 'all sorrow was annihilated, not only for Indians, but for foreigners, birds, caves, railways, and the stars; all became joy, all laughter; there had never been disease nor doubt, misunderstanding, cruelty, fear' (pp. 287–8). The voice of the Marabar is drowned in this festival, in which 'Infinite Love took upon itself the form of Shri Krishna, and saved the world' (p. 287). And Godbole, developing the life of his spirit, in a vision sees Mrs Moore, united in his mind with a wasp seen he forgot where: an echo of an earlier discussion on the all-embracing mercy of God.

It is a prophetic vision, for what happens in 'Temple' is reconciliation on the human level, the cancelling of the effects of the Marabar. Reconciliation, not real union; that is not possible on earth, whatever may be the truth about that universe of which earth is only an atom. The hundred voices of India say, 'No, not yet,' and the sky says, 'No, not there' (p. 322). But the most painful human differences are soothed: Aziz and Fielding resume their friendship, though it can lead no further; Aziz finally makes his peace with Adela.

These things are brought about by Mrs Moore, who returns to India in the guise of her children, Stella, whom Fielding has married, and Ralph, son of her flesh and still more of her spirit. It is the spirit of love, of intuitive understanding, which triumphs at last, in spite of her personal defeat. She had herself told Ronny, 'I think everyone fails, but there are so many kinds of failure' (p. 52). Hers had been a failure of *understanding*, but not of *love*. Her memory, and the presence of her son, Ralph, completely change Aziz's attitude from hostility to homage: 'He knew with his heart that this was Mrs Moore's son, and indeed until his heart was involved he knew nothing' (p. 313). And at Mau, too, Fielding and Stella are brought closer together: 'There seemed a link between them at last – that link outside either participant that is necessary to every relationship. In the language of theology, their union had been blessed' (p. 318). The Marabar has been wiped out.

'All invitations must proceed from heaven perhaps; perhaps it is futile for men to initiate their own unity, they do but widen the the gulfs between them by the attempt' (p. 37). So Forster seems to be saying. *A Passage to India* is a novel of these gulfs, of the bridges thrown across them, of the tensions that hamper and threaten communication, of the failure and the horror of all efforts at union without love, and of whether Oneness when found is Something or Nothing. Since it is a great novel, it is, of course, far more than its dialectical pattern. But a grasp of that pattern in its full detail enables us to evaluate the novel more fully and fairly than has yet been done, and to arrive at an estimate of its author's achievement. We can now appraise Forster's apparently final effort to incarnate his difficult ideas; we can ask whether he has given them satisfactory aesthetic form, has successfully solved the problem which, as a novelist, he has set himself.

A Passage to India is not, as some critics have claimed, an expression of Forster's personal disillusion. Nor is it 'almost unbelievably crude and weak' in its attempt at making a poetic communication about life. It is the last and best of Forster's attempts in that most difficult genre, the novel of ideas. It is an almost-successful attempt at an all-but-impossible task: an attempt to fuse the real world of social comedy and human conflict with the meaning and value of the universe which that world mirrors; to impose on experience the pattern of a moral vision; and out of these disparate elements to create a satisfying aesthetic whole. The wonder is not that it fails of complete success, but that it so nearly succeeds completely.

In *A Passage* appear the recurrent themes, the characteristic attitudes, and the peculiar gifts displayed by its author in his earlier fiction, integrated fully at last into the novel's structure and expressed in its characters, episodes, and atmosphere. Forster has found in it a thesis and a medium that enable him to use his full strength and to minimize or conceal his weaknesses. It is at once the finest and the most typical of his books, revealing most clearly his individual quality and distinction.

This is not to deny that, in some measure, the book is a failure. All good critics of Forster have remarked, in their different ways, upon the 'double vision' apparent in his books: the contrast and often collision between the realistic and the symbolic, the two levels upon which characters and events exist and function. The most serious charge that has been laid at his door is that he is unable 'to create realistic form, credible form, moving form';[6] that his characters are inadequate to the ideas they incarnate; that his preoccupation with these ideas 'leads him outside the limits of consciousness that his comedy would seem to involve' (Leavis); that, in the words of Virginia Woolf, one of his most friendly critics, 'his difficulty is to persuade his different gifts to combine into a single vision'. He is both poet and satirist, both comedian and moralist, both preacher and artist. A mocking spirit of fantasy flouts his reality, poetry ruffles his prim surface, and his books, instead of being artistic wholes, are racked and rent by interior disharmony, the result of the tensions between his ill-assorted gifts and his contradictory aims.

From this charge, *A Passage* cannot wholly be absolved. Mr Trilling, in his full-length study of Forster, has remarked upon the imbalance of its plot to its story. Its characters, he tells us, are right for the plot but not large enough for the story. By 'story' Trilling seems to mean the thought I have just analyzed: the dialectical pattern of the book. The plot, as distinguished from this larger theme, is the story of Aziz; the tale of what goes on in his mind in the course of his tragically unsuccessful attempt to overcome the 'separations and gaps' which divide him from Mrs Moore and Adela. We see him progress from almost total ignorance to complete awareness of the unjust situation in which he is placed, and for which, as he comes to see, there is no remedy in human action. He retreats from Chandrapore to Mau, from the English and their Western science to a remote jungle where he can 'let his instruments rust, [run] his little hospital at half steam, and [cause] no undue alarm' (p. 290). His failure and his disillusionment, humanly speaking, are the real center of interest in the novel.

Yet Aziz, however imaginatively realized as a man and an Indian, is, as Mr Trilling observes, not large enough for the 'story': for the cosmic stage on which his adventures are played. Though he comes to realize the uselessness of attempts at friendship and union, he never apprehends the real significance of his own ordeal nor relates it to the ordeal of India and of the whole world. Not for him, any more than for Ronny, Adela, or Fielding, is the world outside the arch, the silence beyond the echo. 'It is useless discussing Hindus with me,' he tells his friend during their last ride together. 'Living with them teaches me no more' (p. 320).

On the other hand, the two 'redemptive' characters large enough for the cosmic stage move among their human companions awkwardly, not wholly at ease with the world and the flesh. Mrs Moore and Godbole are never really satisfactory as human beings, never vitally related to the people and events around them. Their human features are veiled by the larger-than-life masks they wear, like the actors in Greek tragedy playing at being gods. We perceive their effect without understanding or really accepting it; we take them at the valuation assigned by their author, but we do not put our own valuation upon them nor stamp them with the seal of our affirmation.

Thus, the gulf between symbol and reality, so often noticed in Forster's work, is again the chief feature, and in a sense, the chief failure of *A Passage to India*. The author tries hard to bridge it; but he does not quite succeed. Those who read the book as social comedy, or as an analysis of the Indian question, though they will find much to enjoy and admire, will be baffled and irritated again and again by the suggestion of a meaning far deeper than appears. To them, Godbole will be a nuisance, Mrs Moore incomprehensible, Adela's adventure in the Marabar cave mere hysteria, and the Temple section irrelevant and incoherent. And those who perceive the larger 'story', the immense and mysterious context into which the human adventures of Aziz and Adela are fitted, will also perceive more poignantly the crack between comic manner and cosmic meaning. 'Between the conception / And the creation / Between the emotion / And the response / Falls the Shadow.' The shadow of the double vision falls upon *A Passage*, as it does upon the earlier books: the real and the symbolic worlds co-exist independently instead of blending into one another and becoming a whole.

But only in this ultimate sense does the book fail. In all else it triumphs. Humor and poetry, those unlikely companions, walk arm in arm: tenderness and deep insight offer their balm to the sharp sting of satire. We have heard these themes – we have perceived these attitudes – we have met these people – we have watched these scenes – we have savored this delicate and lyric prose in Forster's earlier books. But we have never seen theme and character and attitude so clear, so free of ambiguity and doubt, we have never seen comedy so deft and light-handed, poetry so poignant. Not as a frieze but as a spirit, Anglo-India, India herself, pass before us. Their hundred voices sound in our ears, their pains and perplexities become our own and those of the whole world.

The value of personal relationships, the holiness of the heart's affections, always important in Forster's novels, is central to the theme, the characters, and the episodes of *A Passage*. Error and evil are the inevitable consequences of the failure of love between human beings: of the disastrous personal failure of Adela, and the no less disastrous social and political failure of the English officials and their wives. And whatever is saved from the wreck – Aziz's life, Adela's reason, Fielding's and Aziz's friendship – is saved by love alone: the love represented by Mrs Moore's spirit. Whatever the level, human or divine, love is the only salvation. 'Kindness, more kindness, and even after that more kindness. I assure you it is the only hope.' This theme is the dominant note of *A Passage*, the keystone of its structural arch.

In the same way, in that 'suspicion of action and of beliefs which sometimes seems to amount to passivity and defeatism' which has been noted as characteristic of Forster, he is here leading from strength rather than weakness. For he here creates a world in which, whether it be on the social, the political, or the philosophical plane, sharply defined beliefs and active policies are productive of nothing but tension, hatred, strife, and disunion. Definite beliefs, Christian, Moslem, or Hindu, English or Indian, do but divide men more sharply from each other; and the world of action is the nightmare world of the English club, the Indian riot, the courtroom, the 'world of telegrams and anger' shown at its most hostile and destructive. Neither beliefs nor action can save us, Forster says, and in *A Passage* compels us to believe, but only 'the secret understanding of the heart', which may fail but can never be really defeated, and is our only answer to the voice of the Marabar.

So too Forster's dissatisfaction with civilization, with that humane and liberal culture which produced him and which he represents is, in *A Passage*, integrated into the plan of the book in a more vital sense than was true of the earlier novels. Did Margaret Schlegel really marry Henry Wilcox? We have never quite believed it. But we can believe in Fielding, in his effort and in his failure, for we see – how clearly! – what Fielding is up against, and we see too that his cultivated agnostic spirit is wholly unable to comprehend the awful mystery or muddle of the world beyond the arch. Fielding believes in good will plus culture and intelligence; but we see him baffled and wistful before the dim apprehension of something, he knows not what – something his wife knows and Mrs Moore had known. *A Passage* shows, far more fully and satisfactorily than Forster's earlier books, the inadequacy, the collapse, of the liberal-bourgeois-agnostic mind face to face with the ultimate mystery at the heart of the universe. The hollowness of Margaret Schlegel's world stands for the first time fully revealed.

Even one of Forster's real weaknesses as a novelist, his 'demurely bloodless gaiety',[7] that embarrassment before the sexual relation which mars his other novels without exception, is a source almost of strength in *A Passage*. For his task here is not to portray a pair of lovers, and to fail at making them lovers, as was true, for example, of George and Lucy in *A Room With a View*. His intention is to show us a young man and woman who

attempt to become lovers and who are temperamentally un-
equipped for their roles. So, while it may be said that Ronny and
Adela are one of the least attractive pairs in fiction, it may also
be said that it is necessary to the purpose and effect of *A Passage*
that this should be so. They are not there to show love and the
life of the senses triumphant, as George and Lucy were – and to
fail, as George and Lucy failed – but to show the horror and
disaster of attempts at union *without* love.

The same thing is true of Forster's gifts of character-drawing,
of social satire, and of that lyrical sensibility so oddly contrasted
with it. A few deft strokes, and the English ladies – Mrs Turton,
Mrs Callendar, Mrs McBryde – are forever impaled in all their
shallow and insular arrogance. Fielding, the holy man minus the
holiness, is both more sympathetic and more vivid than his proto-
type, old Mr Emerson. The portraits of the Indians, Hamidullah,
the Nawab Bahadur, Mahmoud Ali, Mr Das, form a varied
gallery of individuals who never degenerate into types, and are
crowned with that triumph of insight and imaginative sympathy,
the figure of Aziz: most interesting, most human, most believable
of all Forster's characters. Satirist of the collision between the
English middle class and an alien culture, Forster creates in *A
Passage* some unforgettable scenes: the discussions at the English
club; the trial; the Indian riot; both comedy and satire given
sharper edge and more pungent acidity by the deceptive lightness
and grace of touch. And the poet who describes the Marabar
caves, or the festival of Shri Krishna, evokes for us the very
spirit of the Indian earth and conveys a sense of the ineluctable
mystery of human existence.

It is true, as E. K. Brown has reminded us, that the end of fiction is the realistic representation of life, and that a novel is not
saved by a great theme. But a novel which displays such gifts of
political penetration and social comedy, such beauty of language
and depth of character-portrayal, is not rendered less great by a
theme that is worthy of it, and which it manages so very nearly
to subdue into a complete aesthetic pattern. In defiance of all
modern canons of criticism, I believe it is sometimes preferable
to fail of complete success in a great venture than to succeed

wholly in a petty one; and by that token, I believe with Brown that *A Passage to India* is and will remain 'the subtlest effort in our time to write the novel of ideas in English'.

SOURCE: *PMLA* LXVIII (Sept 1953).

NOTES

1. E. K. Brown, 'E. M. Forster and the Contemplative Novel', in *University of Toronto Quarterly*, III (April 1934) 349–61; Morton D. Zabel, 'E. M. Forster', in *Nation*, CXLVII (22 Oct 1938) 413–16; Dorothy M. Hoare, 'E. M. Forster', in *Some Studies in the Modern Novel* (1938) pp. 68–97.

2. Ranjee G. Shahani, 'Some British I Admire', in *Asiatic Review*, XLII (July 1946) 273; F. R. Leavis, 'E. M. Forster', in *Scrutiny*, VII (Sept 1938) 185. This article offers a perfect illustration of the mis-understanding into which even a competent critic may be led by a neglect of the novel's pattern of thought. Mr Leavis selects, for a criticism of Forster's style, the paragraph in chapter XXVI which describes the reactions of Fielding and Hamidullah to the news of Mrs Moore's death, directing particular attention to the 'lapse in taste' responsible for the final phrase of the sentence: 'How indeed is it pos-sible for one human being to be sorry for all the sadness that meets him on the face of the earth, for the pain that is endured not only by men, but by animals and plants, and perhaps by the stones?' This is what he says: 'Once one's critical notice has fastened on it . . . can one do anything but reflect how extraordinary it is that so fine a writer should be able, in such a place, to be so little certain just how serious he is? For surely that run-out of the sentence cannot be justified in terms of the dramatic mood Mr Forster is offering to render?' (pp. 198–9). An understanding of the novel's thought and peculiar method makes it clear, on the contrary, that this phrase is one more echo in a book of echoes; as will be obvious to anyone who troubles to read carefully the account of Godbole's vision of Mrs Moore, the wasp, and the stone in the final section of the novel. What Mr Leavis describes as a fault in style is, in terms of thought, mood, and structure, a con-scious, deliberate, and effective device.

3. E. B. C. Jones, 'E. M. Forster and Virginia Woolf', in *The English Novelists*, ed. Derek Verschoyle (1936) p. 262.

4. *Leaves of Grass*, Incl. ed. (New York, 1924) pp. 343–51.

5. All references are to the Modern Library edition (New York, 1940).

6. E. K. Brown, 'Revival of E. M. Forster', in *Yale Review*, NS XXXIII (June 1944) 668–81.

7. 'Morton D. Zabel, "A Forster Revival" ' (review of Trilling), in *Nation*, CLVII (7 Aug 1943) 158–9.

James McConkey

THE PROPHETIC NOVEL:
A PASSAGE TO INDIA (1957)

[The following discussion of *A Passage to India* occurs in a
section of Mr McConkey's book on *The Novels of E. M. Forster*
in which he argues that in his two last novels Forster 'seems to
be approaching a kind of prophetic utterance' and that in *A
Passage to India* he 'does achieve an effect pure enough to place
him within that select group of writers Forster himself finds (in
Aspects of the Novel) to be prophetic – Dostoevsky, Melville,
Emily Brontë, and D. H. Lawrence'. He points out that Forster is
less prophetic than Dostoevsky because in his work the prophetic
element is found largely *within* the character, while in Forster
'extension in the main comes from *without* the character'; and also
because Forster hesitates to allow himself to be completely immersed and evades faiths, codes, and doctrines.]

FORSTER's prophecy relates rather to . . . the sense of separation
which exists within the Forsterian cosmos. Though the transcendent must perforce be operative on the level of the physical
reality, though there exists one absolute unity which encompasses
all divisions, all shatterings of the temporal world, still that
absolute, so far as the individual person is concerned, remains far
above; for the individual cannot approach the absolute through
reason, nor can he wholly comprehend it through intuition.
Awareness of the separation between actual and ideal is the curse,
the blessed attribute, of the balanced temperament, the temperament of the person who must seek not integration but mediation;
and it is here, in the conscious separation between actual and
ideal, that we find the basis of the prophetic voice in Forster.
    Dostoevsky's characters, Forster finds, convey to us 'the sensa-

tion of sinking into a translucent globe and seeing our experience floating far above us on its surface, tiny, remote, yet ours'. In Forster, the transcendental is implied, extension is gained, but not by our 'sinking' through the characters into it; rather, the transcendental exists at all times as concept, and it is in the relation between that transcendental unity and the characters who are searching for a portion of it that we find the extension to a region where they are 'joined by the rest of humanity'. That region is one in which infinitude may be glimpsed, but only at intervals at best; it is a region haunted by incompleteness, by a people who sense, however obscurely, their limitations – psychological, intellectual, spiritual – and yet in which culture, good will, and intelligence matter. Must matter, for they provide what joys are available. Forster's is, then, a prophetic gift which arises from a compassionate, conscious awareness of the separation between character and transcendent verity, a separation which *ought* to be bridged, but which is not. The author's voice itself originates from a position between the human and transcendent realms, and its own detachment is comment on the theme of human incompletion and separation. . . .

This is not to say, of course, that by the time of *A Passage to India* Forster has been able to construct such a bridge. The last novel is his great novel, the one that most fully realizes its potentialities, and it does so partly at least because in it Forster is most keenly aware that the division does exist, that what he attempted without full success in *Howards End* is totally impossible now. Fielding has supplanted Margaret Schlegel as the protagonist who is concerned with the problem of human relationships; but earth no longer supplies a link between man and the transcendent unity. The voice remains, it can still remind of that unity, but without the aid of earth it cannot give to Fielding a sense of his own connection with it.

For the separation of man from earth and hence from ultimate reality which threatened in 1910 has become accomplished by 1924, a disaster which has had, for Forster as novelist, at least one brighter feature: it has meant that the two commitments which he could never quite reconcile have been divorced fully by forces not his own and that what has been perhaps his individual psychological inability has become the fault of an age; it has meant that Forster's own detachment from human reality has become the only means of sensing, however partially, the divine order. Fielding's achievements in the realm of personal relationships, inconclusive as those achievements finally become, are possible because he, as opposed to Margaret Schlegel, can 'travel light'; he has no roots in society nor place and he desires none; he is associated with no sense of tradition.

Not that all the characters in the novel are completely without root. Aziz, we are told, 'was rooted in society and Islam. He belonged to a tradition which bound him, and he had brought children into the world, the society of the future. Though he lived so vaguely in this flimsy bungalow, nevertheless he was placed, placed'; and it is because he is so placed, because he is aware of such a tradition, that, in spite of the brevity of his acquaintance with Mrs Moore, the two make immediate and lasting connection. For she also is placed: she, like Aziz, has two sons and a daughter, and to her, 'it is the children who are the first consideration'; too, she is equally rooted by tradition – in her case, that of western Christianity.

But Aziz, though placed, 'was without natural affection for the land of his birth' and must make a conscious, willful attempt to love it; and Mrs Moore is in a countryside which is alien, even hostile, to her spirit. That is the difference that the years between *Howards End* and *A Passage to India* finally have forced upon Forster. India is more than a foreign land which the English may leave at their wish: it is the contemporary condition, the separation between all mankind and all earth. In her awareness of continuity and tradition, in her capacity for detachment and resignation, in the greatness of her encompassing love, Mrs Moore is, indeed, Ruth Wilcox once more; but she is a Ruth Wilcox whose intuitive love remains after the major contributing factor to that love – a harmony between her spirit and the earth – has ceased to exist. Although she is fated to failure, we believe in her as we never believed, despite all of Forster's efforts, in Ruth Wilcox.

There is a paragraph in *Howards End* which stands as a fore-shadowing of *A Passage to India* and will even do as a partial statement of the latter novel's intent. Marriage, we are told, 'had not saved' Margaret

from the sense of flux. London was but a foretaste of this nomadic civilization which is altering human nature so profoundly, and throws upon personal relations a stress greater than they have ever borne before. Under cosmopolitanism, if it comes, we shall receive no help from the earth. Trees and meadows and mountains will only be a spectacle, and the binding force that they once exercised on character must be entrusted to Love alone. May Love be equal to the task!

In *A Passage to India*, no longer does man receive 'help from the earth'; quite the opposite is true, for the earth even seems to increase the friction between men: 'It was as if irritation exuded from the very soil. Could one have been so petty on a Scotch moor or an Italian alp? . . . There seemed no reserve of tranquillity to draw upon in India. Either none, or else tranquillity swallowed up everything, as it appeared to do for Professor Godbole.' The English Lake Country is referred to at various times in the novel, and it stands, in its contrast to the land around Chandrapore, as a symbol of the harmony that once existed between man and his surroundings; Wordsworth is in the background, Forster has acknowledged (in a letter to the author of this study), in the reference to Grasmere, whose 'little lakes and mountains were beloved by them all. Romantic yet manageable, it sprang from a kindlier planet.' But in India, beauty is lacking; Fielding 'had forgotten the beauty of form among idol temples and lumpy hills; indeed, without form, how can there be beauty?' With the approach of the hot season, the sun returns 'to his kingdom with power but without beauty – that was the sinister feature. If only there had been beauty! His cruelty would have been tolerable then.'

'*May Love be equal to the task!*' For Mrs Moore, as we have seen, it is not: 'God . . . is . . . love,' He 'has put us on earth to love our neighbours and to show it, and He is omnipresent, even in India, to see how we are succeeding,' she tells Ronnie Heaslop. Yet God has not proved to be the satisfaction to her He was before her arrival in India: 'She must needs pronounce his name frequently, as the greatest she knew, yet she had never found it less efficacious. Outside the arch there seemed always an arch, beyond the remotest echo a silence.' And in the cave, in the unattractive, shapeless hills, she undergoes a psychic experience in which she loses totally the sense of values that her mystical divination of unity, related to the Christian tradition, has afforded her; she loses interest in Aziz, in her own children, in God. Yet Mrs Moore has made a lasting effect, and she acts – *after* her negating vision, after her death – as an influence even more pervasive than that of Ruth Wilcox in *Howards End*. The Hindus at the trial of Aziz invoke her name in an echoing chant, for she has seemed like a goddess to them; she influences Adela toward realization that her accusation of Aziz has been false; her presence is felt throughout the final section of the novel and helps weave the achieved unity – transitory though it may be – that we find there.

In the important essay, 'Art for Art's Sake', Forster, after commenting on the apparent impossibility of man's achievement of harmony 'with his surroundings when he is constantly altering them', finds:

The future of our race is, in this direction, more unpleasant than we care to admit, and it has sometimes seemed to me that its best chance lies through apathy, uninventiveness, and inertia. . . . Universal exhaustion would certainly be a new experience. The human race has never undergone it, and is still too perky to admit that it may be coming and might result in a sprouting of new growth through the decay.

One sees in the depiction of Mrs Moore a concept similar to this. She, who has always inclined toward resignation, must die through spiritual exhaustion – and this is achieved in the cave and not in her actual death on the sea – in order that a new birth, a new growth, may be achieved: the birth and growth which are portrayed for us in the final section of the novel. *Must* die – for the earth has become alien to man; the God, the order, the unity, which had been perceived through that earth must perforce be discovered again.

It is hence as a rebirth after exhaustion that we need to read the final section of *A Passage to India*. The novel's three sections represent, Forster tells us in his notes to the Everyman edition, the 'three seasons of the Cold Weather, the Hot Weather, and the Rains, which divide the Indian year'; it is the recurring cycle of birth through death, commencing, in this novel, with the culmination of the period of fullest realization and maturity, proceeding thence through death to rebirth. The symbolic rites connected with the birth of Krishna, which relate to the Christmas observance in Christian tradition, even if they are primitive, even if they are muddled (perhaps partly *because* they are muddled), reach out in an attempt to encompass everything, to encompass the order which lies beyond chaos; and, because the ceremony is so all-inclusive, it prohibits anyone's discovery of 'the emotional centre of it, any more than he could locate the heart of a cloud'.

Obviously such a rebirth as this last section represents is one to be achieved neither through Christianity nor through the earth-relationship. Though one should not read the novel as a statement that Hinduism as such will solve the Indian dilemma, much less the dilemma of the world, Hindu metaphysics bears a number of definite relationships to the stabilized Forsterian philosophical position, a position which does not require place worship and which has always been hostile to organized Christianity. Certainly the redemptive power that Mrs Moore possesses after death signifies chiefly in regard neither to place nor to her Christian religion; she becomes such a power, indeed, primarily only to the extent that she is merged with the small and elderly Hindu professor, Godbole.

Godbole, the central figure in the last section of the novel and the one most responsible for whatever sense of hope is granted there, is the only truly prophetic *character* in all the novels; for he is the only one who ever becomes the human counterpart of the Forsterian voice. To no locality on earth is Godbole indebted: he 'always did possess the knack of slipping off', and he would be, one assumes, no less tranquil in London or even Chicago than he is in Chandrapore or Mau. For, like the voice, he is detached, though never to the extent of the full mystic. He remains, in his contact with human and transcendent realities, at precisely the mid-point of voice, and his is the same imperfect intuition: he is capable of comprehending the transcendent unity, but not completely. Thus, during the Krishna rites at Mau, he can love a wasp equally with a human figure recollected from his Chandrapore days – it happens to be that of Mrs Moore – but he cannot equally love the stone on which the wasp rests: 'no, he could not, he had been wrong to attempt the stone, logic and conscious effort had seduced, he came back to the strip of red carpet and discovered that he was dancing upon it.'

Basic to the Mau ceremonies and to Godbole's desire 'to attempt the stone' are the dual realities of Hindu metaphysics. Brahman is the unseen metaphysical absolute; the triad of Vishnu, Siva, and Brahma is the manifestation of Brahman. The metaphysical absolute is to be approached through the triad, but since Brahman is devoid of attributes, such an approach is, from the standpoint of logic, impossible. The triad, indeed, as is true of the phenomenal universe itself, offers a reality which is but illusory; hence identification with the absolute comes only with the extinction of individual consciousness, with the final and total separation of soul from the physical realm. One may love other existence within that realm in proportion to the extent of his own remove from the phenomenal universe; thus the detachment and self-abnegation of Godbole are qualities which impart to him his extensive, though necessarily incomplete, sense of love and unity – even as they have always been the qualities of the Forsterian voice, imparting much the same incomplete vision.

And so the rebirth suggested in the final pages of the novel is one to be brought about by a love which, in turn, can be obtained only through as great a denial of self and the physical world as it is possible for mankind to make. Is such a price too dear? Does the cost of the love make that love prohibitive? A recent critic of *A Passage to India*, Glen O. Allen, says that to Forster the Hindu Way of Love is a 'good', although 'not in its extreme nor to the exclusion of all other goods'. The renunciation and loss of individuality which the Hindu must achieve in order to gain

unity is, Allen believes, the 'repugnant extreme'; and he feels that
Forster in *A Passage to India* is asserting, as he did in *Howards
End*, the need for proportion: love is but one of the 'ingredients
of the good life'.

But such a proportion as Margaret Schlegel seeks between seen
and unseen worlds in *Howards End* simply isn't a factor in this
novel, for the seen world has become meaningless through man's
own perversity and decay. The cost of love, to put it simply,
has already been paid; man has already become the alien wanderer
on earth's surface. Fielding and Godbole, those entirely different
men, represent the division that exists between seen and unseen
worlds; and they represent as well the disparity to be found
between Forster's commitment to human relations and his commitment to the insight and love gained through a remove from
those relations. No hope for a spiritual rebirth, for a new awareness of unity, can come from an emphasis upon the values of the
human world; for, without the agency of earth, no valid sense
of connection among men can be obtained. Fielding, despite his
efforts in behalf of Aziz, still is denied brotherhood with him;
thus those efforts, admirable though they may be, can produce no
lessening of the spiritual sterility.

Harmony between man and nature may be gained at some time
in the future, and perhaps once more there will be a reconciliation
of seen and unseen worlds – we are given some slight indication
of this by the landscape at Mau, which, while queer, is less alien
than the rest of India; and we are granted some hope – it is,
however, never stressed – in the as yet unborn child of Stella and
Fielding. Stella, the daughter of Mrs Moore, is her heir, so far as
the possession of intuitive love is concerned; and hence Stella is
also of spiritual kin to Godbole. Through the child of Stella and
Fielding, mankind may once again achieve proportion and a
balance between realms of reality. But, if so, the initiating power
must come from a love which draws no sustenance either from
nature or from human relations. Godbole and the Hindu Way
of Love, absurd though they may seem to the western rationalist,
can provide that power.

As is apparent by now, the major mythological referent of

A Passage to India is that of Hinduism. Since the method whereby this referent is presented to us is primarily that of recurrent symbolism, the intricacies of the subject are best left to the following chapter on 'Rhythm'; here what primarily needs to be noted is that such a referent has given Forster a framework totally in keeping with the implications of his voice and that the prophecy of the novel results from such a relationship.

A word of caution, however, is perhaps necessary. One can easily overemphasize the importance of Hinduism in *A Passage to India*: what we need to recognize, I think, is not that Forster accepts Hinduism, but rather that he selects from its metaphysics and attitudes those things which always have been most congenial to him. Reason, while important to Forster, has always been relegated by him to a position beneath that of love; and man's relationship to the physical world in *A Passage to India* is such that reason no longer can operate in conjunction with a spiritual insight. Other attitudes of Forster's which give him an affinity with Godbole have already been suggested. And clearly the Hindu division of realities – a division which, while affirming the existence of an absolute, makes its approach impossible to conscious man – offers a parallel to Forster's own philosophical view.

Toward the ceremonies of Hinduism, on the other hand, he shows little attraction. One assumes that Forster, with Stella and her brother, likes Hinduism while taking 'no interest in its forms'. Such an assumption is documented by *The Hill of Devi* (1953), an account of Forster's experiences in India in 1921 while he was serving as a personal secretary to the Maharajah of Dewas Senior. The description in *The Hill of Devi* of a Gokul Ashtami festival which he attended, and which provided him with the description of the Mau rites in *A Passage to India*, certainly indicates that the festival itself made no profound religious impression upon him. 'There is no dignity, no taste, no form, and though I am dressed as a Hindu I shall never become one,' he writes concerning his participation in the festival. What he chiefly responded to during the festival was the fact that it 'touches something very deep in their hearts'.[1]

Once we have discovered Forster's attitudes in *A Passage to*

India, we can perceive the thematic progression to be found in his novels, for it is a progression from a complete trust in physical reality to the denial of it in a Marabar cave, that cave, in its lack of attributes, representing the 'nothingness' of the metaphysical absolute itself. It is a progression marked by Forster's choice of redemptive characters, from the elder Emerson to Gino, Wonham, Ruth Wilcox, and finally Godbole; and the disparity that separates the first from the last is, largely, the philosophical distance which Forster has covered within the relatively brief course of five novels.

Yet even the Forster who finds a parallel of his values in a Godbole and in Hindu metaphysics is not a writer who represents what we normally would consider the mystic state of being; he is, rather, a writer most keenly aware of discord and lack of harmony in his world who nevertheless senses, however obscurely, a harmony beyond and strives for identification with it. He never (or rarely) succeeds; it is difficult to determine whether or not Forster has ever attained the mystic vision, and Forster himself could never accurately tell us, as his account of the moment of birth during the Mau ceremonies indicates:

But the human spirit had tried by a desperate contortion to ravish the unknown, flinging down science and history in the struggle, yes, beauty herself. Did it succeed? Books written afterwards say 'Yes'. But how, if there is such an event, can it be remembered afterwards? How can it be expressed in anything but itself? Not only from the unbeliever are mysteries hid, but the adept himself cannot retain them. He may think, if he chooses, that he has been with God, but as soon as he thinks it, it becomes history, and falls under the rules of time.

And, in Forster's belief, if we lose a sense of unity with the earth, if we lose a sense of a divine plan in the stars, the loss, though profound, is ours only; it constitutes no denial of that ultimate order. For Forster's is a Shelleyan view, with the important exception that the veil cannot be fully penetrated to the absolute forms. All that Forster can do is suggest the presence of a transcendent verity. To do more is to absolutize what man cannot decipher;

any absolute would be of man, not of the divine. Such a dissociation between man and ultimate truth is a basic distinction between
Forster and the English Romantics and one reason that Forster's
romanticism, idealism, can exist into the twentieth century while
theirs cannot.

SOURCE: *The Novels of E. M. Forster* (1957).

NOTE

1. *The Hill of Devi* presents many of Forster's experiences which
later were to be incorporated into *A Passage to India*: there is an account
of an automobile accident which becomes the accident involving the
Nawab Bahadur in the novel; there is a description of Mau (the Gokul
Ashtami rites witnessed by Forster actually did not occur there); and
there is always the sense of strangeness and lack of form in India. But
The Hill of Devi, despite its wealth of background material, offers little
new insight into the richness and depth of *A Passage to India*: for it is
what Forster's creative faculty has done to the material which chiefly
matters. In this respect, it is interesting to note in *The Hill of Devi*
a comment on *A Passage to India*:

'I began this novel before my 1921 visit, and took out the opening
chapters with me, with the intention of continuing them. But as soon
as they were confronted with the country they purported to describe, they seemed to wilt and go dead and I could do nothing with
them. I used to look at them of an evening in my room at Dewas,
and felt only distaste and despair. The gap between India remembered and India experienced was too wide. When I got back to
England the gap narrowed, and I was able to resume.'

Frederick C. Crews

A PASSAGE TO INDIA (1962)

A Passage to India (1924), deservedly the best-known of Forster's novels, is also the most difficult to interpret consistently.
Critics have generally recognized that, philosophically, it is
Forster's most ambitious work, but not everyone has professed
to be happy with this fact; the novel's story, we are sometimes
told, is too frail to bear the weight of its supposed metaphysical
implications. Furthermore, what are those implications, and how
do they bear upon the narrower issues of ethics and Empire that
are raised? The novel has inspired some perceptive critics to
reach quite opposite conclusions as to its ethical point of view.
It seems to me, however, that Lionel Trilling [in his *E. M.
Forster*, see pp. 77–92 of this volume] comes closest to the truth
when he says that *A Passage to India*, rather than telling us what
is to be done, simply restates the familiar political and social
dilemmas in the light of the total human situation.

Such a light, of course, must be cast from a great distance;
hence the necessity for extreme detachment in the tone of Forster's narrative and commentary. Hence, too, the incongruity
between the novel's trivial action and its hints of enormous
meaning. This incongruity is essential to Forster's intentions;
indeed, if I were to assign a single theme to *A Passage to India*,
I would call it the incongruity between aspiration and reality.
Religiously, politically, and simply in terms of the characters'
efforts to get along with one another, this incongruity is pervasive. The strands of the novel are unified by the thematic
principle that unity is not to be obtained, and the plot is trivial
because Forster's restatements of the ordinary questions imply
that all of human life, whether great or small in our customary
opinion, is ensnared in pettiness.

It may be difficult at first to adjust our critical focus to this
lofty contemplation of man's helplessness, yet the departure from
Forster's earlier novels is not extreme. Even in *Where Angels
Fear to Tread*, we remember, Philip Herriton's conclusion is that
life is greater but less complete than he has supposed; he discovers
that his humanistic virtues have not really led him to an understanding of the world. *A Room With a View*, though it ends
pleasantly enough for its heroine, suggests, in the Carlylean
agnosticism of the Emersons, a similar uneasiness about the
ultimate order. In *The Longest Journey* all three of the central
male characters suspect that the universe is indifferent or hostile
to humanity. And the satisfactory conclusion to *Howards End* is
reached, not by Margaret Schlegel's having acquiesced in the
providential scheme, but through her striving against the panic
and emptiness of a godless world. In each of the four novels
there *is* a measure of heroism, but it is always strictly bordered
by a sense of human limitation. The difference in emphasis
between these books and *A Passage to India* is simply that the
latter neglects to overcome the latent fear of chaos; it continues
to illustrate the humanistic struggle against meaninglessness, but
fails to affirm that a victory is possible.

The situation of the novel is partly familiar, partly new. In
several ways the basic contrast between India and England, or
between India and Anglo-India, brings us back to the world of
Where Angels Fear to Tread and *A Room with a View*. The
English sexual prudery, the emphasis on duty and good form,
the distrust of everything foreign are all brought into expected
relief against the spontaneity of a manifestly un-English country.
The colonial administrators of Chandrapore and their bigoted
wives stumble through a typically comic series of misinterpreta-
tions of India and individual Indians, just as the earlier tourists
misinterpret Italy; and some of the central English characters –
Adela Quested, Cyril Fielding, Mrs Moore – undergo the customary Forsterian shift of sympathy toward the 'native' point of
view. Socially, however, the novel is much more complicated
than the earlier ones. India, too, has a stratified society, one that is
in fact more rigidly discriminatory than England's; and the Indian

protagonist, Aziz, is only slightly closer to, say, Gino Carella than are the Englishmen in the novel. He, too, is restrained on all sides by barriers of class and race.

Similarly, we look in vain for romantic suggestions that India, like Italy, stands for a passionate release of the human spirit; India is apparently more of a muddle than a mystery, and it distinctly does not embody a tidy moral for the English visitors to ponder on their way home. This brings us to a basic difference in the way Forster now regards his subject-matter. The foreign civilization is no longer a moralized backdrop to the novel's action, but is itself a kind of protagonist. It is not simply that we come to know the Indian Aziz more thoroughly than any of the English characters, but that the image of India as a whole is more important than any of the figures, English or Indian, who move across it. To understand India is to understand the rationale of the whole creation; but the characters do not understand it, and Forster's plot makes us ask whether human faculties are capable of such understanding at all. After each character has made his feeble effort to grasp the total pattern, we are left again with the enormous and irrational presence of India, a riddle that can be ignored but never solved.

The literal plot of *A Passage to India* seems at first to be unrelated to this symbolic level of meaning. Its chief issue is one that is suitable to a detective story: whether or not Aziz has actually attempted to rape Adela Quested in the Marabar Caves. This, however, is bound up with the whole problem of Anglo-Indian misunderstanding, for the occasion of the supposed assault is a picnic organized by Aziz in the interest of interracial friendship. Adela's near-disastrous hallucination is, completely apart from its religious implications, a symbolic breakdown of the effort at mutual sympathy between the two countries. Adela herself has come to Chandrapore not simply to marry Ronny Heaslop, the City Magistrate, but to 'know India' on its own terms. Mrs Moore, too, her traveling-companion and Ronny's mother, has come with a willingness to understand and love the Indians. Much of the early by-play of the plot is taken up with the efforts of Adela and Mrs Moore to be generous toward India

– efforts that are thwarted not by Indians, but by the suspicious
and snobbish colonial officials, including Ronny Heaslop. When
a genuine rapport between East and West seems finally imminent,
however, it is shown to be impossible. Indians and Englishmen
must remain apart, not because Indians are venal and shifty (as
Ronny and his friends believe) but because of fundamental
differences in temperament, social structure, and religious outlook. The one hope for unity is, as we might expect, a trust in the
power of affectionate friendship among individuals; but even this
proves inadequate, as we find in the crumbling of relations between Aziz and Cyril Fielding, the liberal and humane principal
of Chandrapore's Government College.

A Passage to India, then, finally refuses all bids for 'passage'
through the national barriers it defines; the more earnest the
gestures of personal good will, the more thoroughly they are
resented and misconstrued on both sides. Such a novel can have no
hero or villain, since the blame for the failure of communication
rests on the whole conflict of civilizations, indeed upon human
nature generally. Because this is so, the novel dwells less upon
single personalities than its four predecessors; instead of following one character's internal debate between values represented by
a few other characters, we stand before a social panorama in which
a multitude of 'flat' characters are briefly glimpsed.

Thus, on the English side, we shift our main focus continually
among Adela, Mrs Moore, and Fielding, none of whom matches
the complexity of Rickie Elliot or Margaret Schlegel; and after
these, and perhaps Ronny, we become briefly acquainted with a
series of insignificant persons whose natures can be summed up
in a phrase. There is Major Callendar, the Civil Surgeon, who is
rude to Aziz but knows that Aziz is professionally superior to
him; Mr Turton, the well-meaning but jingoistic Collector; his
wife, who speaks Urdu but knows only the imperative mood;
Miss Derek, a prankster chiefly memorable for her expletives
('golly!' 'how putrid!' and so on); the Reverends Graysford and
Sorley, timid missionaries; Mr McBryde, the District Superinten-
dent of Police, whom Forster calls the most reflective and best
educated of the Chandrapore officials, but who firmly maintains

that all persons born south of latitude thirty are criminals at heart; and several others, some of whom appear only for a sentence or a paragraph.

Among the Indians, Aziz and the Hindu Professor Godbole are important and are sharply portrayed, but behind them stand rows of characters whose nearly unanimous contempt for the English tends to blur their individuality. There is the Nawab Bahadur, who argues against superstition but believes in ghosts; Mahmoud Ali, Aziz's genially cynical friend who hates the British but loves the memory of Queen Victoria; Mohammed Latif, 'a gentle, happy and dishonest old man' (p. 14)[1] who humbly but doggedly poaches on his distant relations; Hamidullah, a Cambridge graduate who wistfully deplores the 'wire-pulling and fear' of Chandrapore's political atmosphere (see p. 107); Aziz's servant Hassan, an accomplished shirker; Dr Panna Lal, whose low social position licenses Aziz to make an enemy of him; the magistrate Das, who tries unsuccessfully to befriend Aziz after presiding over the trial; and numerous other figures of incidental importance. Forster underscores the profusion of levels to Indian society. We are told, for example, that in addition to the miserable clients who wait in the dust outside Chandrapore's courthouse, 'there were circles even beyond these – people who wore nothing but a loincloth, people who wore not even that, and spent their lives in knocking two sticks together before a scarlet doll – humanity grading and drifting beyond the educated vision, until no earthly invitation can embrace it' (p. 37).

Sentences like this last one suggest more than they directly say; they lead us to search for some controlling view of life behind the observed fact that is reported. In this case Forster has used two related metaphors that are picked up and elaborated elsewhere with metaphysical overtones. These are the metaphors of *receding circles* and of *invitation*. In *A Passage to India* Forster habitually allows his vision to slide outward from a human 'circle' of perspective to a macrocosmic one, so that we come to see the lives of his characters as a tiny, though possibly central, spot in the total pattern. The very first chapter, which resembles that of *Nostromo* in its portentous fixing of the scale of action, makes striking use of this device. At night over Chandrapore, 'the stars hang like lamps from the immense vault. The distance between the vault and them is as nothing to the distance behind them, and that farther distance, though beyond colour, last freed itself from blue' (p. 9). Forster's syntax here is confusing, but his meaning is sufficiently clear: the scale of measurement suggested by the part of the universe visible to man is insignificantly small compared with the colorless (and hence valueless) realm beyond it.

Later in the novel Forster is more insistent about this dwarfing of humanity. Thus while a group of Englishmen are speaking together at a garden party, 'their words seemed to die as soon as uttered. Some kites hovered overhead, impartial, over the kites passed the mass of a vulture, and with an impartiality exceeding all, the sky, not deeply coloured but translucent, poured light from its whole circumference. It seemed unlikely that the series stopped here. Beyond the sky must not there be something that overarches all the skies, more impartial even than they? Beyond which again. . .' (pp. 39 ff). Here the importance of man is qualified not only by the predatory kites and vulture, suggesting death, but more horribly by the concentric spheres of 'impartiality', that is, of divine indifference to the human world. Mrs Moore, the Christian, begins to doubt whether the name of Jehovah can be meaningful in the vast impersonality of India. 'Outside the arch there seemed always an arch,' she reflects, 'beyond the remotest echo a silence' (p. 52).

Another disquieting feature of India is the constant surrounding presence of the jungle. Unlike England, whose modest proportions and mild climate encourage the illusion of harmony between man and nature (Ronny and Adela, significantly, have had 'serious walks and talks' at Grasmere), India is frankly unimpressed by man. 'Bats, rats, birds, insects will as soon nest inside a house as out; it is to them a normal growth of the eternal jungle, which alternately produces houses trees, houses trees' (p. 35). The animals of England are scarcely more considerate, of course, 'but in the tropics the indifference is more prominent, the inarticulate world is closer at hand and readier to resume control as soon as men are tired' (p. 114).

It is in these conditions that Forster develops his metaphor of
invitation. The offering or withholding of invitations, which is
the Englishman's characteristic means of keeping his life in
proper social order, becomes ineffectual when such 'guests' as
tigers and cobras may drop in at any time. And this fact presents
a challenge to the whole Western Christian mind, as we can see
in the following passage:

All invitations must proceed from heaven perhaps; perhaps it is
futile for men to initiate their own unity, they do but widen the
gulfs between them by the attempt. So at all events thought old
Mr Graysford and young Mr Sorley. . . . In our Father's house
are many mansions, they taught, and there alone will the in-
compatible multitudes of mankind be welcomed and soothed.
Not one shall be turned away by the servants on that verandah,
be he black or white, not one shall be kept standing who approaches with a loving heart. And why should the divine
hospitality cease here? Consider, with all reverence, the monkeys. May there not be a mansion for the monkeys also? Old
Mr Graysford said No, but young Mr Sorley, who was advanced,
said Yes; he saw no reason why monkeys should not have their
collateral share of bliss, and he had sympathetic discussions about
them with his Hindu friends. And the jackals? Jackals were indeed
less to Mr Sorley's mind, but he admitted that the mercy of God,
being infinite, may well embrace all mammals. And the wasps?
He became uneasy during the descent to wasps, and was apt to
change the conversation. And oranges, cactuses, crystals and
mud? and the bacteria inside Mr Sorley? No, no, this is going too
far. We must exclude someone from our gathering, or we shall
be left with nothing. (pp. 37 ff)

Forster is of course being deliberately absurd in pressing the
social metaphor to these lengths. He is implying, with logical
irony, that Christianity cannot afford to slacken its 'inhospitality'
to chaos; as soon as one opens the doors of heaven a crack wider,
the whole idea of bodily resurrection is invaded with contradictions. Human kind, as a Christian poet has put it, cannot bear
very much reality.

On one level the idea of invitation is perfectly literal in *A
Passage to India*; the social tangle of the novel is adumbrated

in the repeated question of whether Englishmen and Indians should entertain one another. Early in the novel, under pressure from Adela and Mrs Moore, the English colonials agree to include Indians in a bridge party, but their continuing suspicion and snobbery prevent any real mingling of the races; the occasion becomes an embarrassing image of apartheid. Again, Aziz's invitation to Adela, Mrs Moore, and Fielding to inspect the Marabar Caves is an ill-starred gesture of friendliness. Even Fielding's private entertainment of Aziz with the two ladies ends in misunderstanding; Ronny, who has the Forsterian egoist's gift of believing precisely the opposite of what is true, arrives on the scene and suggests to Fielding that Aziz cannot be trusted with the delectable Miss Quested. The Indians themselves are divided along religious lines and are no closer to unity at the end of the novel than at the beginning. The flurry of camaraderie following the trial is quickly replaced by the ancient distrust between Moslem and Hindu, while the breach between Indians and English is wider than ever. Fielding, the one character who has temporarily 'belonged' to both sides, understands the futility of his liberalism and departs from India altogether. The very spirit of the Indian earth, Forster says, 'tries to keep men in compartments' (p. 127), and in the final sentence of the novel the sky and earth together are pictured as conspiring against mutual understanding.

On another level of interpretation, this social impasse opens out into the religious question that the Reverends Graysford and Sorley handle so gingerly: whether God's attention extends to all His creatures, to some of them, or to none. It is significant, for instance, that the famous image of the wasp in *A Passage to India* is introduced just after Ronny has tried to discourage his mother from associating with Aziz, and just before Aziz is invited to the bridge party by Mr Turton. Mrs Moore finds a wasp on a coat-peg and, in calling it 'Pretty dear' (p. 35), acknowledges its right to existence; she 'invites' it into the circle of her benevolent interest. The Reverend Sorley, however, draws the line precisely at wasps; he must concede that it is really too much to ask that God should bother with them. Much later in the novel the figure of the wasp is introduced in the mind of Professor Godbole, who remembers Mrs Moore and a wasp with the same spiritual tenderness: 'He loved the wasp equally, he impelled it likewise, he was imitating God'. (p. 286). The Westerners and Moslems in *A Passage to India*, considering themselves distinct from God and from one another, are inhospitable to insects, and the enmity seems mutual. Aziz is repeatedly upset by the presence of flies in his house, and Fielding, the Western rationalist, is pursued by bees (pp. 102, 279, 299). Mrs Moore and Professor Godbole extend their love to wasps because their religions – his is Hinduism, hers a sporadic mysticism overlaying her Christian training – accept the entire creation as an indivisible part of God's being.

Is the novel, then, a covert apology for Hinduism? Many readers have thought so, but at the expense of oversimplifying Forster's attitude. Hinduism is certainly the religion most able to cope with the bewildering contradictions one finds in India, but its method of doing this – accepting everything indiscriminately, obliterating all distinctions – has obvious disadvantages that are brought out in the course of the novel. The tripartite structure of *A Passage to India*, with its formal shifting from 'Mosque' to 'Caves' to 'Temple', suggests that various religious paths to truth are being problematically offered; and the inconclusive and frustrating ending of the book implies that each path, while having particular advantages that the others lack, ultimately ends in a maze.

Those who favor a Hindu reading of *A Passage to India* rest their claims on the final section of the novel, where the setting has changed from Westernized Chandrapore to a Hindu Native State. In these surroundings there is, indeed, occasion for a meeting of East and West. But the meeting, which takes place at the peak of the Hindu festival of Gokul Ashtami, is effected through the capsizing of two boats in a furious rainstorm, and it is a moot question whether the momentarily reconciled parties have been drenched with Hindu love or simply drenched. It is a climax, Forster warns, only 'as far as India admits of one' (p. 315), and in retrospect the festival amounts only to 'ragged edges of

religion . . . unsatisfactory and undramatic tangles' (p. 316). If
Hinduism succeeds, where Islam and Christianity fail, in taking
the entire universe into its view, we still cannot silence the voice
of Western humanism. What about man and his need for order?
Are we to sacrifice our notion of selfhood to the ideal of inclusiveness? 'The fact is,' Forster has said elsewhere, 'we can only love
what we know personally' (*Two Cheers for Democracy*, New
York, 1951, p. 45). And as Fielding thinks when he has quit India
and recovered his sense of proportion at Venice, 'Without form,
how can there be beauty?' (p. 282).

These misgivings about reading *A Passage to India* in a spirit
of orthodoxy are strengthened by an acquaintance with Forster's
private statements of opinion about the religions involved. We
know, of course, that such statements cannot take the place of
internal evidence, but in this case the internal evidence is somewhat ambiguous; the temptation to ask Forster what he really
thinks is irresistible. His attitude toward Christianity is hardly
obscure, but Islam and Hinduism have aroused mixed feelings in
him, and these, I think, find their way into *A Passage to India*. On
his second trip to India, in 1921, Forster was Private Secretary
to the Maharajah of Dewas State Senior, a Hindu Native State;
his letters from there and elsewhere are sometimes revealing. 'I do
like Islam,' he wrote to his mother from Chhatarpur, 'though I
have had to come through Hinduism to discover it. After all the
mess and profusion and confusion of Gokul Ashtami, where
nothing ever stopped or need ever have begun, it was like standing on a mountain' (*The Hill of Devi*, New York, 1953, p. 193).

The nature of this attraction is evident in two essays reprinted
in *Abinger Harvest*, 'Salute to the Orient!' and 'The Mosque'.
Islamic meditation, Forster explains, 'though it has the intensity
and aloofness of mysticism, never leads to abandonment of personality. The Self is precious, because God, who created it, is
Himself a personality. . .' (*Abinger Harvest*, New York, 1936,
p. 273). One thinks immediately of Forster's well-known individualism; the idea of selfhood is indispensable to his entire system
of value. Again, Forster's liberalism and his contempt for superstition seem to govern the following contrasts between Islam

and Christianity: 'Equality before God – so doubtfully pro-
claimed by Christianity – lies at the very root of Islam . . .' and
the Moslem God 'was never incarnate and left no cradles, coats,
handkerchiefs or nails on earth to stimulate and complicate devotion' (ibid. pp. 275, 276). Nowhere does Forster imply that he
actually believes the dogmatic content of Islam; the point is that
he is aesthetically gratified by a religion that is not grossly
anthropomorphic. He is no more of a Moslem than he is a
Christian, but Islam at least does not outrage his con..non sense
and his love of modest form.

A Passage to India, of course, demands more of religion than
this; the central question of the novel is that of man's relationship
to God, and Moslems, Forster says, 'do not seek to be God or
even to see Him' (ibid. p. 273). Thus Islam can hardly lead
Forster's characters to the assurance they need; as Fielding puts
it, ' "There is no God but God" doesn't carry us far through the
complexities of matter and spirit; it is only a game with words,
really, a religious pun, not a religious truth' (*A Passage to India*,
p. 276). And the refusal to abandon personality, which is the
strongest bond between Aziz and the Westerners in the novel,
turns out to be a severe limitation in their apparatus for grasping
transcendent truth.

Forster's opinion of Hinduism is more clearly a dual one: he
finds Hindu ritual absurd but Hindu theology relatively attractive. His letters about Gokul Ashtami are extremely condescend-
ing; he thought the spirit of the festival indistinguishable from
'ordinary mundane intoxication', and he generalized: 'What
troubles me is that every detail, almost without exception, is
fatuous and in bad taste' (*The Hill of Devi*, pp. 160, 159). Yet his
admiration for the Maharajah for whom he was later to work led
him to an early sympathy with Hindu doctrine. The following
excerpt from a letter of 6 March 1913 explains part of the Maharajah's position and Forster's response to it:

His attitude was very difficult for a Westerner. He believes
that we – men, birds, everything – are part of God, and that men
have developed more than birds because they have come nearer
to realising this.

That isn't so difficult; but when I asked why we had any of us ever been severed from God, he explained it by God becoming unconscious that we were parts of him, owing to his energy at some time being concentrated elsewhere. . . . Salvation, then, is the thrill we feel when God again becomes conscious of us, and all our life we must train our perceptions so that we may be capable of feeling when the time comes.

I think I see what lies at the back of this – if you believe that the universe was God's *conscious* creation, you are faced with the fact that he has consciously created suffering and sin, and this the Indian refuses to believe. 'We were either put here intentionally or unintentionally,' said the Rajah, 'and it raises fewer difficulties if we suppose that it was unintentionally' (*The Hill of Devi*, p. 45).

Here again we may observe that Forster is not asserting a religious belief of his own, but is simply trying to be open-minded. Still, we can recognize the congeniality of Hinduism, in this interpretation, to Forster's opinions as we already know them. His disbelief in Providence, his sense of man's ignorance of divine truth, his rejection of the idea of a man-centered universe – all are reconcilable with his summary of the Maharajah's Hinduism. Yet the point at which the correspondence breaks down is even more striking. It is easy enough for Forster to entertain the theory that God is presently unconscious of man, but there is little provision in his philosophy for the moment of awakening; only the negative side of Hinduism accords with his temperament.

There is no escaping the impression that Hinduism is treated with considerable sympathy in *A Passage to India*. Its chief function, however, seems to be to discredit the Christian and Moslem emphasis on personality; the vastness and confusion of India are unsuitable for an orderly, benevolent deity whose attention to individuals is tireless. When the question of mystical union arises, however, Forster becomes evasive in the extreme. Gokul Ashtami, he remarks, presents 'emblems of passage; a passage not easy, not now, not here, not to be apprehended except when it is unattainable. . .' (*A Passage to India*, pp. 314 ff). Although Hinduism offers the most engaging fable to describe our isolation

from meaning, it, too, like Islam and Christianity, seems power-
less before the nihilistic message of the Marabar Caves.

The incidents in the Caves are of course the symbolic heart
of the novel, where India exerts its force of illusion and disillusion
upon the British visitors. These incidents are meaningful on all
levels, making the hopeless misunderstanding between East and
West vivid and complete, but their most important kind of meaning is clearly religious. The Christian Mrs Moore and the Moslem
Aziz, having befriended one another in a mosque, have previously been kept apart by social barriers, but now they are to
meet, with Adela, on the ground of what Adela has called 'the
real India'. The Marabar Caves will offer them an India more
virginal than they bargain for, and will, through utter indifference
to selfhood, challenge their very sense of reality.

The Marabar Hills, 'older than all spirit', date back to an age
long before Hindusim arrived and 'scratched and plastered a few
rocks' (p. 124). They are 'flesh of the sun's flesh', and the sun
'may still discern in their outline forms that were his before our
globe was torn from his bosom' (p. 123). They are thus completely divorced from the works and history of man. Like the
Hindu God, they seem to have no attributes: 'Nothing, nothing
attaches to them,' says Forster (p. 124). And this analogy with
Hinduism is highly suggestive, for Mrs Moore's experience in the
Hills is a kind of parody of the recognition of Brahma. Hinduism
claims that Self and Not-self, Atman and Brahman, are actually
one, and that the highest experience is to perceive this annihilation of value. Value is indeed annihilated for Mrs Moore; the
echoing Caves convince her that 'Everything exists, nothing has
value' (p. 149).

Glen O. Allen has found several references in the *Upanishads*
to the dwelling of Atman and Brahman in caves,[2] and one such
passage seems especially pertinent here. 'The wise who, by means
of meditation on his Self, recognises the Ancient, who is difficult
to be seen, who has entered into the dark, who is hidden in the
cave, who dwells in the abyss, as God, he indeed leaves joy and
sorrow far behind.'[3] In the Marabar Caves Mrs Moore discovers
'the ancient', but it is not Brahma: 'What had spoken to her in

that scoured-out cavity of the granite? What dwelt in the first of
the caves? Something very old and very small. Before time, it was
before space also. Something snub-nosed, incapable of generosity
– the undying worm itself' (p. 208). And though she does,
indeed, leave joy and sorrow behind, the departure is utterly
pedestrian. She has simply been thrust into the disillusion of old
age:

She had come to that state where the horror of the universe and
its smallness are both visible at the same time – the twilight of
the double vision in which so many elderly people are involved.
If this world is not to our taste, well, at all events there is Heaven,
Hell, Annihilation – one or other of those large things, that huge
scenic background of stars, fires, blue or black air. All heroic
endeavor, and all that is known as art, assumes that there is such
a background ... But in the twilight of the double vision, a
spiritual muddledom is set up for which no high-sounding words
can be found; we can neither act nor refrain from action, we can
neither ignore nor respect Infinity. (pp. 207 ff)

Readers who have claimed that Mrs Moore has suddenly been
transformed from a modest Christian to a mystical Brahmin have
had to overlook the prosaic quality of her feelings here. She has
had, in effect, an antivision, a realization that to see through the
world of superficial appearances is to be left with nothing at all.
'The abyss also may be petty, the serpent of eternity made of
maggots ...' (p. 208).

Mrs Moore's inversion of Hinduism is sharpened by the resemblance of the Caves' echoes – 'boum' and 'ou-boum' – to the
mystic Hindu syllable 'Om', which stands for the trinity of the
godhead. He who ponders this syllable, says the *Prasna-
Upanishad*, 'learns to see the all-pervading, the Highest Person'.[4]
This is Mrs Moore's ambition: 'To be one with the universe! So
dignified and simple' (p. 208). In an ironical sense she achieves
this, for she does grasp a oneness underlying everything. Its
monotony, however, is subversive of the moral and ceremonial
distinctions that we require to reconcile ourselves to the Absolute. '... Religion appeared, poor little talkative Christianity,
and she knew that all its divine words from "Let there be Light"

to "It is finished" only amounted to "boum" ' (p. 150). The oneness Mrs Moore has found has obliterated her belief in the categories of space and time, distinctions that are essential to a
religion whose God has a sense of history. This is why she can
be said to have perceived both the horror and the smallness of
the universe; the Marabar Caves 'robbed infinity and eternity of
their vastness, the only quality that accommodates them to
mankind' (p. 150).

If I may digress for a moment, this debasement of the ideas
of infinity and eternity seems to be philosophically suggestive.
The modern Western sense of time, which was once thought to
correspond exactly and immutably with the objective world, and
which kept its 'universality' even after Kant proved it to be sub-
jective, has been challenged from various sides by physicists,
anthropologists, and psychoanalysts. Norman O. Brown, in
summarizing the arguments that time is culturally relative, says
that the progressive and irreversible time of the Newtonian
universe is, in effect, a legacy of religion; it is geared to a day
of redemption at the end of 'history'. Archaic religion, with its
annual atonements, is 'cyclical, periodic, unhistoric'. And at a
still more primitive level we meet Freud's great discovery that the
unconscious mind observes no time schema at all. Our time-sense,
if Brown is correct, is ultimately ruled by repression – by the
effort to manage and spend a primordial unconscious feeling of
guilt. In these terms it seems highly appropriate that both Mrs
Moore and Adela (see below, p. 182) find their sense of time
disrupted in the 'prehistoric' Caves. Both women are gripped by
previously unconscious feelings which their religion customarily
placates or denies; in both cases Forster strikes an oblique blow
at Christianity by implying that its time-sense is dependent on
repression.[5]

· We may well ask at this point why Mrs Moore, who seems to
have a kind of second sight on occasion and who is certainly a
morally sympathetic character, is visited with disillusionment.
One answer may simply be that she *does* have second sight, that
she perceives what truly subsists behind the veil of Maya; in this
case her experience would constitute a thorough disavowal of

Hindusim on Forster's part. Remembering Adela's hallucination, however, we may question whether Mrs Moore has penetrated anything at all. Perhaps she has merely heard echoes of her own unvoiced misgivings about the significance of life.[6] It is impossible, in any case, to support the popular reading that she has experienced the merging of Atman and Brahman. Atman is the presence of the *universal* ego in the individual, the 'God dwelling within', and the properly disciplined Hindu will find Brahman, the supreme soul, echoed in this 'Self'. Mrs Moore, however, is unprepared to relinquish her selfhood in the narrow sense of personality. Instead of blending her identity with that of the world-soul, she reduces the world-soul to the scale of her own wearied ego; her dilettantish yearning for oneness with the universe has been echoed, not answered. Whether or not Forster considers the serpent of eternity to be made of maggots is a question we cannot answer on the basis of *A Passage to India*; in view of his skepticism it is doubtful that he would feel himself qualified to make any assertion at all on the subject. What does emerge clearly from the novel is that the Marabar Caves have not brought us into the presence of ultimate truth. The last words of India to Mrs Moore, as she sails away to die, may serve also as a caveat to eager critics: 'So you thought an echo was India; you took the Marabar caves as final? . . . What have we in common with them, or they with Asirgarh? Good-bye!' (p. 210).

Adela's experience in the Cave, though it has religious implications, lends itself more readily to analysis in psychological terms. This agrees with the Caves' function of echoing only what is brought to them, for Adela's yearnings are sexual, not mystical. As she climbs upward with Aziz her conscious thoughts are occupied with her approaching marriage to Ronny, but she is increasingly troubled by misgivings, until she realizes with vexation that she is not in love with her fiancé. Before entering the Cave, however, she commits the Forsterian heresy of deciding that love is not essential to a successful marriage; she will marry Ronny anyway. As in the case of Mrs Moore, the Marabar Caves thrust to the surface a conflict between conventional and suppressed feelings. The echo that is metaphorically sounded in

Adela's hallucination (if it is a hallucination) of sexual attack is that of her unvoiced desire for physical love.

That this problematic assault should be attributed to Aziz is perhaps the central irony of plot in *A Passage to India*. Forster takes pains to let us know that Aziz's thoughts about sex are 'hard and direct, though not brutal' (p. 102) – exactly the reverse of Adela's. Though he generally 'upheld the proprieties ... he did not invest them with any moral halo, and it was here that he chiefly differed from an Englishman' (p. 103). As for Adela, he finds her sexually repellent ('She has practically no breasts,' he tells Fielding; p. 120), whereas Adela, for her part, is attracted to him ('What a handsome little Oriental he was ...'; p. 152). Just before she enters the Cave, whose significance is apparently Freudian as well as metaphysical, Adela enviously ponders Aziz's physical advantages: 'beauty, thick hair, a fine skin' (p. 153). She asks him, in what Forster calls 'her honest, decent, inquisitive way: "Have you one wife or more than one?"' (p. 153). And when the monogamous widower Aziz passes into a Cave to hide his embarrassment over her question, Adela enters a different Cave, 'thinking with half her mind "sight-seeing bores me," and wondering with the other half about marriage' (p. 153). It is this other half, this wondering about physical gratification, that accosts her in the Cave; and, since Self and Not-self are confused there, she assigns her thoughts to Aziz.

An important difference between Adela's crisis and Mrs Moore's is that Mrs Moore adjusts her whole view of life to accord with the annihilation of value in the Cave, while Adela continues for a while to be torn between accepting and rejecting her experience. Mrs Moore knows intuitively that Aziz is not a rapist, but she is weary of legalistic distinctions; the alleged crime 'presented itself to her as love: in a cave, in a church – Boum, it amounts to the same' (p. 208). She does not stay to testify for Aziz, for the moral issue of the trial cannot interest her; if there is no value in the universe, there is surely none in distinctions between sanctioned and illicit love. Yet this very indifference makes it proper that Mrs Moore, after she has withered out of bodily existence, should be resurrected as a Hindu goddess in the minds of the Indians at Aziz's trial. 'When all the ties of the heart are severed here on earth,' says the *Katha-Upanishad,* 'then the mortal becomes immortal. . . .'[7] The parallel is in one sense ironic, as we have seen: Mrs Moore has been the victim of a travesty of Hindu enlightenment. On the other hand, the Mrs Moore who originally befriended Aziz and who is remembered fondly by Professor Godbole has believed in loving everything that enters her consciousness, and such a love is the cornerstone of Hinduism.

Unlike Mrs Moore, Adela lacks the imagination to be permanently shattered by her irrational experience. 'In space things touch, in time things part' (p. 192), she repeats to herself, attempting to re-establish the categories that were imperiled by the Caves. Though she has been a freethinker, she turns to Jehovah for redress: 'God who saves the King will surely support the police,' goes her reasoning (p. 211). From the day of the hallucination until the climax of the trial she continually seeks to reconstruct the incident in direct logical terms. The dark savage has attacked her – but who has been the savage, Aziz or herself? Her virtue has been threatened – or has she simply rebelled against her starched prudery? Justice will be exacted upon the guilty one – but who is to cast the first stone in matters of sex? The psychological complexity of Adela's situation lends a kind of realistic support to Professor Godbole's doctrinal view: 'All perform a good action, when one is performed, and when an evil action is performed, all perform it' (p. 177).

Forster would not assert this as a fixed principle, but we have often enough observed him recoiling from its opposite, the black-and-white attribution of guilt and innocence to separate parties. Before Adela can be freed from the echo of the Cave she must retreat a little from her simplistic Western notion of cause and effect. She is finally able to retract her charge because she has achieved a 'double relation' to the controversial event: 'Now she was of it and not of it at the same time . . .' (p. 227). In other words, she has begun to feel the limitations of a knowledge that is strictly bounded by her personality, her discrete selfhood. If she is never to know what occurred in the Cave, at least she will

remember that there may be an order of truth beyond the field
of her rational vision. Like Fielding, whose empiricism has
brought him no closer to knowledge than her own resort to
prayer, Adela has reached 'the end of her spiritual tether ...
Were there worlds beyond which they could never touch, or did
all that is possible enter their consciousness? They could not
tell.... Perhaps life is a mystery, not a muddle; they could not
tell. Perhaps the hundred Indias which fuss and squabble so tiresomely are one, and the universe they mirror is one. They had
not the apparatus for judging' (p. 263).

A Passage to India, then, is a novel in which two levels of truth,
the human and the divine, are simultaneously explored, never
very successfully. Epistemological conclusions are reached, but
they are all negative ones. Christian righteousness, we discover,
helps us to misconstrue both God and man; Moslem love can
scarcely reach beyond the individual personality; rational skepticism is wilfully arid; and the Hindu ideal of oneness, though it
does take notice of the totality of things, abolishes the intellectual
sanity that makes life endurable to the Western mind. The in-
escapable point of this demonstration is that God cannot be
realized in any satisfactory way. It is a point that Forster dwelt
upon at some length in his earlier novels, but always with a note
of smugness; there was always the facile warning that we should
restrict our interest to the world that we know. In *A Passage to
India*, however, Forster's characters are given no choice; if they
are to understand themselves and one another they must grapple
with metaphysics. They do their best, but it is very little – not
because they are exceptionally weak, but simply because they are
human. Forster implies that we ourselves, his readers, are equally
blocked off from meaning. We cannot fall back on reason and the
visible world, for we see how these are falsely colored by personality. Even if we could, we ought not seek Mrs Moore's 'dignified
and simple' identification with the universe, for this is nihilism in
disguise. Nor can we assert with humanistic piety that our whole
duty is to love one another; this, too, proves more difficult than
we might have gathered from Forster's previous books. What

finally confronts us is an irreparable breach between man's powers and his needs.

It is perhaps significant that Forster's career as a novelist comes to an apparent end at this moment of development, for the characters of a novel, as he has said elsewhere, 'suggest a more comprehensible and thus a more manageable human race; they give us the illusion of perspicacity and power' (*Aspects of the Novel*, New York, 1927, p. 99). *A Passage to India*, though it tells us more about its characters than they themselves know, tries to refute the very thought that our race is comprehensible and manageable; it casts doubt upon the claim of anyone, even of the artist, to supply the full context of human action. In writing one novel which pays full deference to the unknown and the unknowable, Forster thus seems to announce the end of the traditional novel as he found it; between pathetic futility and absolute mystery no middle ground remains for significant action.

SOURCE: '*A Passage to India*', in *E. M. Forster: The Perils of Humanism* (1962).

NOTES

1. [*Editor's note.*] Page references to the Harcourt Brace American edition, 1924.
2. Glen O. Allen, 'Structure, Symbol, and Theme in E. M. Forster's *A Passage to India*', in *PMLA* LXX (Dec 1955) 934–54.
3. *The Sacred Books of the East*, ed. F. Max Müller (Oxford, 1884) vol. XV: *The Upanishads*, p. 10.
4. Quoted by Allen, p. 943.
5. See Norman O. Brown, *Life Against Death; the psychoanalytical meaning of history* (New York, 1959) pp. 273–8. If Brown is right in treating the Newtonian sense of reality as a stepchild of religion, Forster also seems vindicated in his treatment of the rationalist, Fielding. Fielding has little to offer in the ontological debate of the novel, for his religious outlook is simply the Christian one minus God and the Savior. Though Fielding and Adela seem dissimilar, they are philosophically quite close, and it is proper that they should recognize their common impasse in trying to 'understand India'.

6. The Caves not only deliver a dull echo in reply to every sound, they also offer reflections of light on their polished walls. The flame of a match and its reflection, we are told, 'approach and strive to unite, but cannot, because one of them breathes air, the other stone' (p. 125). In symbolic terms this seems to support the idea that one will 'see' his own thoughts imprisoned in Marabar stone, i.e. robbed of their context of human illusion.

7. *The Sacred Books of the East*, XV 23.

John Beer
THE UNDYING WORM (1962)

FORSTER visited India twice, in 1912–13 and 1921. He has recalled some of his impressions, and included letters written at the time, in *The Hill of Devi*. But the seeds of *A Passage to India* lie scattered still further back. They were growing when [in *The Longest Journey*] Herbert Pembroke, addressing his house at Sawston School, pointed to portraits of empire-builders on the wall and quoted imperial poets.

There is an inevitability in the choice of theme for this culminating novel. In the earlier ones, Sawston never quite found an antagonist worthy of its powers. In England, it was faced on one side by an aristocracy which patronized and used it, on the other by a working class with which it had long ago compromised. It existed only with the connivance of other classes of society which in their turn kept some check on it. Even when it set itself against the more spontaneous life of Italy, it was facing a society which in its treatment of women and relatives was even-more rigid than itself.

But in India, Sawston could flourish with greater freedom. As a class it was single and distinct, not subject to checks from above or below: and the opposition to it came from a separate civilization which although more comprehensive, more venerable and more alive to the human condition than itself, was seen by its blinkered vision as naïve and primitive. The characteristics of Sawston were bound to become exaggerated in a situation where it lived both complacently assured of its own rightness and consciously embattled against forces which could easily, through some error or miscalculation, overwhelm it. A novel with such a setting is necessarily alive with dramatic tensions.

Into this precarious situation, as localized in the small station of Chandrapore, step Mrs Moore and Adela Quested, two visitors from England. Adela has come because a marriage is being arranged between her and Ronny Heaslop, the district magistrate; Mrs Moore in order to accompany her. Adela expresses a desire to see the 'real' India, and in order that she may do so Dr Aziz, a young doctor, arranges a trip to the famous Marabar caves. But during the expedition Adela enters a cave and on emerging has the impression that Aziz followed her in and assaulted her. Her accusations are made publicly, an explosive situation is created in the small town, and a trial is arranged at which she is to be called as a witness. Then, when the tension is at its height during the trial, Adela suddenly declares that no one followed her into the cave. The trial collapses; there is a temporary crisis during which there are fears for the breakdown of public order, and then life resumes its normal tenor. Adela, who has incurred universal dislike for her action, returns to England without marrying Ronny. The novel concludes with a long section devoted to an Indian festival which is attended by Mrs Moore's son and daughter. Mrs Moore herself, who stood throughout the novel as a reconciling power between English and Indians, has died on the voyage home after an illness which began, like Adela's crisis, with her experiences in a Marabar cave.

The dramatic situation of the novel, involving as it does an explosive human situation which can be ignited by the failure of a single individual, is finely conceived. If one regards plot as a means for manipulating the reader's expectations and responses, on the other hand, the novel is less successful. It is a major disappointment to readers who have been brought up on detective stories to find that there is no spectacular dénouement, no final revelation concerning the events in the cave, only Adela's denial that Dr Aziz followed her. And if this negation is all that is to be offered, the key events of the trial ought to come at the end of the novel. Why is there a long sequence dealing with irrelevancies such as the festival?

Forster has explained his introduction of the Hindu festival in his *Writers at Work* interview. [See p. 28 of this volume.]

Interviewers. 'What was the exact function of the long description of the Hindu festival in *A Passage to India?*' *Forster.* 'It was architecturally necessary. I needed a lump, or a Hindu temple if you like – a mountain standing up. It is well placed; and it gathers up some strings. But there ought to be more after it. The lump sticks out a little too much.' But this answers one question only to raise another. Why, when the climax of the book has been passed, should such a lump be 'architecturally necessary'? The answer can only be that it is there for some purpose other than the dramatic demands of the plot. In other words, we have to cope with the possibility that the structure of the novel does not consist simply of an arrangement of events. Behind that structure there is another, an arrangement of the novel's meaning.

A reader who is looking for further meaning in the novel may well be attracted to the idea that it is intended as a piece of anti-imperialist propaganda, polemic against British rule in India. As a picture of that rule, however, it contains some major distortions. Some of the characters could be typical only of the sort of Princely State in which Forster spent most of his time, not of modern India. And as both Nirad Chaudhuri and George Orwell have pointed out, little attention is paid to the sheer vastness of the political and economic forces at work there. But the novel ought never to have been read as an essay in *realpolitik.* It is at once too local and too universal. As a contribution to a 'practical' solution of the Indian problem as it existed at that time its value was limited, and the last chapter acknowledges the fact.

Beyond these immediate questions, the pettinesses of officials in a small Government station do have their relevance: for racial and economic questions are, ultimately, questions of human relations and it can never be out of place to say so. And Forster's satire is not directed only against the British: as so often in his work, we are being presented not with propaganda, but with a dialectic, of which the British and the Indians furnish respective limbs. The British may act badly in Forster's India, but so do the Indians. There is never any doubt that they need the justice and fair administration that the British give them. It is the hostility and lack of communication between the two sides that marks the failure – the old failure to 'connect'.

The gap between the two sides is, roughly speaking, the gap between head and heart. In his 'Notes on the English Character', Forster says that it is the 'undeveloped heart that is largely responsible for the difficulties of Englishmen abroad'.[1] Forster's Indians, on the other hand, make up for any failure in cold judicial reasoning by their highly developed hearts. Between the two groups there is a failure. But if the British are to be blamed for the failure, that is only because they were the group from which any initiative must necessarily have come.

Throughout his novel, Forster is at pains to stress the quality of achievement of the British and in particular their desire that justice be done. His central points both for and against the régime are made in his account of the work of Ronny as City Magistrate at Chandrapore:

Every day he worked hard in the court trying to decide which of two untrue accounts was the less untrue, trying to dispense justice fearlessly, to protect the weak against the less weak, the incoherent against the plausible, surrounded by lies and·flattery.

Adela listening to his defence of his behaviour, is not satisfied however:

His words without his voice might have impressed her, but when she heard the self-satisfied lilt of them, when she saw the mouth moving so complacently and competently beneath the little red nose, she felt, quite illogically, that this was not the last word on India. One touch of regret – not the canny substitute but the true regret from the heart – would have made him a different man, and the British Empire a different institution. (ch. v, p. 54)[2]

Throughout the novel, this failure of connection between British and Indians is a running theme. There is no need to illustrate in detail what every reader can see for himself. Towards the end of the novel it is symbolized perhaps in the temple at Mau which has two shrines – the Shrine of the Head on the hill, the Shrine of the Body below. At all events, the separation is strongly emphasized in the last chapter, when the two characters who have tried hardest to come together, Fielding and Aziz, are out riding. The final passage, in which the whole landscape confirms Aziz's words about the impossibility of friendship between British and Indians, finely epitomizes this element in the novel:

But the horses didn't want it – they swerved apart; the earth didn't want it, sending up rocks through which riders must pass single file; the temples, the tank, the jail, the palace, the birds, the carrion, the Guest House, that came into view as they issued from the gap and saw Mau beneath: they didn't want it, they said in their hundred voices, 'No, not yet,' and the sky said, 'No, not there.'

For Fielding, a moderate man who is content with friendliness and sweet reasonableness in his dealings with other men, there can be no solution in India. He finds what he is looking for only when he visits Italy on his way home to England and rediscovers the beauty of its cities. 'He had forgotten the beauty of form among idol temples and lumpy hills.' The account of his visit concludes:

The Mediterranean is the human norm. When men leave that exquisite lake, whether through the Bosphorus or the Pillars of Hercules, they approach the monstrous and extraordinary; and the southern exit leads to the strangest experience of all. (ch. XXXII, p. 293)

This observation is sometimes taken to be Forster's final message in the novel: and it is true that in so far as it is a study of the conflict between two civilizations, at extreme poles from each other and separated by the Mediterranean, the passage offers the only hint of a solution. But it also has to be read in conjunction with another statement of Forster's: 'though proportion is the final secret, to espouse it at the outset is to insure sterility'.

The point of the novel lies not in an assertion of normality, but in an exploration of extremes. And this exploration is not simply social and political. Further issues are involved, which reflect Forster's basic preoccupations as a thinker, and his own experiences in India.

The relationship between Forster's experiences and the final shape of his novel is a good deal more subtle than one might at first imagine. If one turns to *The Hill of Devi*, the later factual record of his visits, some points of contact with the novel stand out immediately. . . . And longer incidents sometimes find their way into the novel, when some important purpose is to be served. There was, for example, his adventure during a walk:

> There we had an exciting and typical adventure. Our train of villagers stopped and pointed to the opposite bank with cries of a snake. At last I saw it – a black thing reared up to the height of three feet and motionless. I said, 'It looks like a small dead tree', and was told 'Oh no', and exact species and habits of snake were indicated – not a cobra, but very fierce and revengeful, and if we shot it would pursue us several days later all the way to Dewas. We then took stones and threw them across the Sipra . . . in order to make snake crawl away. Still he didn't move and when a stone hit his base still didn't move. He *was* a small dead tree. All the villagers shrieked with laughter. (*HD* 63)

During the ascent to the caves in *A Passage to India*, there is a corresponding incident:

> Again, there was a confusion about a snake which was never cleared up. Miss Quested saw a thin, dark object reared on end at the farther side of a watercourse, and said, 'A snake!' The villagers agreed, and Aziz explained: yes, a black cobra, very venomous, who had reared himself up to watch the passing of the elephant. But when she looked through Ronny's field-glasses, she found it wasn't a snake, but the withered and twisted stump of a toddy-palm. So she said, 'It isn't a snake.' The villagers contradicted her. She had put the word into their minds, and they refused to abandon it. Aziz admitted that it looked like a tree through the glasses, but insisted that it was a black cobra really, and improvised some rubbish about protective mimicry. Nothing was explained, and yet there was no romance. (ch. xiv, p. 147)

In *The Hill of Devi* there is also an account of an incident which puzzled Forster a good deal, and led him to wonder whether his Maharajah might possess super-normal faculties. A couple described how they had been motoring from Dewas to Indore,

and how their car had been hit by some animal just as they crossed
the Sipra so that it swerved and nearly hit the parapet of the
bridge:

His Highness sat up keenly interested. 'The animal came from
the left?' he asked.
'Yes.'
'It was a large animal? Larger than a pig but not as big as a
buffalo?'
'Yes, but how did you know?'
'You couldn't be sure what animal it was?'
'No we couldn't.'
He leant back again and said, 'It is most unfortunate. Years ago
I ran over a man there. I was not at all to blame – he was drunk
and ran on to the road and I was cleared at the enquiry, and I
gave money to his family. But ever since then he has been trying
to kill me in the form you describe.' (*HD* 89–90)

Forster relates that he was left with the sense of 'an unexplained
residuum'. In *A Passage to India* there is a similar incident, which
takes place when Adela and Ronny are out driving. An estrangement between them is just being resolved by their consciousness
of physical attraction when the car is brought to a standstill by
the impact of something against it. They get out and decide that
a hyena has hit them. Shortly afterwards, Adela tells Ronny that
she has no intention of breaking with him after all. When the
incident is recounted to Mrs Moore, she shivers and says, 'A
ghost!' No one can explain why she says this, least of all herself:
but we later learn that the Nawab had hit a drunken man there
some years before, just as Forster's Maharajah had done in real
life.

An examination of the use of these incidents shows that Forster is not simply putting in useful local colour. A more subtle
purpose is being served. Both help to suggest Adela's state of
mind during the expedition to the Marabar caves, as we shall see
later.

A good.deal of Forster's experience must have been used in
producing the details which give the novel its deceptively causal
appearance – its air that 'this is how things usually happen, one

after another'. But the fact that some of the most important incidents appear, not at random but in order to subserve a particular effect, harmonizes with a statement by Forster in *The Hill of Devi*, in which he tries to explain the relationship between his Indian experiences and his Indian novel:

> I began this novel before my 1921 visit, and took out the opening chapters with me, with the intention of continuing them. But as soon as they were confronted with the country they purported to describe, they seemed to wilt and go dead and I could do nothing with them. I used to look at them of an evening in my room at Dewas, and felt only distaste and despair. The gap between India remembered and India experienced was too wide. When I got back to England the gap narrowed, and I was able to resume. But I still thought the book bad, and probably should not have completed it without the encouragement of Leonard Woolf. (*HD*, 155)

Only away from India could the patterns which were being woven to interpret his Indian experiences flourish without being swamped by the sheer mass of meaningless experience in everyday life there.

II

In the early part of the novel the 'pattern' consists mainly of a suggestive atmosphere. There is a constant emphasis upon the existence, side by side, of attractiveness and hostility in the Indian scene. The two interweave constantly. They are represented with particular strength in the tension between sky and earth – the sky benevolent, the earth hostile. The most important statement of this tension comes at the end of the first chapter:

> The sky settles everything – not only climates and seasons but when the earth shall be beautiful. By herself she can do little – only feeble outbursts of flowers. But when the sky chooses, glory can rain into the Chandrapore bazaars or a benediction pass from horizon to horizon. The sky can do this because it is so strong and so enormous. Strength comes from the sun, infused in it daily, size from the prostrate earth. No mountains infringe on

the curve. League after league the earth lies flat, heaves a little, is flat again. Only in the south, where a group of fists and fingers are thrust up through the soil, is the endless expanse interrupted. These fists and fingers are the Marabar Hills, containing the extraordinary caves.

The juxtaposition of beauty and hostility continues. When Aziz is on his way to the beautiful mosque where he first meets Mrs Moore, Forster comments on the difficulty of walking in India. 'There is something hostile in that soil. It either yields, and the foot sinks into a depression, or else it is unexpectedly rigid and sharp, pressing stones or crystals against the tread' (ch. II, p. 20). Mrs Moore notices the sky continually and feels a kinship with it. 'In England the moon had seemed dead and alien; here she was caught in the shawl of night together with earth and all the other stars' (ch. III, pp. 32, 37–8). But at the end of the chapter, when she murmurs a vague endearment. to a wasp which she finds sleeping on a clothes peg, it is against a sinister background. '. . . jackals in the plain bayed their desires and mingled with the percussion of drums.' Her voice floats out, 'to swell the night's uneasiness'. The double theme persists throughout the novel. At the climax, in the Hindu festival, there is a momentary reconciliation, symbolized when Aziz looks down on the tank from the road above. 'Reflecting the evening clouds, it filled the netherworld with an equal splendour, so that earth and sky leant toward one another, about to clash in ecstasy' (ch. XXXVI, pp. 318–319). But this is the nearest approach to fusion. In the last episode of the novel, earth and sky alike are made to agree in the impossibility of reconciliation between English and Indians here and now.

The discussion so far might suggest that the sky is only associated with benevolence, the earth only with hostility. This is not so, however. Forster's symbolism has to be referred back to his purposes in *Howards End*. Here, as there, Forster is concerned with the finite and the infinite. The earth represents the finite, the sky the infinite. But both are morally ambivalent. When the moonlight shines on the mosque, it offers 'acceptable hints of infinity' (ch. XVI, p. 166). But when the sun beats down on a parched landscape, infinity becomes unbearable. In the same way, the finite earth can either harden to the hostility of rock, or relax to the benevolence of a fertile plain.

This moral ambivalence provides the warp and woof of the novel. But at its extreme points, the utmost of hostility is found in the finite intractability of rock, the utmost of benevolence in the infinite sun – not the unbearable sun which beats down on noonday India, but the gentler, more glorious sun which is seen for a moment at sunrise and which symbolizes the splendour of true love.

The two poles of the novel are narrowed and focused into more precise symbols. The hostility of rock is particularized in the Marabar caves. As Professor Frank Kermode has pointed out,[3] Forster achieves a good deal of his effect here by an insistent use of the word 'extraordinary'. The first sentence of the whole book reads, 'Except for the Marabar Caves – and they are twenty miles off – the city of Chandrapore presents nothing extraordinary.' The last sentence of the first chapter ends with a mention of 'the Marabar Hills, containing the extraordinary caves'. The innocent word recurs in a later dialogue, when Aziz tries to make Godbole explain why the Marabar caves are famous – but at each move in the conversation the listeners are further from discovering 'what, if anything, was extraordinary about the Marabar Caves' (ch. VII, pp. 79–80). Even when the visitors are on their way, no one will tell them exactly why they are going or what they are going to see. In the meantime, however, there has intervened a description of the caves. Nothing, says Forster, distinguishes one cave from another: 'It is as if the surrounding plain or the passing birds have taken upon themselves to exclaim "extraordinary", and the word has taken root in the air, and been inhaled by mankind' (ch. XII, p. 130).

This peculiar atmosphere, where all is ordinary to the point of being extraordinary, where nullity hardens into hostility, where lack of value turns dully malignant, is crystallized in another image. Elsewhere Forster has described the sinister atmosphere of the Grand Canyon, where the Colorado River 'rages like an infuriated maggot between precipices of granite, gnawing at them and cutting the Canyon deeper'.[4] In 'The Machine Stops', there is a horrifying scene where the hero, ⌐ying to escape, finds himself seized by hideous long white worms which overcome his struggles and suck him back from the surface of the earth into the Machine beneath.[5] This image-pattern is used by Forster to describe Mrs Moore's experience of the Marabar caves (ch. XXIII, p. 217). The echoes in the cave are little worms coiling, ascending and descending. What speaks to her there is 'something snub-nosed, incapable of generosity – the undying worm itself'. In this negative vision, the serpent of eternity is 'made of maggots'.

Against the nightmarish nullity of the caves there is to be set another voice which rings insistently in the novel. Professor Godbole represents the old Hindu tradition of love. At one point he sings a song expressing the earth's yearning for the heavens – the song of the milkmaid calling to Krishna, who refuses to come. In answer to a question from Mrs Moore, he explains that the god never comes in any of his songs. ' "I say to Him, Come, come, come, come, come, come. He neglects to come" ' (ch. VII, pp. 83–4).

When Ronny and Adela pass through the countryside in the car, their estrangement unresolved, the landscape is described as too vast to admit of excellence. 'In vain did each item in it call out, "Come, come." There was not enough god to go round' (ch. VIII, p. 92). The outward scene here expresses their own inward landscape, from which the visionary sun-god of love is absent. Again, when the train is steaming towards the Marabar caves, there is a long passage on India, culminating in the statement, 'She knows of the whole world's trouble, to its uttermost depth. She calls "Come" through her hundred mouths, through objects ridiculous and august. But come to what? She has never defined. She is not a promise, only an appeal' (ch. XIV, p. 143).

Godbole's song may express the yearning of India, but the spirit of love which he also represents cannot cope with the intractability of the caves. As we have seen, he insistently refrains from specifying exactly what is 'extraordinary' about the caves: in particular, he does not mention the echo. Similarly, after the disastrous expedition, his lack of concern about it disconcerts

Fielding. He explains that his unconcern is due to the fact that good and evil are 'both aspects of my Lord':

'He is present in the one, absent in the other, and the difference between presence and absence is great, as great as my feeble mind can grasp. Yet absence implies presence, absence is not non-existence, and we are therefore entitled to repeat, "Come, come, come, come." ' (ch. XIX, p. 186)

A similar limitation is apparent in his dance-ecstasy at the festival. As he dances his love, he brings more and more things into his vision, but when at last he imagines a stone, he finds that he cannot include it. Certain things always resist the harmonizing vision, which can only ignore them.

Yet, if the caves represent one extreme of India, its 'reality' in one sense, Godbole's spirit of love, rising to ecstasy, expresses its other extreme, its other 'reality'. And if the two extremes cannot quite meet, that does not mean that mankind ought to turn away from both and seek a compromise halfway between them. One is reminded again of that vehement assertion in *Howards End*:

No; truth, being alive, was not halfway between anything. It was only to be found by continuous excursions into either realm, and though proportion is the final secret, to espouse it at the outset is to insure sterility.[6]

III

By this time, it will be observed, symbolic implications have transformed the pattern of the novel. What seemed at first sight to be only a conflict between British and Indians has broadened into a conflict between earth and sky – which in its turn veils the conflict between spirit and matter, between love and the intractable.

The title of the novel might have suggested these depths to us. Walt Whitman's poem, 'Passage to India', from which it is taken, begins as a poem about human voyaging. But as it proceeds, it turns into a poem about the voyage of the soul to God.

O thou transcendant!
Nameless – the fibre and the breath!
Light of the light – shedding forth universes – thou centre
     of them!
Thou mightier centre of the true, the good, the loving!
Thou moral, spiritual fountain! affection's source!
     thou reservoir![7]

The poem continues with the reiterated cry, 'Passage to more
than India!' Forster's use of Whitman's title has a distinctly
ironical flavour, however, for if his two visitors are to find in
India 'more than India', it will also be something very far removed from the transcendent or the Ideal: Mrs Moore will find
herself confronted by the very negation of her values. The main
events of Forster's novel are dominated not by the 'Light of
light' but by an oppressive and hostile sun. Yet Whitman's ideal
is not irrelevant. The symbolic events of Forster's first section,
at least, are lit by a gentle moon, and throughout the novel there
is suggestion of a greater power, a sun-like spirit of love which
never quite manages to become incarnate. And Godbole's point
becomes relevant: 'absence implies presence, absence is not non-
existence. . . .'
     Moreover, if Forster has not Whitman's full optimism, his
central point is the same. Mrs Moore and Adela Quested, who
think that they are making an ordinary tourist's trip to India,
and that they know what they mean when they ask to see the
'real' India, are to find that they are making a spiritual passage,
and that they will be brought face to face with 'reality' in a very
different form. This confrontation reverberates throughout the
novel, shedding light on and affecting everything else that
happens in it.
     It is here that the boldness of the novel becomes apparent. At
the level of events, the plot which promises so much fizzles out in
a negation. To find positiveness we have to move behind the
simple action – first to the moral significance of the events and
then, quite naturally, to a pattern of symbolism which rises
behind the plot just as the Marabar caves rise silently against the
sky behind the busy little station of Chandrapore.

We have already touched upon some of the symbolic themes. Their point of interaction with the plot, however, lies chiefly in the experiences of Mrs Moore and Adela Quested, and we cannot do justice to the subtlety of the interweaving without examining those experiences more closely.

There is one important respect in which an appreciation of what is going on at the symbolic and psychological level helps to unravel the plot itself. A point which troubles many readers is whether Aziz actually assaulted Adela or not. At first she declares that she was assaulted; then at the trial she says with equal conviction that Aziz did not follow her into the cave. Either or both statements as they stand might be the result of hysterical delusion. Which are we to believe? Even as close a friend as Goldsworthy Lowes Dickinson asked Forster, 'What did happen in the caves?'[8]

Confusion on this point has to do with a confusion concerning the place of 'reality' in this novel. Here, as in *The Longest Journey*, 'reality' is on the anvil. We are back with Forster's idea that its importance consists not only in its objective nature, but also in its psychological function. Whatever philosophical position they take up, men will normally agree that reality is one and unchanging. But a sense of reality can fluctuate: and according to Forster all men lose their sense of reality to a greater or lesser extent when they fail to connect head and heart.

This was what happened to Lucy Honeychurch when she entered the 'armies of the benighted', and to Rickie when he married Agnes and taught in Sawston School: it is also what happens to Adela Quested in this novel. She has arrived with the double intention of seeing the 'real' India and settling the question of her proposed marriage to Ronny Heaslop. Early in the novel, having observed the effect of India on Ronny, she has decided that she will not marry him after all. But the incidents just afterwards when they go out for a drive and are thrust together first by the jolting of the car then by the impact of collision with an animal, restore the relationship for the time being by reminding them of their physical attraction towards each other.

So the relationship stands until the day when Adela is climbing up towards the Marabar caves. Two incidents affect her state of mind on this occasion: first the confusion over the snake, then, as she is thinking about her marriage, a reminder of the animal impact:

But as she toiled over a rock that resembled an inverted saucer, she thought, 'What about love?' The rock was nicked by a double row of footholds, and somehow the question was suggested by them. Where had she seen footholds before? Oh yes, they were the pattern traced in the dust by the wheels of the Nawab Bahadur's car. She and Ronny – no, they did not love each other.

She considers the position, pausing thoughtfully:

Vexed rather than appalled, she stood still, her eyes on the sparkling rock. There was esteem and animal contact at dusk, but the emotion that links them was absent. (ch. xv, pp. 158–9)

Like Rickie at a corresponding moment, however, she fails to respond to the symbolic moment and decides to go through with the marriage. To break it off would cause too much trouble, and she is not at all sure that love is necessary to a successful union. She dismisses the thought and enters on a discussion of marriage with Aziz. Like Lucy Honeychurch, she is in the process of muddling herself: and it is in this state of muddle that she enters the cave.

The clue to her subsequent behaviour lies not in any outward event but in this muddled state of her mind at the crucial moment. It is still the vital clue when, after a long period of illness, she arrives at the trial to give her testimony. In the intervening period one important event has taken place. She has visited Mrs Moore, talking to her first about the persistent echo in her head, then about love and marriage. Afterwards, although in fact nothing has been said about the subject directly, she emerges with a conviction that Aziz is innocent and that Mrs Moore has said so. Questioned later, Mrs Moore denies having mentioned Aziz – but also says irritably, 'Of course he's innocent' (ch. xxii, pp. 206–13).

The remark does not deter Adela from going forward, but it has disturbed her. It has cracked, without breaking, the state of unreality in which she has been living since the day of the expedition. The state was created because she muddled herself about her relationship with Ronny, and Mrs Moore's ramblings have probed the muddle without exposing it. The exposure does not come until she is standing in the courtroom: and then, significantly, she thinks immediately of Mrs Moore:

The Court was crowded and of course very hot, and the first person Adela noticed in it was the humblest of all who were present, a person who had no bearing officially upon the trial: the man who pulled the punkah. Almost naked, and splendidly formed, he sat on a raised platform near the back, in the middle of the central gangway, and he caught her attention as she came in, and he seemed to control the proceedings. He had the strength and beauty that sometimes come to flower in Indians of low birth. When that strange race nears the dust and is condemned as untouchable, then nature remembers the physical perfection that she accomplished elsewhere, and throws out a god – not many, but one here and there, to prove to society how little its categories impress her. This man would have been notable anywhere: among the thin-hammed, flat-chested mediocrities of Chandrapore he stood out as divine, yet he was of the city, its garbage had nourished him, he would end on its rubbish heaps. Pulling the rope towards him, relaxing it rhythmically, sending swirls of air over others, receiving none himself, he seemed apart from human destinies, a male fate, a winnower of souls. Opposite him, also on a platform, sat the little assistant magistrate, cultivated, self-conscious, and conscientious. The punkah wallah was none of these things: he scarcely knew that he existed and did not understand why the Court was fuller than usual, indeed he did not know that it was fuller than usual, didn't even know he worked a fan, though he thought he pulled a rope. Something in his aloofness impressed the girl from middle-class England, and rebuked the narrowness of her sufferings. In virtue of what had she collected this roomful of people together? Her particular brand of opinions, and the suburban Jehovah who sanctified them – by what right did they claim so much importance in the world, and assume the title of civilization? Mrs Moore – she looked round, but Mrs Moore was far away on the sea; it was the kind of question they might have discussed on the voyage out before the old lady had turned disagreeable and queer.

While thinking of Mrs Moore she heard sounds, which gradually grew more distinct. The epoch-making trial had started. . . .
(ch. xxiv)

At this, the crisis of the novel, there has been an irruption from
an old world, the world of Forster's mythologies. The figure who
catches Adela's attention is an incarnate god, an Indian Apollo.
He is as real as the garbage-heaps of the city, yet he is also a
visionary figure. His glory outshines the muddle which has made
her confuse a mixture of desire and esteem with love, and releases
a power which reminds her again and again of Mrs Moore, dis-
solving the cloud of unreality which has shrouded her since the
day of her muddle, and restoring her sense of reality.

Looking at Aziz in the courtroom, she is once again wondering
whether she has made a mistake, when the memory of Mrs Moore
is unexpectedly reinforced. Her name is mentioned in court, and
the defence suggests that she has been deliberately hidden in
order that her witness may not clear Aziz. The grievance spreads
to the crowd outside, who begin chanting

> Esmiss Esmoor
> Esmiss Esmoor
> Esmiss Esmoor

in the way that at a festival they would chant 'Radakrishna
Radakrishna'.

Just afterwards, Adela rises to give her evidence. She has
always been shy of this moment, because in spite of her desire to
tell the truth, she remembers that her entry into the cave was
associated with thoughts about marriage, and thinks that her
question to Aziz on the subject might have roused evil in him.
Yet she would find it hard to recount a matter so intimate in open
court. By the time that she rises, however, the 'naked god' and
Mrs Moore have done their work.

But as soon as she rose to reply, and heard the sound of her
own voice, she feared not even that. A new and unknown sensation protected her, like magnificent armour. She didn't think
what had happened, or even remember in the ordinary way of
memory, but she returned to the Marabar hills, and spoke from

them across a sort of darkness to Mr McBryde. The fatal day recurred, in every detail, but now she was of it and not of it at the same time, and this double relation gave it indescribable splendour. Why had she thought the expedition 'dull'? Now the sun rose again, the elephant waited, the pale masses of the rock flowed round her and presented the first cave. . . .

Because her head has once again made contact with her heart (the 'Mrs Moore' in her) her sense of reality has been restored, and the memory of what happened is not only clear but magnificent. Imagination and perceptions have been reunited to make that state which is commonly acknowledged to be the true 'reality', where the universe of the heart and the universe presented to the senses form a single pattern. She is no longer separate from the scene – instead, the masses of the rock 'flow round her' in a symphony of experience.

The reality so presented to her governs her testimony, which brings the trial to its abrupt close. And at the close of the trial, the chief symbol in it is left in full possession of the scene.

. . . before long no one remained on the scene of the fantasy but the beautiful naked god. Unaware that anything unusual had occurred, he continued to pull the cord of his punkah, to gaze at the empty dais and the overturned special chairs, and rhythmically to agitate the clouds of descending dust.

Once one has observed the symbolism of this figure, coupled with the train of mental development that has elapsed, it becomes clear that Adela's new state of mind is not and cannot be another hysterical state: it is a recovery from hysteria. The important thing is not what happened in the cave but what has been happening to Adela.

In the eyes of British India she is now finished. She has committed the unforgivable sin of betraying her fellow-countrymen and bringing about the possibility of rebellion. Certainly there can now be no question of her marrying Ronny Heaslop, even if she wanted to. She can only return to England, lucky that Dr Aziz does not press for heavy damages.

For her as an individual, however, the events have a decisive and formative effect. As Fielding talks to her later, he is impressed by her new attitude. 'Although her hard school-mistressy manner remained, she was no longer examining life, but being examined by it; she had become a real person.' Nevertheless, the progress has been made within strict limitations. She remains a creature dominated by her head, and so her behaviour cannot impress the Indians:

> For her behaviour rested on cold justice and honesty; she had felt, while she recanted, no passion of love for those whom she had wronged. Truth is not truth in that exacting land unless there go with it kindness and more kindness and kindness again, unless the Word that was with God also is God. And the girl's sacrifice – so creditable according to Western notions – was rightly rejected, because, though it came from her heart, it did not include her heart. (ch. XXVI, pp. 254-5)

We are reminded again of that husband and wife in the story 'The Point of It': the wife who loved truth and grew hard, and the husband who loved humanity and went soft.[9] The limitations of Adela's experience in the courtroom have now been exposed – her heart came into play in the service of truth but did not become engaged. The vision of the 'naked god' was a temporary stimulus, not a lasting revelation. The crisis of the novel over, Adela, now realized as a person but still a creature of the head, emerges in contrast to Mrs Moore, whose heart is developed, but who cannot face the nakedness of truth.

This gives us the cue for an examination of Mrs Moore's experiences in India. In the early part of the novel, when the atmosphere is not oppressive and the two women are merely two travellers who are seeing the sights of the state, Mrs Moore figures in an incident which sets the tone of her character for the rest of the novel. Venturing into a mosque one evening she encounters Aziz, who is still smouldering under recent insults from the British. He speaks to her sharply, but she replies with friendliness, establishing a bond with him which is never afterwards broken. It is a peaceful, moonlit night as she returns to the club, but she is soon given to understand that she has behaved

in an un-English way by speaking to Aziz. After an argument
with her son Ronny she emerges from the club to find a small
wasp on the peg where her cloak is hanging. ' "Pretty dear," said
Mrs Moore to the wasp. He did not wake, but her voice floated
out, to swell the night's uneasiness' (ch. III, p. 38).

Mrs Moore's kindness to Aziz, and her treatment of the wasp,
introduce one of the novel's main themes. Where is love to end?
Mrs Moore has a developed heart and is kind to those whom she
meets, but what is she in the face of India's teeming millions and
manifold sufferings? Love in India: is it not like a snow-flake
dropping into the ocean? It is not even simply a question of
people, for India is shown to be a country which human beings
have not quite dominated. In mentioning the wasp, Forster
comments on the fact that no Indian animal has any sense of an
interior. The animal and vegetable kingdoms have a prominence
which they have lost in Western Europe and behind them
stretches something still more intractable – the hardness of rock
itself.

At the moment, however, we are still at the more manageable
level of animals and insects, and this theme is reinforced in the
next chapter, where there is an account of Mr Graysford and Mr
Sorley, the two missionaries of Chandrapore. Mr Sorley, who is
more advanced than his older companion, considers that God's
hospitality may extend to the animal kingdom, to monkeys for
example. Even jackals might be included. But he is less sure about
wasps.

He became uneasy during the descent to wasps, and was apt
to change the conversation. And oranges, cactuses, crystals and
mud? and the bacteria inside Mr Sorley? No, no, this is going too
far. We must exclude someone from our gathering, or we shall
be left with nothing.

The uneasiness about extending love to wasps foreshadows the
more sinister atmosphere of the next section, which is dominated
by the Marabar caves. The description of the caves at the beginning of the section is no mere chunk of local colour, but a statement of significance which 'places' the caves before they begin

to act in the narrative. Their rockiness is not merely beyond the
reach of civilization: there is a sense that they extend behind the
time process itself, untouched by any human quality.

They are older than anything in the world. No water has ever
covered them, and the sun who has watched them for countless
æons may still discern in their outlines forms that were his before
our globe was torn from his bosom. If flesh of the sun's flesh
is to be touched anywhere, it is here, among the incredible
antiquity of these hills. (ch. XII, p. 129)

Hostility is a keynote of the whole section. The main scene of
the first section took place in moonlight, a moonlight which
helped to establish the atmosphere of human kindness. But even
in that section the Marabar hills were always 'fists and fingers'.
In this section, where they come into their own, the sun is the
dominating presence, always hostile. This part of India is 'flesh
of the sun's flesh'. On the morning of the ill-fated expedition to
the Marabar caves, the sunrise which the visitors are looking
forward to fails them.

They awaited the miracle. But at the supreme moment, when
night should have died and day lived, nothing occurred. It was
as if virtue had failed in the celestial fount. . . . Why, when the
chamber was prepared, did the bridegroom not enter with trum-
pets and shawms, as humanity expects? The sun rose without
splendour. (ch. XIV, p. 144)

Symbolic interpretations press hard here. Like Blake and
Coleridge, Forster sees the moment of sunrise as the nearest
approach in the universe at large to the splendid birth of love in
human experience. For one moment an almost transcendent glory
is revealed. But on this occasion, an unglamorous sunrise only
serves to stress the hostility of a sun in which heat predominates.
During the day the presence of the sun is mentioned again and
again, always as a hostile presence. The experiences undergone
by both Mrs Moore and Adela are ascribed partly to sunstroke
and correspond to recorded case-histories of it.

The sun beats down on them as they toil up towards the caves
and banks the oppressiveness that pervades the scene. It bars

escape from the experiences that await them. Mrs Moore, entering a cave, finds the interior unpleasant and even horrifying. The cave is immediately filled by their retinue and begins to smell. Some 'vile naked thing' (which later turns out to have been a baby, astride its mother's hip) strikes her face and settles on her mouth. For an instant she goes mad, hitting and gasping like a fanatic, alarmed not merely by the crush and stench, but by the unexpected and terrifying echo.

The echo is the culminating horror of the novel. It reminds one directly of the echo that oppressed Margaret Schlegel in St Paul's and indirectly of the 'goblin footfalls', also in *Howards End*. It has the same nullity, the same ability to deny value: it is 'entirely devoid of distinction'.

Whatever is said, the same monotonous noise replies, and quivers up and down the walls until it is absorbed into the roof. 'Boum' is the sound as far as the human alphabet can express it, or 'bou-oum', or ou-boum' – utterly dull. Hope, politeness, the blowing of a nose, the squeak of a boot, all produce 'boum'. Even the striking of a match starts a little worm coiling, which is too small to complete a circle but is eternally watchful. And if several people talk at once, an overlapping howling noise begins, echoes generate echoes, and the cave is stuffed with a snake composed of small snakes, which writhe independently. (ch. XIV, pp. 154, 156–7)

The echoes turn swiftly into worms and serpents, which reinforce the hint that their significance is reaching out beyond the cave. The worm and serpent have associations with an evil which is characterized more closely later, when Mrs Moore comes to reflect upon her experience:

She minded it much more now than at the time. The crush and smells she could forget, but the echo began in some indescribable way to undermine her hold on life. Coming at a moment when she chanced to be fatigued, it had managed to murmur, 'Pathos, piety, courage – they exist, but are identical, and so is filth. Everything exists, nothing has value.' If one had spoken vileness in that place, or quoted lofty poetry, the comment would have been the same – 'ou-boum'. If one had spoken with the tongues of angels and pleaded for all the unhappiness and misunderstanding in the world, past, present, and to come, for all the misery men must undergo whatever their opinion and position, and however much they dodge or bluff – it would amount to the same, the serpent would descend and return to the ceiling. Devils are of the North, and poems can be written about them, but no one could romanticize the Marabar because it robbed infinity and eternity of their vastness, the only quality that accommodates them to mankind.

She tried to go on with her letter, reminding herself that she was only an elderly woman who had got up too early in the morning and journeyed too far, that the despair creeping over her was merely her despair, her personal weakness, and that even if she got a sunstroke and went mad the rest of the world would go on. But suddenly, at the edge of her mind, Religion appeared, poor little talkative Christianity, and she knew that all its divine words from 'Let there be Light' to 'It is finished' only amounted to 'boum'.

The moment is a crucial one in Forster's writings, and Mrs Moore becomes here an allegorical figure. She possesses within herself all the virtues of the heart, only to find at this moment that her values are nullified by an echo.

There have been many visionary moments in the novel, but this is a moment of anti-vision – a vision of the horror of the universe which contrasts completely with Adela's moment of vision in the court-house. Mrs Moore passes into what Forster describes as 'that state where the horror of the universe and its smallness are both visible at the same time – the twilight of the double vision in which so many elderly people are involved'. And he goes on to work out the significance of the echo:

What had spoken to her in that scoured-out cavity of the granite? what dwelt in the first of the caves? Something very old and very small. Before time, it was before space also. Something snub-nosed, incapable of generosity – the undying worm itself. Since hearing its voice, she had not entertained one large thought, she was actually envious of Adela. All this fuss over a frightened girl! Nothing had happened, 'and if it had', she found herself thinking with the cynicism of a withered priestess, 'if it had,

there are worse evils than love'. The unspeakable attempt presented itself to her as love: in a cave, in a church – Boum, it
amounts to the same. Visions are supposed to entail profundity,
but – Wait till you get one, dear reader! The abyss may also be
petty, the serpent of eternity made of maggots. . . . (ch. XXIII,
p. 217)

It would be easy to see this moment of nightmare vision as the
core of the novel. For many readers, it leaves a deeper impression
than anything else, and it 's not therefore surprising that they
should invest it with central significance. Such centrality, however, is not assigned by Forster, who has called it 'a moment of
negation . . . the vision with its back turned'.[10] Nor is it assigned
in the novel itself, for as Mrs Moore leaves India, other voices
speak to her. The train passes a place called Asirgarh, which
consists of bastions and a mosque. Ten minutes later, Asirgarh
reappears, the mosque now on the other side of the bastions. The
train has described a complete semicircle round it. She has
nothing with which to connect it: 'But it had looked at her twice
and seemed to say: "I do not vanish." ' It evidently reminds her
of the moonlit mosque of the first section, which had offered a
more agreeable India, a less hostile infinity. Similarly, the hostility of the caves is contrasted with the scene where her boat
moves out of the harbour and thousands of coconut palms wave
her farewell. ' "So you thought an echo was India; you took the
Marabar caves as final?" they laughed. "What have we in common with them, or they with Asirgarh? Good-bye!" ' (ch. XXIII,
pp. 218–19).

The echo, after all, does not undermine Adela, who also experiences it. It enters her only for a time, echoing and re-echoing in
her head during her illness, but disappears during her conversation with Mrs Moore. Mrs Moore's failure, on the other hand,
is the physical enforcement of a psychical lack. She is old, and
after a lifetime of developing her heart rather than her head, she
cannot stand against a re-orientation of reality. When this basis
is gone, the cave becomes the universe, her values are destroyed
and she dies. Nevertheless, even then her spirit is not extin-
guished. It can still, even when she is rambling, suggest to Adela

that Aziz is innocent. And it survives in the memories of those who have known her. As with Rickie and Mrs Wilcox, her vicarious survival is a form of redemptive immortality. She is resurrected in the mind of Adela during the trial and the crowd outside chant her name. She is resurrected again towards the end of the novel, when Professor Godbole is dancing himself into an ecstasy of love at the Hindu festival. The image of Mrs Moore then comes into his mind:

Chance brought her into his mind while it was in this heated state, he did not select her, she happened to occur among the throng of soliciting images, a tiny splinter, and he impelled her by his spiritual force to that place where completeness can be found. Completeness, not reconstruction. His senses grew thinner, he remembered a wasp seen he forgot where, perhaps on a stone. He loved the wasp equally, he impelled it likewise, he was imitating God. And the stone where the wasp clung – could he . . . no, he could not, he had been wrong to attempt the stone, logic and conscious effort had seduced, he came back to the strip of red carpet and discovered that he was dancing upon it. (ch. XXXIII, pp. 298, 303)

Later, the ecstasy over, he steps out of the temple into the grey of a pouring wet morning, thinking, 'One old Englishwoman and one little, little wasp. It does not seem much, still it is more than I am myself.'

The images that occurred in his ecstasy reiterate themes of the novel. Unlike the two missionaries, but like Mrs Moore, Godbole can extend his love to include the wasp. His failure to include the stone is equally significant. There is always something that resists and denies love, and the stone is reminiscent of the intractable Marabar caves.

Forster's inclusion of this intractable element even in Godbole's ecstatic dance is another indication of its importance in the novel as a whole. Once again, he insists on having a Caliban on his island. But the Marabar caves, which make no pretensions at all to humanity, are better than Caliban or Leonard Bast for his purpose. As symbols, their excellence can be measured by the number of significances which critics have found in them. They have been respectively described as 'bare, dark, echoing', echoing 'eternity, infinity, the Absolute'; 'the very voice of that union which is the opposite of divine; the voice of evil and negation'; 'wombs'; and 'it may be, the soul of India'.[11]

Forster's own account of them in his *Writers at Work* interview helps to point their significance:

> When I began *A Passage to India* I knew that something important happened in the Marabar Caves, and that it would have a central place in the novel – but I didn't know what it would be. ... The Marabar Caves represented an area in which concentration can take place. A cavity. They were something to focus everything up: they were to engender an event like an egg.

Everything in the novel has to be confronted by the caves. The head of Adela and the heart of Mrs Moore are equally challenged by the negation of a cave which can only reflect sights and sounds. For them it is a confrontation with 'reality' in the worst sense of the word: matter without mind, substance devoid of imaginative appeal. But this is not full reality even if it is an element without which reality cannot exist. The attempt to love a stone breaks into Professor Godbole's ecstasy and brings him back to the strip of red carpet where he is dancing, but it does not stop him dancing. Similarly the existence of the Marabar caves in India does not prevent thousands of palm-trees from waving farewell to Mrs Moore, nor does the hostility of the sun invalidate the hints of a more benevolent infinity offered in the first section of the novel.

The Marabar caves are not a revelation of reality, but a touchstone by which reality is tested. They are a 'vortex', in the sense in which Blake used the word. The forces of the novel are attracted towards the experience which they offer, and in passing through it are transformed. They are drawn in and englobed, to emerge with form and new life. Adela becomes a person. Mrs Moore is destroyed in the body but, as we have seen, her spirit lives on in the lives and spirits of others: and in the last section of the novel it is actually reincarnate in physical form, when her children Ralph and Stella visit India.

At this point, moreover, the spirit of Mrs Moore is absorbed

into the total spirit of Love which is shadowed, however un-
certainly, by the Hindu festival of the same section. We have
already mentioned Forster's reference to this as 'architecturally
necessary', meeting the need for 'a lump, or a Hindu temple if
you like – a mountain standing up'. The image which he is here
using may well derive·from a wartime experience which he
described in a broadcast talk and later in a book review. Writing
of an exhibition of Indian temples which .Stella Kramrisch
(together with Dr Saxl) devised in London in 1940, he says:

> Briefly she showed me the temple as the World Mountain on
> whose exterior is displayed life in all its forms, life human and
> superhuman and subhuman and animal, life tragic and cheerful,
> cruel and kind, seemly and obscene, all crowned at the moun-
> tain's summit by the sun. And in the interior of the mountain she
> revealed a tiny cavity, a central cell, where, in the heart of the
> world complexity, the individual could be alone with his god.
> Hinduism, unlike Buddhism, Islam and Christianity – is not a
> congregational religion: it by-passes the community and despite
> its entanglement with caste it by-passes class. Its main concern
> is the individual and his relation to reality, and however much it
> wanders over the surface of the world mountain it returns at last
> to the mountain's heart. This happens to appeal to me.[12]

In retrospect, the Hindu festival evidently seems to him to
possess some of the same qualities. It is a final image of all-inclusive reality, through which some of the chief characters must pass
before his novel can be concluded.

Together with Fielding, to whom Stella is now married, Mrs
Moore's children come to take part in the festival. They take a
boat on the water when the festival is at its height and are joined
grudgingly by Aziz, who has been moved by Ralph's resemblance
to his mother to set aside, at least for an evening, the hatred for
English people which has possessed him since his trial.

Unfortunately, a slight gale is running on the tank, heralding a
storm: and the result is that they lose control of the boat, which,
having collided with another boat, drifts towards the servitor
with his tray and strikes it. Stella, by shrinking first towards her
husband, then flinging herself against Aziz, capsizes the boat and

plunges them all into the warm shallow water. Meanwhile there is a crescendo of noise from artillery, drums and elephants, culminating in an immense peal of thunder. The climax, 'as far as India admits of one', has been reached, and rain sets in steadily to wet everything and everybody (ch. xxxvi, p. 329).

Symbolic meaning surges again at this point. It is significant that the capsizing is caused by Stella throwing herself at both Fielding and Aziz in quick succession; it is significant that afterwards letters from Ronny and Adela float on the water. This mêlée at the feast of Krishna, prince of love, is the nearest approach to a birth of brotherly love in the novel – it at least marks the release of Aziz from the hatred which has confined him since his trial. It is equally typical of Forster's firm realism in this novel that the approach should only be made in the middle of the upsetting of a boat, and that the accompanying climax of the festival should immediately dissolve in rainy confusion. If there is a mystery of love in India, it subsists only at the heart of a huge muddle.

Unlike the civilization of Sawston, which has gradually selected a manageable segment of human experience to be its world, India represents the whole of human experience. It contains at one extreme the ecstasy of human and divine love, at the other the sort of basic stony 'reality' which baffles an undeveloped head and challenges an undeveloped heart. When someone remarked earlier in the novel that India was a muddle, Mrs Moore recoiled. Her 'undeveloped head' could not deal with muddles:

'I like mysteries but I rather dislike muddles,' said Mrs Moore.
'A mystery is a muddle.'
'Oh, do you think so, Mr Fielding?'
'A mystery is only a high-sounding term for a muddle. No advantage in stirring it up, in either case. Aziz and I know well that India's a muddle.'
'India's – Oh, what an alarming idea!' (ch. vii, p. 73)

Fielding represents the British attitude which has done so much for India in clearing away administrative inefficiencies and giving her improved communications, but which is dead to other perceptions. Yet he, too, can still recognize other possibilities. When he is saying good-bye to Adela later, they sense a certain similarity in their outlooks and gain satisfaction from it.

Perhaps life is a mystery, not a muddle; they could not tell. Perhaps the hundred Indias which fuss and squabble so tiresomely are one, and the universe they mirror is one. They had not the apparatus for judging. (ch. xxix, p. 274)

After that it is fitting that when they part, 'A friendliness, as of dwarfs shaking hands, was in the air.' They seem for a moment to see their own gestures from a great height – there is a wistfulness, the shadow of a shadow of a dream.

Adela and Fielding for their part have missed something great: and so, for her part, has Mrs Moore. The familiar broken dialectic between head and heart is still operative. The final events of the novel confirm the impression that Fielding has failed by his disregard of mystery, Mrs Moore by her dislike of muddles. In this way, they have each shown that they are still half in touch with the Sawston which tries to evade both muddles and mysteries at one and the same time. India, on the other hand, because it contains the extremes of human experience, is both a vast muddle and a concealed mystery.

In his culminating view of India, Forster thus achieves his greatest fusion of vision and realism, for each quality has its objective correlative in this great panorama. India's muddle needs all the efficiency which British administrators brought to it: at the same time its mystery asks for the reverence of a fully developed heart. In presenting the situation, moreover, Forster is able to present the 'muddle' with a completeness which Virginia Woolf, like most readers, finds highly attractive:

We notice things, about the country especially, spontaneously, accidentally almost, as if we were actually there; and now it was the sparrows flying about the pictures that caught our eyes, now the elephant with the painted forehead, now the enormous but badly designed ranges of hills. The people too, particularly the Indians, have something of the same casual, inevitable quality. (Virginia Woolf, *The Death of the Moth and Other Essays* (1942))

D. A. Traversi has commented on the fact that this casualness becomes an essential part of the novel's meaning: Godbole

declares that Krishna '*neglects* to come'; the echo comes upon
Mrs Moore when she '*chanced* to be fatigued'; '*chance*' brings Mrs
Moore into Godbole's mind while he is dancing, and so on.[13]
The casualness is an essential part of the Indian mind, as compared with the English. And so the 'reality' which is so broad and
casual and attractive can also be refined to the point where echoes
and reflections in a cave mirror the terrifying, casual, incompre-
hensibility of the entire universe: the 'Pan' of Forster's early
short stories, the 'earth' of *The Longest Journey*, which is best
avoided unless it can be met with a fully developed head and
heart. In the same way, 'vision' can be presented broadly in the
spirit that informs the actions of Fielding and Mrs Moore, but it
can also be intensified to the ecstatic love which is still to be
found in the old Hindu traditions of Forster's India.

Vision and reality are not at one, even in India, and Forster is
at pains to emphasize the fact. But his last words on the festival
are a way of suggesting that somehow, somewhere, India, at least,
manages to preserve a connection between them:

Looking back at the great blur of the last twenty-four hours, no
man could say where was the emotional centre of it, any more
than he could locate the heart of a cloud. (ch. XXVI, p. 329)

SOURCE: *The Achievement of E. M. Forster* (1962).

NOTES

1. *Abinger Harvest* (1936) pp. 4–5.
2. References to *A Passage to India* (pocket edition, 1947).
3. Frank Kermode, 'The One Orderly Product', see pp. 216–23.
4. *Two Cheers for Democracy* (1951) p. 340.
5. *Collected Short Stories* (1947) pp. 143–4.
6. *Howards End* (pocket edn. 1947) p. 206.
7. Sec. XI, *Leaves of Grass* (1907) p. 352.
8. *Goldsworthy Lowes Dickinson* (1934) p. 216.
9. *Collected Short Stories* (1947).
10. Angus Wilson, 'A Conversation with E. M. Forster', in
Encounter (Nov 1957) p. 54.
11. Quotations from G. O. Allen, 'Forster's *A Passage to India*',
PMLA LXX (Dec 1955) 941.
12. *Listener* (2 Dec 1954) 977–8.
13. D. A. Traversi, 'The Novels of E. M. Forster', *Arena*, I 36–9.

Frank Kermode

THE ONE ORDERLY PRODUCT
(1958)

'A TRULY great novel is a tale to the simple, a parable to the wise, and a direct revelation of reality to the man who has made it a part of his being': so Middleton Murry, in a piece called 'The Breakup of the Novel' which was published in 1924, the year of *A Passage to India*. A story, a parable, and at the same time an intuited truth, an image: anything less, it appeared, was only a bundle of fragments.

Whether or not *A Passage to India* provides 'a direct revelation of reality', it certainly tells a story, and it also speaks, as it were in parable, for tolerance and liberalism. Indeed it does these things so well that it is admired by people who regard talk of 'direct revelations of reality' as empty nonsense, and regret, as Roger Fry regretted, Mr Forster's mystical tendencies. I think such readers are unlucky – I mean in their art rather than their religion – because, like Mr Forster's character Fielding, they have the experience but miss the meaning. They miss a designedly inexplicable wholeness. Having, perhaps, every other gift, they want love – which, for Mr Forster, can mean the power to read a book properly. 'Our comprehension of the fine arts', he says, 'is, or should be, of the nature of a mystic union. But, as in mysticism, we enter an unusual state, and we can only enter it through love.' Love is the only mediator of meaning, because it confers and apprehends unity. The author in the act of composition is, according to Mr Forster, in a condition of love. And clearly he had no difficulty in understanding the Rajah who said to him, 'Love is the only power that can keep thought out.' For 'thought' here means that which analyses in this connection, douses reality in time, and misses the meaning.

To translate this into convertible critical currency, Mr Forster is a kind of Symbolist. He declares for the autonomy of the work of art; for co-essence of form and meaning; for art as 'organic and free from dead matter'; for music as a criterion of formal purity; for the work's essential anonymity. Like all art, he thinks, the novel must fuse differentiation into unity, in order to provide meaning we can experience; art is 'the one orderly product that our muddling race has produced', the only unity and therefore the only meaning. This is Symbolist. But there are interesting qualifications to be made; they bear on the question of differentiation, of stresses within the unity – a question that would have interested the Cambridge Hegelians of Mr Forster's youth, when the enemy, Bertrand Russell, was at their gates, brandishing what the Rajah called 'thought'.

The first qualification arises from Mr Forster's celebrated insistence on the point that the novel tells a story – a low, atavistic thing to be doing if you claim the power to make direct revelations of reality. In the novel, the matter which seeks pure form is itself impure. This sounds like the old Symbolist envy of music; but we soon learn that Mr Forster really values this impurity. He dislikes novels of the sort H. G. Wells attributed to James: 'On the altar, very reverently placed, intensely there, is a dead kitten, an eggshell, a piece of string.' He agrees with Wells that 'life should be given the preference, and must not be whittled or distended for a pattern's sake'. If 'life' in this sense is pattern-resisting, impure, nevertheless our direct revelation of reality, pure as it is, must somehow include it. One thinks of Valéry, who said that no poem could be pure poetry and still be a poem. Unity implies the inclusion of impurity.

The second qualification again brings the French Symbolist to mind. 'Organic unity' – art's kind of unity – has to be produced by a process coarsely characterised by Mr Forster himself as 'faking'. 'All a writer's faculties,' he says, 'including the valuable faculty of faking, do conspire together . . . for the creative act.' 'Faking' is the power he so greatly admired in Virginia Woolf. From the author's point of view the organism can look rather like a machine – a machine, as Valéry said, for producing poetic

states. Eventually the author withdraws and lets the work lead its
own anonymous life; but he must not do so too soon. The burden
of Mr Forster's criticism of Gide is that one can withdraw too
soon, 'introducing mysticism at the wrong stage of the affair'.
Later, the author may stand back and see what he has said; but
first he must do his faking intelligently. Faking is what Valéry
did in his multitudinous drafts; it is what makes the work of art
different from oracular raving. 'How shameful to write without
a conception of the work's structure, caring little for *why* and still
less for *how*! *Rougir d'être la Pythie!*' Organic and free of dead
matter this direct revelation may be; but it contains impurity, and
intelligence helped to make it. It is faked.

In this sense of the word, a novel not only fakes human relationships but also, working against muddle and chance, fakes an
idea of order without which those relationships could have no
significance. The fraud committed is, in fact, a general benefaction
of significance. Nowadays, so far as I know, nobody attempts
faking on anything like Mr Forster's scale, and to this difference
between then and now I will return. But first I must have some
sort of a shot at the task of illustrating how, in *A Passage to India*,
where it is almost inconceivably elaborate, the faking is done.
The events it describes include the coming of Krishna, which
makes the world whole by love; and the novel's own analogous
unity is achieved by faking.

One can start at the opening chapter, indeed the opening sentence. 'Except for the Marabar Caves – and they are twenty miles
off – the city of Chandrapore presents nothing extraordinary.'
Easy, colloquial, if with a touch of the guide-book, the words set
a scene. But they will reach out and shape the organic whole. Or,
to put it another way, they lie there, lacking all rhetorical emphasis, waiting for the relations which will give them significance to
the eye of 'love'. But they are prepared for these relations. The
order of principal and subordinate clauses, for instance, is inverted, so that the exception may be mentioned first – 'Except for
the Marabar Caves'. The excepted is what must be included if
there is to be meaning; first things first. First, then, the extraordinary which governs and limits significance; then, secondly,

we may consider the city. It keeps the caves at a distance; it is free of mystery till nightfall, when the caves close in to question its fragile appearance of order – an appearance that depends upon a social conspiracy to ignore the extraordinary. Henceforth, in this novel, the word 'extraordinary' is never used without reference to the opening sentence. It belongs to the caves. The last words of the first chapter speak once more of 'the extraordinary caves'. Miss Quested's behaviour in relation to the caves is 'extraordinary'.

It is a characteristically brilliant device; the word occurs so naturally in conversation that its faked significance cannot disturb the story. The characters say 'extraordinary' but the novelist means 'extra-ordinary'. In a sense, Fielding can measure the extraordinariness of Marabar by the Mediterranean, the norm of his civilisation. But nobody can actually say in what this extraordinariness consists. 'Nothing, nothing attaches to them, and their reputation – for they have one – does not depend upon human speech. It is as if the surrounding plain or the passing birds have taken upon themselves to exclaim "extraordinary", and the word has taken root in the air, and been inhaled by mankind.' Perhaps Professor Godbole can explain in what they are extraordinary; Miss Quested asks him at Fielding's tea-party:

'Are they large caves?' she asked.

'No, not large.'

'Do describe them, Professor Godbole.'

'It will be a great honour.' He drew up his chair and an expression of tension came over his face. Taking the cigarette box, she offered to him and Aziz, and lit up herself. After an impressive pause he said: 'There is an entrance in the rock which you enter, and through the entrance is the cave.'

'Something like the caves at Elephanta?'

'Oh no, not at all; at Elephanta there are sculptures of Siva and Parvati. There are no sculptures at Marabar.'

'They are immensely holy, no doubt,' said Aziz, to help on the narrative.

'Oh no, oh no.'

'Well, why are they so famous? We all talk of the famous Marabar Caves. Perhaps that is our empty brag.'

'No, I should not quite say that.'
'Describe them to this lady, then.'
'It will be a great pleasure.' He forewent the pleasure. . . .

We find out why he had to. The caves are the exception that menaces the city, the city of gardens and geometrical roads made by the English, the Indian city of unholy muddle. And sometimes it is possible to exclude them, to ignore them like the distance beyond distance in the sky, because, like God in the song of the beautiful ecstatic girl, they are without attributes.

In a sense, they *are* God without attributes; because his absence implies his presence. Therefore, says the Professor, we are entitled to repeat to Krishna, 'Come, come, come.' Without them there is no whole by which we may understand the parts. Fielding rejects them, and will never understand; he believes in 'thought'. Mrs Moore accepts them, seeing a whole, but one in which love is absent; all distinctions obliterated not by meaning but by meaninglessness, the roar of the Marabar echo. Including the excepted does not necessarily result in felicity. But when we know the worst of Marabar – that it is of the very stuff of life, flesh of the sun, thrusting up into the holy soil of Ganges – we still have to observe that `the last explicit mention of Marabar in the book, at the end of a petulant remark of Aziz, is drowned in the noise of rejoicing at Krishna's coming. An ordinary conversational remark, of course, with its place in the story, bears the weight of this piece of faking. Similarly, in the last pages, the rocks which, as in a parable, separate the friends Aziz and Fielding, are thrust up from the Indian earth like the fists and fingers of Marabar. Story, parable, coexist in the wholeness of the revelation.

Privation, the want of wholeness, may entitle us in life to say 'Come, come, come'; but in the novel this appeal has also to be faked. Godbole first uses the words at the tea-party, after his statement concerning Marabar. In his song, the milkmaid asks Krishna to come; but he neglects to come. At Marabar the need of him is absolute; and even the road to the caves, where everything calls out 'Come, come,' remains what it is because 'there is not enough god to go around.' Resonant with the absence of

Krishna, it confuses distinctions like that between love and animal feeling; so Miss Quested discovers. But it is not only Marabar; nothing is proof against the god's neglect, not even Aziz' poetry, for all it says about the Friend who never comes. What comes instead is the sun in April, the source of life and of Marabar; and the sun spreads not love but lust and muddle. Or, instead of Krishna, a British magistrate arrives: 'He comes, he comes, he comes,' says a satirical Indian. The lack of this coming is felt by the guests at the party who heard Godbole's song; they are unwell, with some malaise of privation; they are suffering from a deficiency of meaning, which cannot be cured until Love takes upon itself the form of Krishna and saves the world in the rain. The unity he makes is an image of art; for a moment at least all is one, apprehensible by love; nothing is excepted or extraordinary. The novel itself assumes a similar unity, becomes a mystery, a revelation of wholeness; and does so without disturbing the story or the parable.

But after this, does it, like the rejoicing at Krishna's coming, 'become history and fall under the rule of time'? Like the birth of the god, the novel is contrived as a direct revelation of reality, of meaning conferred by a unifying and thought-excluding love; as – leaving gods out of it – the one orderly product. But does it still fall under the rule of time? Perhaps this mystical conception of order in art *was* more accessible to Mr Forster than to his younger contemporaries. I rather bluntly called him a Symbolist; in fact the doctrines of that great sect were mediated to him in a peculiar way. Think how valuable, for instance, to a writer with this idea of order, was the ethics of G. E. Moore! I mean, in particular, the notion of overall unity analogous to that which gives significance to art; without such unity friendship itself is mocked by exception – beyond and beyond – and is only dwarfs shaking hands. All that civilisation excepts or disconnects has to be got in for meaning to subsist. Moore calls this unity 'organic' – an analogy that surely reached ethics through aesthetics. Perhaps the *Principia* are never realisable except in novels; however this may be, a belief of this sort about human life as dependent on the orderly inclusion of the extraordinary, is clearly valuable to a novelist who holds the analogous aesthetic doctrine. The 'one orderly product' can include life entire; good and evil, privation and plenitude, muddle and mystery – seen, for a moment, whole. The wholeness is made by love; nothing is excepted except what the Rajah called 'thought'.

The feeling that a work of art, a novel for instance, must be in this exalted sense orderly, survives; but, for whatever reasons, it seems less potent now. Perhaps you cannot have it very fully unless you have that 'conviction of harmony' of which the Cambridge philosopher McTaggart used to speak in Mr Forster's youth. For him, too, all meaning depended upon oneness. He had an argument to prove that it could never inhere in inductive thought; on the contrary, it depended upon what he called 'love', meaning not sexual love nor benevolence nor saintliness nor even the love of God, but something like full knowledge and the justice and harmony this entails. McTaggart even allows the possibility of one's experiencing a mystic unity which is not benevolent, not indeed anything but 'perfectly simple Being' – without attributes – 'difficult, if not impossible, to distinguish from Nothing'. He is thinking of Indian mysticism. Marabar is perhaps Being under that aspect; however, Godbole can distinguish between presence and absence, and it is Mrs Moore who cannot, and who therefore becomes a saint of Nothingness.

These remarks about the intellectual climate at the relevant period are meant to be suggestive, but not to suggest that Mr Forster as a novelist is a conscious disciple of any philosopher. I do think, though, that the wonderful years at Cambridge enabled him to prepare the ground for a creation of order – gave him the secure sense of organic unity that made possible those feats of faking, and allowed him to see that, properly viewed, the human muddle could itself be mystery. Only in some such way can I account for the marvellous ease with which story, parable and image here coexist. There was a 'conviction of harmony', a belief in order. Perhaps that has fallen under the rule of time.

We, in our time, are, I think, incapable of genuinely supposing a work of art to be something quite different from *A Passage to India*; it is, in this sense, contemporary and exemplary. In another sense, though, it does fall under the rule of time, because any conviction of harmony we may have will be differently grounded. Of these two facts, the first seems to me of incomparably greater importance. It is a consequence that we cannot know too much about the remarkable *inclusiveness* of the book. We continue to have our illusions of order, and clever faking; but this book reminds us how vast the effort for totality must be; nothing is excepted, the extraordinary is essential to order. The cities of muddle, the echoes of disorder, the excepting and the excepted, are all to be made meaningful in being made one. This will not happen without the truth of imagination which Mr Forster calls 'love'; love cheats, and muddle turns into mystery: into art, our one orderly product.

SOURCE: *Puzzles and Epiphanies: Essays and Reviews 1958–1961* (1962).

Malcolm Bradbury

TWO PASSAGES TO INDIA: FORSTER AS VICTORIAN AND MODERN (1969)

I

THERE are major writers whose work seems to us important as
a contribution to the distinctive powers and dimensions of art;
there are others whose work represents almost a personal appeal
to value, and who therefore live – for certain of their readers, at
least – with a singular force. There have not been many English
novelists of our own time who have established with us the
second function, but E. M. Forster is certainly one of them. He
has served as an embodiment of the virtues he writes about; he
has shown us their function and their destiny; he has left, for
other writers and other men, a workable inheritance. Partly this
is because he has always regarded art as a matter of intelligence
as well as passion, honesty as well as imagination. In making such
alliances he has given us a contemporary version of a once-
familiar belief – that art can be a species of active virtue as well
as a form of magic – and has thus sharply appealed to our sense
of what man can be. Literary humanist qualities of this sort are
not always easy to express today within the impersonal context
of modern literary criticism – which tends, more and more, to
ascribe virtue to structural performance within the text and to
neglect what lies beyond. In fact, they are crucial virtues, and we
fortunately have enough personal testimony – particularly from
writers like Christopher Isherwood and Angus Wilson – to see
the kind of inheritance he has left. At the same time, what Tony
Tanner has called the 'trace of totemism'[1] with which Forster has
been and is still regarded – and I must assert here my own sense
of indebtedness, intellectual, moral, and literary – has its dangers,

and to his role and his influence may be ascribed certain slightly odd and uneasy features of Forster's present reputation. That he is a major writer I have no doubt, yet criticism has repeatedly expressed an unsureness about him, has wondered, time and time again, whether he really stands with the other great writers of the century we feel sure of – with Joyce or Conrad or Lawrence.

Why is this? One reason is surely that Forster stands much exposed to our modern predilection for historicist thinking – our inclination to substitute, in Karl Popper's phrase, 'historical prophecy for conscience'. Forster once told us that he belongs to 'the fag-end of Victorian liberalism' and the phrase is often taken with complete literalness and applied against him. As a result his intellectual and his literary destiny has been too readily linked with that strange death of liberal England which historians have dated around 1914, when the equation of economic individualism with social progress lost political force. Since it is easy to explain the exhaustion of political liberalism as a historical necessity, as the inevitable failure of a synthesis proven unworkable by the new social conditions of the second-stage industrial revolution, then it is also possible to see Forster's ideas and faith as historically superannuated, too. This view, indeed, has taken root – even though Forster recognises the ironies of the situation and works with them, even though he raises all the crucial questions about elevating social determinism above value; and we often overlook the fact that the liberalism he speaks for so obliquely has had a longer history as a moral conviction than as a political force, that it has as much to do with our idea of man and culture as with our political solutions, that it speaks for a recurrent need for the criticism of institutions and collectivities from the standpoint of the claims of human wholeness. But coupled with this there has been another distrust: distrust of the entire idea of art and culture as Forster suggests or expresses it.

In this century critics have increasingly accepted modernist norms for the judgement of literature, even though, of course, many of our writers have not been modernists in the strict sense. Forster is a paradox here; he is, and he is not. There is in his work the appeal to art as transcendence, art as the one orderly product, a view that makes for modernism; and there is the view of art as a responsible power, a force for belief, a means of judgement, an impulse to spiritual control as well as spiritual curiosity. The point perhaps is that Forster is not, in the conventional sense, a modernist, but rather a central figure of the transition into modernism; and that is surely his interest, the force of his claim. He is, indeed, to a remarkable degree, the representative of two kinds of mind, two versions of literary possibility, and of the tensions of consciousness that exist between them. He stands at the beginning of the age of the new, speaking through it and against it. In this way his five novels – and particularly his last two – can be taken as reflecting the advantages and disadvantages of the humanist literary mind in an environment half hostile to it; they clearly and often painfully carry the strain of a direct encounter with new experience. Forster has been, by training and temperament, sufficiently the historian to see the irony: that culture itself is in history, that a humanist view of the arts as a way of sanely perceiving and evaluating is itself conditioned, for it has its own social environment and limits. So Forster is at once the spokesman for the transcendent symbol, the luminous wholeness of the work of art, out of time and in infinity, and for its obverse – the view that a proper part of art's responsibility is to know and live in the contingent world of history.

If Forster is indeed a Victorian liberal, as some of his critics charge, he is also deeply marked by the encounters that the moralised romantic inheritance must make with those environments which challenge it in matters of belief, technique, and aesthetics. Of course, Forster's confession that he belongs to the fag-end of Victorian liberalism does express a real inheritance; but that end is also the beginning of new forms of belief and of new literary postures and procedures. My point is that he emerges not as a conventionally modernist writer, but rather as a writer who has experienced, in a full way, the impact of what modernism means for us – a hope for transcendence, a sense of apocalypse, an *avant-garde* posture, a sense of detachment, a feeling that a new phase of history has emerged – while holding on (with tentative balance that turns often to the ironic mode) to much that modernism would affront.

Forster's traditional literary inheritance, which reaches back through the Victorian period to roots in English romanticism, is something which he himself has sketched clearly and well in books like *Marianne Thornton*. He has shown us the formative influence of the world of the Victorian upper-middle-class intelligentsia in its liberal radical mode – that world of 'philanthropists, bishops, clergy, members of parliament, Miss Hannah More' which reached into evangelical Christianity and into agnostic enlightenment, that world which he draws upon and values, and against which he also reacts. To the cultural historian, its interest lies in its unconditioned spirit, its sense of disinterestedness, its capacity to act beyond both self and class interest and to transcend its economic roots without losing its social standing. Its view of the critical intelligence working in society is therefore accompanied by no strong sense of disjunction, and it takes many of its terms from the moralised line of English romantic thought. What Forster inherits from it is apparent – something of the flavour of that engaging marriage made by the most influential English romantics, Wordsworth and Coleridge in particular, between the claims on the one hand of the imagination and the poet's transcendent vision, and on the other of right reason and moral duty; something of its power, therefore, to make a vision of Wholeness which embraces the social world in all its contingency. So the personal connection between inner and outer worlds – a connection forged through the powers of passion and imagination – has its social equivalent, in the notion of an obligation on society that it, too, be whole; that it grant, as Mill stresses, 'the absolute and essential importance of human development in its richest diversity',[2] that it sees, in Arnold's terms, that perfection can be both an *inward* condition of mind and spirit and a *general* expansion of the human family. Forster draws on the full equation for his fiction, taking as his proper field the social realm of action as well as the life of individuals in their personal relations, and criticising his characters and their society now from the standpoint of right reason and culture, now from that of the heart, the passions, the power of visionary imagination that can testify, however inadequately, to the claims of the infinite. Thus there come under fire 'the vast armies of the benighted, who follow neither the heart nor the brain' (*Room With a View*); and the connective impulses embrace not only man and man, and man and infinity, but the social order, too.

But if Forster is undoubtedly an inheritor of that world of value, he inherits with a due sense of difficulty. In *Howards End* he touches in with deep force those powers and forces in history which are process, and can't be gainsaid; the pastoral and vividly felt landscape of England is turned by the demanding processes of urbanisation and industrialism into a civilisation of luggage; while the very economics of the intelligentsia he belongs to become a matter for ironic exposure. In *A Passage to India* the final nullity of romanticism is exposed in the cave, where the worlds within us and without echo together the sound of *boum*; this is the extreme beyond Coleridgean dejection, for the visionary hope is lost in the face of an unspeaking and utterly alien nature, a nature only self-reflecting. The will to vision and the liberal thrust to right reason, the desire to connect both with infinity and all mankind, are placed against unyielding forces in nature and history – obstructing the movement of Forster's visionary themes and producing, particularly in these two last novels, a countervailing, ironic reaction. This countervailing sense, this sense of historical apocalypse coupled with spiritual abyss, is surely recognisably modernist. And what in the early novels appears as a species of social comedy – a comedy exercising the claims of moral realism against the liberal wish to draw clear lines between good and bad action – emerges in these latter novels as an essential irony of structure: indeed, as a direct challenge to the values Forster is so often supposed to represent. If, to cite Lionel Trilling (who writes so well of this ironic aspect of Forster), there is an ironic counterpart in the early work whereby while 'the plot speaks of clear certainties, the manner resolutely insists that nothing can be quite so simple',[3] these complexities increase in the later work into the mental and aesthetic possession of two colliding views of the world.

Forster's way of assimilating two modes of thought – one an inheritance, the other an urgent group of ideas about contemporary necessity – is matched by the curious aesthetic implications of his techniques in fiction. He is often considered as a writer technically a coeval of his Victorian predecessors (Walter Allen calls him a 'throwback'),⁴ and in asserting his own debts has particularly named three writers: Jane Austen, Samuel Butler, and Marcel Proust. The indebtedness to the first two of his species of moralised social irony hardly needs elaborating; it is the third name which suggests that the 'traditionalist' account of his technique is misleading. Of course, in his novels the omniscient author mediates, with the voice of the guide-book or essay or sermon, the proffered material – though as much to sustain fiction's place in the field of intelligence and thought as to establish the authenticity of fact. But at the same time he offers his work as the symbolist or autotelic artefact; a work of art is 'the only material object in the universe which may possess internal harmony' (*Two Cheers for Democracy*). What is so fascinating about his most extended aesthetic statement, *Aspects of the Novel*, is its attempt to place the modes of symbolism and post-impressionism in the context of what might be considered the more 'traditional' story-telling function; the novel *tells* (rather than *is*) a story, and it lives in the conditioned world of stuff, of event, of history. (So, finally, Forster puts Tolstoy above Proust.) Yet it has transcendent purposes; art, 'the one orderly product which our muddling race has produced', has Platonic powers to touch infinity, reach to the unity behind all things, prophesy (in the Shelleyan sense).

In this respect Forster is as post-impressionist or post-Paterian as anyone else in Bloomsbury, and the ultimate field of action for the arts is that of the 'unseen'. Procedurally this symbolist power seems to lie in the analogue with music, and is gained from aspects of the novel outside and beyond story, in thematic recurrences, leitmotifs, pattern and rhythm, prophetic song. The problem of whether art can redeem life by transcending it is crucial to modernism; the encounter between the formally transcendent – the epiphany, the unitary symbol – and the world of history recurs throughout its works. And Forster's view is, like that of most modernism, dualistic: art may reach beyond the world of men and things – the world of 'story' – but it can never leave that world behind, and must seek meanings and connections in it. What distinguishes Forster is the faint hope which he entertains on behalf of history: the hope that by understanding and right relationship men may win for it a limited redemption.

I have suggested that Forster is deeply involved in some of the largest intellectual, cultural, and aesthetic collisions that occur in the transition into this century; and it is his sharp sense of the contingent, of the powers that rule the world of men, that makes him so. The result is a complex version of modern literary disquiet. An intermediary between those two literary traditions of 'moderns' and 'contemporaries' that Stephen Spender[5] sees as the two main lines of modern English writing, he bears these burdens so as to expose the crucial choices that a writer of this transitional period might make. Divided as he is between infinite and contingent, he is none the less more available to the offered pressures than most of the more confirmed modernists. This is because his sense of the 'crisis' of infinity is so much bound up with his sense of the divisive and changing forces of the world of time. For he is increasingly concerned with the problems of the infinite view within the cultural movements of the modernising world; and in his growing sense of the need to synthesise an ever more eclectic experience he testifies to the new multiverse, the chaotic welter of values, which has confounded the modern mind. Hence his visions, though they may suggest an order or unity in the universe, are defined, increasingly from novel to novel, in terms of an anarchy that they must always comprehend. Thus they are never fully redemptive, since the world of time persistently enlarges our feelings of intellectual, moral, social, and spiritual relativism, creating a world in which no one philosophy or cosmology accounts for the world order – where it is possible to believe with Mrs Moore that 'Everything exists; nothing has value' (*PI* 156).[6] This, with its suggestion that in seeing life whole one may see nothing except multiplicity, is the obverse of the unitary vision; and in *A Passage to India*, his fullest and most eclectic book, Forster gives us in full that possibility – and its sources in social relations, personal relations, and the realm of spirit.

Forster may have an ideal of unity, a will to a whole solution, but we mistake him if we see only that in him. For he is characteristically not a novelist of solutions, but rather of reservations, of the contingencies and powers which inhibit spirit. The power of sympathy, understanding, and community with all things is for him an overriding power; but its claim to wholeness is always conditioned, and mystery, to which we must yield, co-exists with muddle, which we must try to redeem, or even accept in its nullity. Indeed, it is because Forster is so attentive to the forces in our culture and world-order which induce the vision of anarchy – and threaten through its very real powers not only the will to but the very insights of the whole vision – that he seems so central a writer; a novelist whom we in our turn have not always seen whole.

II

Forster is a difficult and ambiguous writer, a writer who has often made his critics uneasy and caused them to feel how strangely elusive his work is. His observation of his materials, and his way of making his structures, usually involves two tones that come into perplexing relationship. There is the instinct towards 'poetry', which goes with the view of art as a symbolist unity; and there is the comedy and the irony, the belittling aspect of his tone, which brings in the problems and difficulties of the contingent world. Because of this it is often possible simultaneously to interpret his work positively and negatively, depending on the kind of critical attentiveness one gives.

Thus for some critics, like Wilfred Stone, *A Passage to India* is Forster's most affirmative and optimistic novel, the one which most suggests, as Stone puts it, that 'unity and harmony are the ultimate promises of life'.[7] 'The theme which this book hammers home', says Stone, 'is that, for all our differences, we are in fact *one. . . .* Physically of one environment, we are also psychically

one, and it is reason's denial of our commonality, the repression
of that *participation mystique*, which has caused man to rule his
Indias and himself with such futility and blindness.'⁸ But other
critics like James McConkey and Alan Wilde have come to precisely the opposite view, seeing the work as a novel of the final
dissociation between the chaotic life of man and an intractable
eternal reality. In part the decision depends upon whether one
insists, like Trilling, on a relatively realistic reading of the book,
or whether, as E. K. Brown does, one reads it as a 'symbolist'
novel. If the world of men and manners, of politics and human
behaviour, which it depicts suggests divisiveness, the world of
the work itself as single 'orderly product' suggests profound
correspondences within it, a power to resolve its meanings which
lies beyond any given character. Of this aspect of the book, Frank
Kermode has remarked that it depends upon faking – faking a
universe of promised wholeness, of rhetorical and structural
unity, of a testing of the world of men from the standpoint of
total coherence: 'All that civilisation excepts or disconnects has
to be got in for meaning to subsist.'⁹ What this means is that the
world of men and the world of order must exist in paradoxical
relationship, and this is what Lionel Trilling seems to imply, too,
when he remarks that the novel has an unusual imbalance between plot and story: 'The characters are of sufficient size for the
plot; they are not large enough for the story – and that indeed is
the point of the story.'¹⁰ But it is typically in such contrasts of
time and transcendence that Forster deals, and to clarify the
relationship between them one needs to look very closely at the
overall working of the novel.

To a considerable extent, the book deals in themes and matters
we have learned to associate with Forster from his previous
novels. Here again are those rival claims upon men and nature
which dichotomise the universe – the claims of the seen and the
unseen, the public and the private, the powers of human activities
and institutions and of the ultimate mysteries for which the right
institutions and activities have yet to be found. And here again
Forster's own sympathies are relatively apparent. The book is
focused upon the testing-field of human relationships, with their

various possibilities and disasters; on the 'good will plus culture and intelligence' (p. 65) which are the necessary conditions of honest intercourse; on the clashes of interest and custom which divide men but which the liberal mind must hope, as Fielding hopes, to transcend. Its modes of presentation are familiarly complex – moving between a 'poetic' evocation of the world of mystery and a 'comic' evocation of the world of muddle, which is in a sense its obverse and refers to the normal state of men.

But what is unmistakable, I think, is that in this book Forster reveals new powers and resources – of a kind not previously achieved in his fiction – and that this extension of resource is linked with an extension of his sensibility, and above all with a new sense of complexity. For instance, *A Passage to India* is not simply an international novel – in the Jamesian sense of attempting to resolve contrasting value-systems by means of a cosmopolitan scale of value – but a global novel. The contrast of England and India is not the end of the issue, since India is schismatic within itself; India's challenge is the challenge of the multiverse, a new version of the challenge that Henry Adams faced on looking at the dynamo. What the city is as metaphor in *Howards End*, India is in *Passage*; it is a metaphor of contingency. Forster is not simply interested in raising the social-comic irony of confronting one social world with the standards of another; he stretches through the social and political implications to religious and mystical ones, and finally to the most basic question of all – how, in the face of such contingency, one structures meaning.

The geographical scale of the novel is, in short, supported by a vast scale of standpoint. Forster attempts a structure inclusive of the range of India, and the judgements of the book are reinforced by the festivals and rituals of three religions, by the heterodoxy – racial, political, cultural, religious, and mystical – of this multiple nation, and by the physical landscape of a country which both invites meaning ('Come, come') and denies any. 'Nothing embraces the whole of India, nothing, nothing,' says Aziz (p. 151); the landscape and the spirit of the earth divide men ('Trouble after trouble encountered him [Aziz], because he had challenged

the spirit of the Indian earth, which tries to keep men in compartments' (p. 133)); and even the sects are divided within themselves just as the earth is: 'The fissures in the Indian soil are
infinite: Hinduism, so solid from a distance, is riven into sects
and clans, which radiate and join, and change their names
according to the aspect from which they are approached' (p. 304).

Forster's social comedy works to provoke, among a variety of
different and sympathetically viewed groups, those ironic international and intra-national encounters that come when one value-
system meets another and confusion and muddle ensue. But his
other aim is to call up, by a poetic irradiation, the ironies lying
within the forces of mystery and muddle in the constituted universe of nature itself. For here, too, are deceptions, above all in
the absence of Beauty, which is traditionally a form for infinity,
so that the very discourse of Romanticism becomes negative
under the hot sun – who is 'not the unattainable friend, either of
men or birds or other suns, [who] was not the eternal promise,
the never-withdrawn suggestion that haunts our consciousness;
he was merely a creature, like the rest, and so debarred from
glory' (p. 120). There is much in India that invites a cosmic
meaning, but it places both man and infinity:

Trees of a poor quality bordered the road, indeed the whole scene
was inferior, and suggested that the countryside was too vast to
admit of excellence. In vain did each item in it call out, 'Come,
come.' There was not enough god to go round. The two young
people conversed feebly and felt unimportant. (p. 92)

All this stretches the Whitmanesque enterprise called up by the
title to a vast level of inclusiveness. It also involves Forster in a
placing of the social and human world of his novel in a way he
has never approached before. One way of putting the situation
is to say that the human plot of the novel is set into singular
relation to the verbal plot, with its radiating expansiveness of
language. The human plot of the novel is essentially a story hing-
ing on Adela Quested, who comes to India to marry, has doubts
about her marriage when she sees what India has made of her
fiancé, and tries herself to create a more reasonable relationship

between British and Indians. She takes part in an expedition, arranged by an Indian, to the Marabar caves, in one of which she believes she is attacked by him. She accuses him of attempted rape, and, although at the trial she retracts her accusation, the incident has sown dissent and discord, and has exposed the political and institutional tensions of the country.

The plot moves us from the world of personal relationships to the social world (which in this case involves political relationships), and is set largely in and around the city of Chandrapore, at a time not stated but evidently intended to be in the 1920s. The dense social world that Forster delineates so skilfully consists primarily of racial or religious groups with their own customs and patterns. The English, whom we see largely through the eyes of Adela Quested and Mrs Moore, visiting India together, are identified with their institutional functions. Mostly professional middle-class people, they have gone through a process of adaptation to their duties, which are, as Ronny says, 'to do justice and keep the peace' (p. 53). They have learned the importance of solidarity, conventions, rank, and standoffishness; and their judgements and their social order are those of a particular class in a particular situation. Their ethics are dutiful and serious; they have a deep sense of rational justice; they are distrustful of mysticism and lethargy; their deep Englishness has been reinforced by their situation. They operate at the level of political and social duty, and their relationships – the ties that bind the characters together and enable Forster to thread the way from one to another – are those of the political and social roles they play.

The other group, which we see first largely through the eyes of Aziz, consists of Indians, though these are themselves divided by religions and castes. Here again what we see are primarily the professional classes, linked to the British by their duties and to their own people by their familial and friendly relationships. The two main groupings that emerge here are, of course, the Hindus and the Moslems, and Forster differentiates carefully between them, and their respective versions of India. Where they differ radically from the English is in their long and adaptive response to the confusions of their country, a response which obscures the firm lines of value that the British in their isolation can protect, and permits lethargy, emotionalism, and mysticism. Forster explores Indian custom and faith in great detail, noting its own patterns of classification, its own way of making and not making social and moral distinctions, above all recognising that Indians have adapted to a different physical environment by being comprehensive or passive rather than orderly or rationalistic.

These worlds – Anglo-Indian (to use the phrase of the day), Hindu, Muslim – are given us in full as they connect and draw apart, and Forster enters imaginatively into each of them. And to a large extent what interests him is not the relations between people, the normal matter for the novelist, but their separation. In the novel's social scenes we are always conscious of those who are absent, and much of the discussion in the early part of the novel is devoted to those not present – the whites are talked of by the Indians, the Indians by the whites. And this suggests the vast social inclusiveness of the novel, which spreads beyond the communities established for the sake of the action into a cast of thousands: nameless marginal characters who appear for a moment and are gone, like the punkah wallah or the voice out of the darkness at the club, and the inhabitants of Chandrapore who seem made of 'mud moving' (p. 9).

Out of this complex social world derives a complex moral world, in which the values of no one group are given total virtue, The English may have thrown the net of rationalism and 'civilisation' over the country, but India's resistance to this – 'The triumphant machine of civilisation may suddenly hitch and be immobilised into a car of stone' (p. 220) – puts them in ironic relation to Indian reality; they scratch only the surface of its life, and theirs is a feeble invasion. On the other hand, the passive comprehensiveness of India is seen as itself a kind of social decay, debased as well as spiritual, leading to a potential neglect of man. The traditional repositories of Forsterian virtue – goodwill plus culture and intelligence – function only incompletely in this universe; and Forster's own liberal passion for social connection motivates a large section of the action, but does not contain its chief interest. In the deceptively guide-bookish opening chapter Forster establishes an appeal beyond the social world, to the overarching sky; it looks, at first, like a figure for the potential unity of man, the redemption that might come through breaking out of the social institutions and classifications that segregate them into their closed groupings, but the gesture has an ambiguous quality. The civil station 'shares nothing with the city except the overarching sky' (p. 10), but the sky itself is an infinite mystery, and reaching away into its 'farther distance . . . beyond colour, last freed itself from blue' (p. 11). Certainly, beyond the world of social organisation is that world of 'the secret understanding of the heart' (p. 22) to which Aziz appeals; this is the world that is damaged when Ronnie and Mrs Moore discuss Aziz and she finds: 'Yes, it was all true, but how false as a summary of the man; the essential life of him had been slain' (p. 37).

Forster is, as usual, superb at creating that 'essential life' and showing what threatens it, and much of the book deals with its virtues and its triumphs. So at one level the social world *is* redeemed by those who resist its classifications – by Adela and Mrs Moore, Fielding, Aziz, Godbole. Forster does not belittle their victories directly except in so far as he sees their comedy. But he does place beyond them a world of infinitude which is not, here, to be won through the personal. For this is not the entire realm of moral victory in the novel; indeed, these acts of resistance, which provide the book's lineal structure, are usually marked by failure. Adela's is a conventional disaster; she makes the moral mistake of exposing the personal to the social. Fielding's is more complicated; he is an agent of liberal contact through goodwill plus culture and intelligence, but he, like Mrs Moore, meets an echo:

'In the old eighteenth century, when cruelty and injustice raged, an invisible power repaired their ravages. Everything echoes now; there's no stopping the echo. The original sound may be harmless, but the echo is always evil.' This reflection about an echo lay at the verge of Fielding's mind. He could never develop it. It belonged to the universe that he had missed or rejected. And the mosque missed it too. Like himself, those shallow arcades provided but a limited asylum. (pp. 286–7)

As for Mrs Moore, who does touch it, she encounters another
force still – the moral nihilism that comes when the boundary
walls are down. Her disaster dominates the novel, for it places
even moral and mystical virtue within the sphere of contingency;
it, too, is subject to spiritual anarchy. Beyond the world of the
plot, the lineal world of consequences and relationships, there
lies a second universe of fictional structure, which links spiritual
events, and then a third, which in turn places these in history and
appeals to the infinite recession of the universe beyond any human
structure that seeks to comprehend it.

This we may see by noting that in this novel, as compared with
the earlier ones, the world of men is clearly granted reduced
powers. The universe of time and contingency is made smaller,
by the nature that surrounds man, by the scale of the continent on
which man's presence is a feeble invasion, by the sky which over-
arches him and his works. It is a world of dwarfs and of dwarfed
relationships, in which the familiar forces of romantic redemption in Forster's work – personal relationships as mirrors to
infinity, a willingness to confront the unseen – undertake their
movements toward connection without the full support of the
universe. The theme recurs, but Mrs Moore expresses it most
strongly in chapter XIV, when she reflects on her situation and
grows towards her state of spiritual nullity in the cave:

She felt increasingly (vision or nightmare?) that, though people
are important, the relations between them are not, and that in
particular too much fuss has been made over marriage; centuries
of carnal embracement, yet man is no nearer to understanding
man. And today she felt this with such force that it seemed itself
a relationship, itself a person who was trying to take hold of her
hand. (p. 141)

The negative withdrawal is, of course, an aspect of that 'twilight
of the double vision in which so many elderly people are involved' (p. 216), and it is not the only meaning in the book. But
it is the dominant one. It is by seeking its obverse that Adela
compounds her basic moral error:

It was Adela's faith that the whole stream of events is important and interesting, and if she grew bored she blamed herself severely and compelled her lips to utter enthusiasms. This was the only insincerity in a character otherwise sincere, and it was indeed the intellectual protest of her youth. She was particularly vexed now because she was both in India and engaged to be married, which double event should have made every instant sublime. (p. 139)

Human relationships are dwarfed not only by the scale of the historical and social world, which is potentially redeemable, but by the natural world, which is not.

III

Of course, intimations of transcendence are present throughout the novel. Structurally they run through the seasonal cycle, from decisive hot sun to the benedictive healing water at the end, and from Mosque to Caves to Temple. By taking that as his order, Forster is able poetically to sustain the hope of a spiritual possibility, a prefiguring of the world beyond in the world below. The climax of this theme is Godbole's attempt at 'completeness, not reconstruction' (p. 298). But what happens here is that divine revelation is shifted to the level of the comic sublime; Forster's rhetoric now puts what has been spiritually perplexing – the webs, nets, and prisons that divide spirit as well as society – back into the comic universe of muddle. The Mau festival is the celebration of the formlessness of the Indian multiverse, seen for a moment inclusively. The poetic realm of the novel, in which above all Mrs Moore and Godbole have participated, and which has dominated the book's primary art, is reconciled with the muddle of the world of men, in an emotional cataract that momentarily repairs the divisions of the spiritual world (through Godbole's revelation) and the social world (through the festival itself). It satisfies much of the passion for inclusiveness that has been one thread in the novel, the desire that heaven should include all because India *is* all. Earlier the two Christian missionaries have disagreed: Mr Sorley, the more advanced,

admitted that the mercy of God, being infinite, may well embrace all mammals. And the wasps? He became uneasy during the descent to wasps, and was apt to change the conversation. And oranges, cactuses, crystals and mud? and the bacteria inside Mr Sorley? No, no, this is going too far. We must exclude someone from our gathering, or we shall be left with nothing. (p. 41)

Godbole's universe of spirit is much more inclusive:

Godbole consulted the music-book, said a word to the drummer, who broke rhythm, made a thick little blur of sound, and produced a new rhythm. This was more exciting, the inner images it evoked more definite, and the singers' expressions became fatuous and languid. They loved all men, the whole universe, and scraps of their past, tiny splinters of detail, emerged for a moment to melt into the universal warmth. Thus Godbole, though she was not important to him, remembered an old woman he had met in Chandrapore days. Chance brought her into his mind while it was in this heated state, he did not select her, she happened to occur among the throng of soliciting images, a tiny splinter, and he impelled her by his spiritual force to that place where completeness can be found. Completeness, not reconstruction. His senses grew thinner, he remembered a wasp seen he forgot where, perhaps on a stone. He loved the wasp equally, he impelled it likewise, he was imitating God. And the stone where the wasp clung – could he ... no, he could not, he had been wrong to attempt the stone, logic and conscious effort had seduced, he came back to the strip of red carpet and discovered that he was dancing upon it. (p. 298)

His doctrine – 'completeness, not reconstruction' – is, of course, a species of transcendence, a momentary vision of the whole, the invocation of a universe invested with spirit. It links up with the symbolist plot of the novel, its power as a radiant image, rather than with plot in the linear sense, with its world of 'and then ... and then ...' Threading its way through the novel, to an old woman and a wasp, it takes these 'soliciting images' and puts them in new association – not with all things, but with each other and with what else comes almost unbidden into the world of spirit. But the stone is left, and equally spirit may or may not invest the universe in any of its day-to-day affairs: 'Perhaps all these things! Perhaps none!' (p. 302). Things, in freeing themselves from their traditional associations, social and historical, form a new order, beyond dialogue, beyond human plot, in the realm where poetic figures function on their own order of consciousness. Yet here, too, irony is at work: mystery is sometimes muddle, completeness is sometimes the universe where 'everythings exists, nothing has value' (p. 156). If history ultimately obstructs, and does not give us a final, rounded structure in terms of human events, if the horses, the earth, the clutter of human institutions say, 'No, not yet,' then like obstructions dwell in the realm of spirit and symbol, too: the sky says, 'No, not there' (p. 336).

The linear, social plot, then, has stretched a long way in search of a structure of its own that will provide coherence in the world, but if it finds one it is in the form of an oblique, doubtful, and ironic promise; personal relations only go so far to solve the muddle of history. As for the symbolist plot, it transcends but it does not redeem; it is there but 'neglects to come' (p. 84). The power of the novel lies, of course, in the Whitmanesque ambition to include multitudes, to find eternity in some order in the given world. But is this ambition realised? Intimations of eternity may have their symbols in the world of men (in love and relationship) and in the world of nature (in the force of mystery that resides in things); the social and the natural worlds have in them touches that promise wholeness. But they do not of themselves have unity; they are themselves afflicted by the double vision which is all that man can bring to them, grounded as he is in history and hope at once. The world stretches infinitely about us, and there is infinity beyond us. But questions bring us only to the unyielding hostility of the soil and the unyielding ambiguity of the sky.

The universe, then, is less intimation than cipher; a mask rather than a revelation in the romantic sense. Does love meet with love? Do we receive but what we give? The answer is surely a paradox, the paradox that there are Platonic universals beyond, but that the glass is too dark to see them. Is there a light beyond the glass, or is it a mirror only to the self? The Platonic cave is even darker than Plato made it, for it introduces the echo, and so leaves us back in the world of men, which does not carry total meaning, is just a story of events. The Platonic romantic gesture of the match in the cave is the dominating ambiguity of the book. Does it see *itself* in the polished wall of stone, or is the glimmer of radiance a promise?

There is little to see, and no eye to see it, until the visitor arrives for his five minutes, and strikes a match. Immediately another flame rises in the depths of the rock and moves towards the surface like an imprisoned spirit: the walls of the circular chamber have been most marvellously polished. The two flames approach and strive to unite, but cannot, because one of them breathes air, the other stone. A mirror inlaid with lovely colours divides the lovers, delicate stars of pink and grey interpose, exquisite nebulae, shadings fainter than the tail of a comet or the midday moon, all the evanescent life of the granite, only here visible. Fists and fingers thrust above the advancing soil – here at last is their skin, finer than any covering acquired by the animals, smoother than windless water, more voluptuous than love. The radiance increases, the flames touch one another, kiss, expire. The cave is dark again, like all the caves. (pp. 130–1)

Isn't it less the transcendence of a Whitman, uniting all things through the self and the ongoing lines of history, than the ambiguous and narcissistic transcendence of Melville, where the universe is a diabolical cipher, where the desire to penetrate meaning ends only in our being swallowed up in the meaning we have conferred? Isn't the novel not Forster's *Passage to India*, but rather, in the end, Forster's *Moby-Dick*?

SOURCE: *Aspects of E. M. Forster*, ed. Oliver Stallybrass (1969).

NOTES

1. Review of *The Cave and the Mountain*, by Wilfred Stone, in *London Magazine*, VI, no. 5, NS (Aug 1966) p. 102.
2. This quotation from Wilhelm von Humboldt, *Sphere and Duties of Government*, forms the epigraph to John Stuart Mill's *On Liberty* (1859).
3. *E. M. Forster* (1944) p. 13.
4. *The English Novel* (1954) p. 319.
5. *The Struggle of the Modern* (1963).

6. References to *A Passage to India* are to the English pocket edition (Arnold, 1947).

7. Stone, *The Cave and the Mountain* (Stanford and London, 1966) p. 344.

8. Ibid. p. 339.

9. 'The One Orderly Product (E. M. Forster)', in *Puzzles and Epiphanies* (1962) p. 84. This essay is reprinted in this volume, pp. 216–23.

10. Trilling, *E. M. Forster*, p. 126. Reprinted in this volume; see p. 81.

SELECT BIBLIOGRAPHY

The following books and articles are, in the editor's opinion, of particular interest and value in the criticism of *A Passage to India*, though it was not possible for reasons of space to include them in this book.

Glen O. Allen, 'Structure, Symbol and Theme in E. M. Forster's *A Passage to India*', in *PMLA* LXX (Dec 1955) 934–54.
  A challenging close reading of the book, stressing its Hindu features.

Nirad C. Chaudhuri, 'Passage to and from India', in *Encounter*, II (June 1954) 19–24.
  An interesting discussion of the impact of *A Passage to India* in forming attitudes toward imperial politics and to India, which seeks to emphasize that the novel overlooks larger political significances through its stress on the problems of personal relationships.

John Colmer, *E. M. Forster: A Passage to India* (Edward Arnold, 1967).
  An excellent introduction to the novel, giving a detailed reading by exploring certain central themes ('the importance of personal relations, the sanctity of the emotional life, the problems of reconciling worldly success and spiritual salvation, the importance of the relationship of man and nature'). In the 'Studies in English Literature' series.

C. B. Cox, *The Free Spirit: a study of liberal humanism in the novels of George Eliot, Henry James, E. M. Forster, Virginia Woolf, Angus Wilson* (Oxford U.P., 1963).
  Contains a good chapter on Forster with an interesting and

analytical questioning of some of the moral and artistic consequences of Forster's liberal presumptions.

K. W. Gransden, *E. M. Forster* (Oliver & Boyd and Grove
Press, New York, 1962).
A very good general introduction to Forster containing a
useful discussion of *A Passage to India*.

Dennis Hickley, 'Ou-Boum and Verbum', in *Downside Review*,
LXXII (Spring 1954) 172–80.
A good exploration of the religious dimensions of Forster's
novel from a critically Catholic point of view.

Ellin Horowitz, 'The Communal Ritual and the Dying God in
E. M. Forster's *A Passage to India*', in *Criticism*, VI, no. i
(Winter 1964) 70–88.
An interesting exploration of the view that the book 'can
profitably be interpreted within the context of myth and ritual',
and in particular with relation to the pattern of vegetation
ritual.

Arnold Kettle, *An Introduction to the English Novel*, vol. II
(Hutchinson, 1953).
This study contains an excellent chapter giving a reading of
the novel.

Hugh Maclean, 'The Structure of *A Passage to India*', in *University of Toronto Quarterly*, XXII, no. ii (Jan 1953) 157–71.
An 'optimistic' reading of the novel which suggests that the
book is closer to the approach and mood of Whitman than
has been previously suggested by critics, and that 'the effect
of the novel is to make us feel that the glimpses available to all
may, though with difficulty, be converted to full and active
vision'.

Herbert Marshall McLuhan, 'Kipling and Forster', in *Sewanee
Review*, LII (Summer 1944) 332–42.

SELECT BIBLIOGRAPHY

A lively, perverse essay which suggests that both writers
are melodramatic and hence are incapable of producing really
new insights; the answers are already mechanically pre-
determined.

H. J. Oliver, *The Art of E. M. Forster* (Melbourne U.P., 1960).
A useful study containing a good discussion of the novel.

David Shusterman, *The Quest for Certitude in E. M. Forster's
Fiction* (Indiana U.P., 1965).
A good study which questions some of the more positive
views of the novel.

Wilfred Stone, *The Cave and the Mountain: A Study of E. M.
Forster* (Stanford U.P., 1966).
A large and central study of Forster which offers an extended
and very 'positive' reading of *A Passage to India* of a fascinat-
ingly thorough kind, with a psycho-analytic bias.

George H. Thomson, *The Fiction of E. M. Forster* (Michigan
U.P., 1967).
This interesting study makes use of the manuscript of
A Passage to India in its reading of the novel.

Alan Wilde, *Art and Order: A Study of E. M. Forster* (New
York U.P., 1964, Peter Owen, 1965).
Contains a good reading of the novel stressing the problem
of relating an extensive vision of chaos to a notion of aesthetic
order.

Richard R. Werry, 'Rhythm in Forster's *A Passage to India*', in
Studies in Honor of John Wilcox, ed. A. Dayle Wallace and
Woodburn O. Ross (Wayne State U.P., 1958).
An interesting development and extension of the argument
used by E. K. Brown, stressing the 'self-generating' creativity
of the novel.

NOTES ON CONTRIBUTORS

JOHN BEER. Fellow of Peterhouse, and Lecturer in English at Cambridge. His publications include works on Blake, Coleridge and Milton.

MALCOLM BRADBURY, Professor of American Studies in the University of East Anglia; novelist (*Eating People is Wrong, Stepping Westward, The History Man*) and critic, author of *Evelyn Waugh, The Social Context of Modern English Literature, Possibilities: Essays on the State of the Novel,* etc. Editor of *E. M. Forster: A Collection of Critical Essays.*

REUBEN A. BROWER. Professor of English at Harvard University until his death in 1975. His books include *Alexander Pope: the poetry of allusion.*

E. K. BROWN. Formerly Professor of English at the Universities of Toronto, Manitoba, Cornell, and Chicago. His books include *Matthew Arnold: a study in conflict.* He died in 1951.

PETER BURRA. English critic and journalist, author of studies of Van Gogh and Wordsworth. He died in 1937.

FREDERICK C. CREWS. Professor of English at the University of California, Berkeley. His books include *Tragedy Of Manners: moral drama in the later works of Henry James, The Pooh Perplex* (parody) and works on Nathaniel Hawthorne.

L. P. HARTLEY (1895–1972). Celebrated novelist and journalist.

FRANK KERMODE. Fellow of King's College, Cambridge, and formerly King Edward VII Professor of English Literature at the University of Cambridge. His books include *Romantic Image* and *The Sense of an Ending.*

JAMES MCCONKEY. Formerly Professor of English at Cornell University. His books include *The Novels of E. M. Forster.*

248 NOTES ON CONTRIBUTORS

OLIVER STALLYBRASS. Successively teacher, librarian, publisher and freelance writer. Editor of *Aspects of E.M. Forster* and of the Abinger edition of Forster's works. He died in 1978.

LIONEL TRILLING. Professor of English at Columbia University until his death in 1975. Famous critic and novelist. His books include *Matthew Arnold* and *The Liberal Imagination*.

GERTRUDE M. WHITE. Formerly Professor of English in America; well known as a Forster critic.

INDEX

250

INDEX